direct experience 13, 84, 1

truth 30, 45 61, 141

signs 39,
human 39,

Sign ad infinitum 50

+ Foucault.
65 power vs. meaning

War vs language

Wittgenstein, language, disease 88, 140
to cure language of its disease

plato's cave 131

Peirce's 3 axioms 138

*Charles S. Peirce's*
*Philosophy of Signs*

**Advances in Semiotics**
Thomas A. Sebeok, *General Editor*

# Charles S. Peirce's Philosophy of Signs

## ESSAYS IN COMPARATIVE SEMIOTICS

## Gérard Deledalle

*Indiana*
*University*
*Press*

BLOOMINGTON AND INDIANAPOLIS

This book is a publication of

*Indiana University Press*

601 North Morton Street

Bloomington, IN 47404-3797 USA

HTTP://WWW.INDIANA.EDU/~IUPRESS

*Telephone orders* 800-842-6796
*Fax orders* 812-855-7931
*Orders by e-mail* iuporder@indiana.edu

MANUFACTURED IN THE UNITED STATES OF AMERICA

**Library of Congress Cataloging-in-Publication Data**

Deledalle, Gérard.
Charles S. Peirce's philosophy of signs : essays in comparative semiotics / Gérard Deledalle.
p. cm.
Includes bibliographical references and index.
ISBN 0-253-33736-4 (hardcover : alk. paper)
1. Peirce, Charles S. (Charles Sanders), 1839–1914. 2. Semiotics.   I. Title: Charles Sanders Peirce's
philosophy of signs.   II. Title.
B945.P44 D434 2000
121'.68—dc21
00-024320

1 2 3 4 5   05 04 03 02 01 00

# CONTENTS

vi                              Contents

# INTRODUCTION
## Peirce Compared: Directions for Use

Although the present book is a collection of essays written over fifty years, either in French or in English, according to circumstances, my way of approaching Peirce has always followed the same line which allows me to call them *Essays in Comparative Semiotics.* As to the title, *Charles S. Peirce's Philosophy of Signs,* I am not responsible for the fact that Peirce's theory of signs is philosophical, rather than "ethnological" like that of Claude Lévy-Strauss, or "linguistic" like that of Roman Jakobson. That is why not only philosophy in general, including ideology, but metaphysics in particular, play a part in Peirce's semiotics, and consequently in my book.

In spite of the fact that my papers were written to introduce Peirce to a French public, and perhaps thanks to it, my book has a unity of method which explains itself. First, writing for French readers, I could not refer them to English or American authors whom they were not supposed to know. I could resort only to French authors or French translations of English-speaking authors, dealing with the same semiotic subject matter. Unfortunately, or rather fortunately, their approach was so different that I could stress only the differences and not the resemblances. That is why my "comparative" method is *differential.* Peirce stands alone of his kind. Second, I had to compare Peirce, not only to French authors or foreign authors translated into French, but to himself both chronologically and contextually.

As a reader of Peirce myself, I wanted to be fair and read Peirce's writings *chronologically.* One cannot reject an argument, developed, let us say in 1906, by quoting a text from 1867 or 1877–1878. Between 1867, when Peirce proposed his new list of categories, or 1877–1878 when he proposed his "pragmatic maxim," and 1904–1911 when he was corresponding with Lady Welby, he changed his mind. The new logic of relatives which he invented around 1875 led him to abandon the Western "dualistic" way of thinking as promoted from Aristotle to Kant, for a "triadic" and "anti-inductive" way of reasoning which experimental method and evolutive sciences first practiced. That is why I sometimes, when necessary, give the date of my quotations from Peirce.

To be fair, one has also to read an author *in context.* The vocabulary of a philosopher is not the same as that of a mathematician or a biologist. When a philosopher is also a mathematical logician and pragmatist, as was the case with Peirce, one has to specify the public to which a given text (already dated) is addressed. For instance, Peirce uses the concept of "degenerate" when he wants to be understood by mathematicians or logicians. When he addresses philosophers, he uses other concepts, such as the three phenomenological or rather phanero-scopical categories. In the first instance, he would say that a "proposition" is a degenerate case of "argument" ("argument," in Peirce's sense, i.e., any ordered system). In the other instance, he would say that a Third is "vague and empty," a mere "structure" and that a Second is a single, singular, and unique replica of a Third, the best example being the relation between "type" and "token." But it would be nonsense to speak here in terms of "degeneracy," because, as a First, the type is not a "genuine" category, but an "accretive" sign.

Let us give another more simple and general case. In a paper published in the *Times Literary Supplement* on August 23, 1985, Jonathan Cohen insists on what he thinks to be a contradiction in what he calls Peircean "anti-realism": The Peircean anti-realist "assumes that scientific method [ . . . ] is sufficient to guarantee the convergence" between scientific consensus and truth, because "he takes such convergence to be an *a priori* philosophical truth." "So though the Peircean is a fallibilist in relation to science itself, he is an infallibilist in relation to methodology" (Cohen 1985: 929). Jonathan Cohen is mistaken here because his conception of truth is out of context. "Inquiry" has nothing to do with "truth" and certainly not with "an *a priori* philosophical truth." According to Peirce, "inquiry" can give birth only to "warranted assertibility," to use the ex-pression coined by John Dewey and quoted by Cohen. The same mistake was made by the analytic philosophers when they were orthodox and by the rene-gades of the next generation, whether they were "realists" or "neo-pragmatists."

Of course, the reader may be tempted to unify Peirce's thought and may be successful, provided the two conditions of chronology and contextualization are respected. For instance, chronologically and contextually, a concept may have been dealt with by Peirce at *one period* and in *one context*. For example, consider the concept of "object" in his correspondence with Lady Welby between 1904 and 1911, and in the context of semiotics. The distinction between the concept of immediate object and the concept of dynamic object applies only to the idea of "semiosis." The immediate object (Oi) is the name of the object *within* a given semiosis, the dynamic object (Od) is the name of the same object *without* the same semiosis. In other words, dynamic object (Od) and immediate object (Oi) can be separated only analytically. The object is existentially one and the same, only, like a coin, with a reverse (Od) and an obverse (Oi). While the nature of Oi is easy to define because it is psychologically apprehended, the nature of Od can-not be with certainty semiotically described. Is it an "essence" or the totality of immediate objects solidified in a transparent ideal object produced by all the in-terpretants as habits in a given social group for a given individual of this group?

Generalization is thus in this case and other similar cases, according to Peirce's own ethics of terminology, to be limited to their respective proper time and context.

But when one wants to systematize a concept which Peirce discussed several times at *different periods* and in *different contexts*, it is more risky, because two cases have to be distinguished: the meaning of the concept may be either *changed* or *enlarged.*

When the object of the concept is *changed,* things are relatively easy. It is the case of the new conception of inference we mentioned earlier. The "anti-inductive" attitude that Peirce adopted at the turn of the century rested on the fact that no theory of change could prove that singular, concrete facts by themselves give birth to "universals" or rather "generals" to use Peirce's term. The abductive process that Peirce advanced instead was that facts can only suggest hypotheses which have to be experimentally tested. In consequence, if this is acknowledged, facts and ideas cannot be thought as opposed as Mill's empiricism is opposed to Descartes's idealism.

When the concept is *enlarged,* the whole system has to be looked at in another way. For instance, the two main Peircean protocols: the *phaneroscopical protocol* and its mathematical foundation and incidentally the so-called *protocol of degeneracy,* with which we will deal later on.

The main Peircean protocols or principles will serve in the present book as references:

Phaneroscopy: the principle of the hierarchy of categories;

Epistemology: primacy of Thirdness over Secondness, but necessity of Secondness for "instantiating" Thirdness;

Semiotics: three kinds of references to signs: Triadic symbol, dyadic index, and monadic icon: no symbolic sign without index and icon; no indexical sign without icon; the iconic sign refers to itself.

To sum up, my approach is philosophical in the two senses of the word: ideological and metaphysical. I shall insist on ideology in the two sections devoted respectively to Peirce's pragmatism (Part I) and Peirce's metaphysics (Part IV). Part II will deal with Peirce as semiotician. Part III is, properly speaking, comparative in the sense I gave to the term above.

The first part: "Semeiotic as Philosophy," deals respectively with Peirce's philosophical paradigms as opposed to European paradigms and especially with the first two pragmatic papers which were published in French in the *Revue philosophique* in 1878 and 1879. The circumstances of their being written in French by Peirce and subsequently rewritten, suggest an ideological influence which is worth stressing.

The second part: "Semeiotic as Semiotics," insists on semiotics as the theory of sign-action. Without rejecting the formal aspect of the sign, the accent is put on time and terminology, on *semiosis* as the action of "making-sign": objects or words.

The third part: "Comparative Semiotics," contrasts Peirce's triadic semiotics with the theories of signs—most of them dualistic—as dealt with by nearly every contemporary human science: formal logic, linguistics, semiology, theory of communication, epistemology, etcetera.

The fourth part: "Comparative metaphysics," discusses the two ideological foundations of triadicity in the context of the quarrel of the Holy Trinity:

equalitarian with the West and hierarchical with the East. Peirce's hierarchical triadicity not only conforms to experimental evolutionary sciences and sheds light on all the semiotic processes, but provides a new approach to the mystery of the Trinity, and saves metaphysics. It is as if metaphysics, which was born with the Roman Church and of which the end was not long ago announced, can now be reborn thanks to Peirce's hierarchically triadic philosophy of signs.

## ABOUT THE TEXT

### Repetitions

Over fifty years, one is bound to repeat oneself, by way of routine or necessity of the subject matter. I have suppressed all the repetition of the first kind, and kept the second kind, to make my ideas, or rather Peirce's ideas, clear. As Schopenhauer said: "The author may sometimes repeat himself. He should be excused on the ground of the difficulty of the subject-matter. The structure of the set of ideas he introduces is not that of a chain but of an organic whole, which obliges him to touch twice on certain aspect[s] of it" (Schopenhauer 1888: Preface).

### Translations

All the translations from Latin, Greek, French, and German are mine, except when otherwise specified.

### Bibliography

The bibliography serves as reference and indications for further reading. As a list of references, it gives all the details necessary to find a text quoted. For instance, (Santayana 1920: 107) refers to "Santayana, George. 1920. *Character and Opinion in the United States.* New York: Charles Scribner's Sons (p. 107)." As a guide for reading, it may be used to complement my essays: by way of example, the comparison of Peirce with Marx and Lenin (Deledalle 1990: 59–70), with Rossi-Landi and Morris (Petrilli, ed. 1992), with Sherlock Holmes (Sebeok and Umiker-Sebeok 1979: 203–250), with Eco (Tejera 1991), and others.

The French or, in a few recent cases, English papers I wrote on the various topics which are discussed in the present book are given chronologically in the following list.

## ORIGINAL PAPERS BY THE AUTHOR

*The papers totally or partially used are referred to the corresponding chapters of the book.*

1964. "Charles S. Peirce et les maîtres à penser de la philosophie européenne d'aujourd'hui." *Les Études philosophiques,* April–June: 283–295.

1970. "États-Unis, La pensée américaine." Pp. 637–642 in *Encyclopaedia Universalis,* vol. VI. Paris: Encyclopaedia Universalis France.

1973. "Peirce (C. S.), 1839–1914." Pp. 719–720 in *Encyclopaedia Universalis*, vol. XII. Paris: Encyclopaedia Universalis France.

1973. "Pragmatisme." Pp. 441–443 in *Encyclopaedia Universalis*, vol. XIII. Paris: Encyclopaedia Universalis France.

1976. "Peirce ou Saussure." *Semiosis* 1: 7–13.—Chapter 9.

1976. "Saussure et Peirce." *Semiosis* 2: 18–24.—Chapter 9.

1979. "Les pragmatistes et la nature du pragmatisme." *Revue philosophique de Louvain*, November: 471–486.

1980a. "Les articles pragmatistes de Charles S. Peirce." *Revue philosophique*, January–March: 17–29.—Chapter 3.

1980b. "Avertissement aux lecteurs de Peirce." *Langages*, n° 58: 25–27.—Chapter 3.

1981a. "English and French Versions of Charles S. Peirce's 'The Fixation of Belief' and 'How to Make Our Ideas Clear.'" *Transactions of the Charles S. Peirce Society*, Spring: 140–152.—Chapter 3.

1981b. "Charles S. Peirce, Un argument négligé en faveur de la réalité de Dieu." Présentation et traduction, *Revue philosophique de Louvain*, August: 327–349.—Chapter 17.

1981c. "Le representamen et l'objet dans la *semiosis* de Charles S. Peirce." *Semiotica*, 3/4: 195–200.

1983. "L'actualité de Peirce: abduction, induction, déduction." *Semiotica*, 3/4: 307–313.—Chapter 13.

1986a. "La sémiotique peircienne comme métalangage: Eléments théoriques et esquisse d'une application." Pp. 49–63 in *Semiotics and International Scholarship: Towards a Language of Theory*, ed. Jonathan D. Evans and André Helbo. Nato Asi Series. Dordrecht: Martinus Nijhoff.

1986b. "La sémiotique de Peirce *sub specie philosophiae*." *Estudis Semiotics/Estudios Semioticos*, 6/7: 7–15.—Chapter 2.

1987. "Quelle philosophie pour la sémiotique peircienne? Peirce et la sémiotique grecque." *Semiotica*, 3/4: 241–251.—Chapter 7.

1988a. "Epistémologie, logique et sémiotique." *Cruzeiro Semiotico*, n° 8: 13–21.—Chapter 13.

1988b. "Morris lecteur de Peirce?" *Degrés*, n° 54–55, Summer–Autumn: c 1–7.—Chapter 10.

1989a. "Victoria Lady Welby and Charles S. Peirce: Meaning and Signification." Pp. 133–149 in *Essays on Significs*, ed. H. Walter Schmitz. Amsterdam/Philadelphia: John Benjamins.—Chapter 8.

1989b. "Peirce: *The Nation*'s Philosophy." [Harvard] (*unpublished*)—Conclusion.

1990. "Traduire Charles S. Peirce." *TTR: Traduction, Terminologie, Rédaction*, 3–1: 15–29.—Chapter 5.

1991. "Reply to Jerzy Pelc's Questions of a Logician to a Philosopher." (VS 55/56: 13–28) (*unpublished*).—Chapter 6.

1992a. "La triade en sémiotique." Pp. 1299–1303 in *Signs of Humanity/L'homme et ses signes,* ed. Michel Balat, Janice Deledalle-Rhodes, and Gérard Deledalle, vol. III. Berlin/New York: Mouton de Gruyter.

1992b. "Percevoir et connaître." *Cruzeiro Semiotico,* 8: 65–76.—Chapter 14.

1992c. "Charles S. Peirce et les Transcendantaux de l'Être." *Semiosis,* 65–68: 36–47.—Chapter 15.

1993. "Charles S. Peirce. Les ruptures épistémologiques et les nouveaux paradigmes." Pp. 51–66 in *Charles Sanders Peirce, Apports récents et perspectives en épistémologie, sémiologie et logique,* ed. Denis Miéville.—Chapter 1.

1996. "Peirce and Jakobson: Cross-Readings." Prague (*unpublished*).—Chapter 11.

1997a. "The World of Signs Is the World of Objects." Pp. 15–27 in *World of Signs/World of Things,* ed. Jeff Bernard, Josef Wallmannsberger, and Gloria Withalm. Vienna: ÖGS.—Chapter 4.

1997b. "Media between Balnibarbi and Plato's Cave." Pp. 49–60 in *Semiotics of the Media,* ed. Winfried Nöth. Berlin: Walter de Gruyter.—Chapter 12.

1998a. "Peirce's Semiosis and Time." Pp. 247–251 in *Signs & Time / Zeit & Zeichen,* ed. Ernest W. B. Hess-Lüttich and Brigitte Schlieben-Lange. Gunter Narr Verlag Tübingen.—Chapter 4.

1998b. "Peirce, Theologian." Pp. 139–150 in *C. S. Peirce: Categories to Constantinople,* ed. Jaap van Brakel and Michael van Heerden. Leuven: Leuven University Press.—Chapter 17.

1999. "No Order without Chaos." Pp. 38–46 in *Caos e Ordem na Filosofia e Nas Ciências,* ed. Lucia Santaella e Jorge Albuquerque Vieira. São Paulo, Edição especial (n° 2) da revista *Face.*—Chapter 16.

# PART ONE

# *Semeiotic as Philosophy*

Philosophy is the attempt,—for as the word itself implies it is and must be imperfect—is the attempt to form a general informed conception of the *All.* [ ... ] Those who neglect philosophy have metaphysical theories as much as others— only they [have] rude, false, and wordy theories.

—Peirce (7.579)*

[I]t has never been in my power to study anything, [ ... ] except as a study of semeiotic.

—Peirce (Hardwick 1977: 85–86)

Just as Saussure's semiology is a branch of linguistics, Peirce's semeiotic is a branch of philosophy. Not of any philosophy, but a new philosophy, the paradigms of which are to be clearly defined if one wants to take full advantage of Peirce's theory of signs. The question will be approached from three sides. First, from the new philosophical paradigms which Peirce has proposed to replace the classical paradigms of Aristotle, Descartes, and Kant. Second, from a descriptive point of view, as the new theory of signs derived from Peirce's new paradigms. Third, in a comparative way, from the ideological aspect of pragmatism in the historical context of its conception in the seventies.

* References in the text by volume and paragraph to the *Collected Papers,* vols. 1–6, ed. Charles Hartshorne and Paul Weiss (Boston: Harvard University Press, 1931–1935), vols. 7–8, ed. Arthur W. Burks (Boston: Harvard University Press, 1958).

# - 1 -

# Peirce's New
# Philosophical Paradigms

Right from the beginning, the relations of America as New England with Europe were, from the philosophical view, ambiguous, when they were not simply difficult and, in the end, impossible. Peirce is in himself the *résumé* of this story which I plan to sum up, from the rejection of the European philosophical paradigms to the creation of a new set of paradigms which are not only Peirce's, but the new philosophical paradigms of America, and slowly but inevitably the new paradigms of the global world of tomorrow.

## PARADIGM SHIFTS

### *Against Aristotle*

#### The Syllogism: Against the Reduction to the First Figure (1866)

In *Memoranda Concerning the Aristotelean Syllogism (1866),* Peirce proves that no syllogism of the second or third figure can be reduced to the first, contrary to what Aristotle maintained.

> It is important to observe that the second and third figures are *apagogical,* that is, infer a thing to be false in order to avoid a false result which would follow from it. That which is thus reduced to an absurdity is a Case in the second figure, and a Rule in the third. (W1: 506–507)*

* References in the text by volume and page to the *Writings of Charles S. Peirce,* Peirce Edition Project, Bloomington and Indianapolis, Indiana University Press, vol. 1 (1982), vol. 2 (1984), vol. 3 (1986).

Of course, the second and third figures involve the principle of the first figure, "but the second and third figures contain other principles, besides" (W2: 514).

### For Another Conception of the Figures of the Syllogism

In the last article of the series "Illustrations of the Logic of Science" (1878), which was revised in 1893 as chapter XIII of *Search for a Method* (W3: 325-326), Peirce concludes that the three figures are therefore original and correspond to the three following types of inferences:

Fig. 1: Deduction (in the classical sense),
Fig. 2: Induction (in the classical sense),
Fig. 3: Hypothesis (Peircean abduction).

DEDUCTION

Rule.—All the beans from this bag are white.
Case.—These beans are from this bag.
∴  Result.—These beans are white.

INDUCTION

Case.—These beans are from this bag.
Result.—These beans are white.
∴  Rule.—All the beans from this bag are white.

HYPOTHESIS

Rule.—All the beans from this bag are white.
Result.—These beans are white.
∴  Case.—These beans are from this bag.

At this time, Peirce's classification is still Aristotelian, and even worse, if one may say so, since the three figures of the syllogism are no longer reducible and constitute three different types of inference. At this stage, Peirce's classification is Kantian (W3: 326).

We, accordingly, classify all inference as follows:

Inference

Deductive or Analytic                    Synthetic

Induction          Hypothesis

(2.623)

*Against Kant*

## Critique of Kant's Categories (1866 and 1867)

In his article of 1867 entitled *On a New List of Categories,* Peirce asks himself Kant's question: "How can the manifold of sensuous impressions be reduced to unity?" At first he gives a Kantian answer: "The unity to which the understanding reduces impressions is the unity of the proposition" (W2: 49). But he then immediately broaches the question of the passing from being to substance. Thus in the proposition "The stove is black," the stove is the *substance,* from which its blackness has not been differentiated and the copula "*is*" only explains that the blackness is confused with the substance of the stove "by the application to it of *blackness* as a predicate" (W2: 50). So being does not affect substance. Being and substance are indeed "the beginning and end of all conception," but "substance is inapplicable to a predicate, and being is equally so to a subject" (W2: 50).

How can we pass from being to substance? The question is no longer Kantian, but Peircean. Peirce here introduces a notion on which all his subsequent thinking will hinge: the notion of "prescission" (1.353), which is not a reciprocal process, unlike "discrimination" and "dissociation."

In an article dated 1866, but not published until long afterwards, Peirce drew up a table showing the difference between the three possible types of distinction, of which we give here a modified version in which 1 takes the place of "yes," 0 the place of "no":

| Can we think | | | | |
|---|---|---|---|---|
| | blue without red? | space without color? | color without space? | red without color? |
| By discrimination | 1 | 1 | 1 | 0 |
| By prescission | 1 | 1 | 0 | 0 |
| By dissociation | 1 | 0 | 0 | 0 |

Table 1.1. The three types of distinctions

It must be noted that it is not mathematical space nor Kantian space which is in question here, but the physical, in the sense of quantitative, space that Aristotle opposed to the intelligible, and the *étendue* that Descartes opposed to *pen-*

*sée*. At this stage of the development of Peirce's philosophy, an abstract concept like color could be classified in the same way, i.e., in the order of Aristotle's passive intelligible and of Descartes's *pensée*.

In 1867, Peirce applied the process of precision to the conceptions or categories which he shows to be indispensable for the passing from being to substance: quality, which he here calls a "ground," the relation with a correlate, and the mediating representation which he already calls "an interpretant." Let us remark that the Peircean categories owe nothing either to Kant nor to Aristotle.

To say "the stove is black" is to say that the stove embodies blackness (W2: 52). But a quality is what it is because it is different from another. Hence the conception of relation to a correlate (here: color). The conception of relation to a correlate itself requires that of representation. Now a comparison can be made only by a "mediating representation which represents the relate (quality) as standing for a correlate with which the mediating representation is itself in relation" (W2: 53).

Prescission shows that the three conceptions are *hierarchical*. The mediating representation or interpretant (a Third) presupposes the reference or relation (a Second) which itself presupposes quality or a ground (a First). But this relation is not reciprocal: quality or ground (First) is what it is in itself, whether there are many other qualities or not, or whether they are compared or not, if there are. Relation (Second) does not change, whether it be interpreted or not in a mediating comparison (Third). But relation will nonetheless imply the totality of qualities (Second) and there can be no mediating comparison (Third) without relation (Second) nor quality (First). In short, Peirce's categories are *ordinal* and not cardinal. A Third is triadic, a Second dyadic, and a First monadic (W2: 55). Which can be expressed in the following table:

| Can we prescind | | | |
|---|---|---|---|
| quality (a First) from relation (a Second)? | relation (a Second) from the interpretant (a Third)? | the interpretant (a Third) from relation (a Second)? | relation (a Second) from quality (a First)? |
| 1 | 1 | 0 | 0 |

Table 1.2. Prescission

In 1867, Peirce is still Aristotelian. The three conceptions or categories he proposes are "intermediate" (W2: 54–55): between the conceptions or categories of being and substance which he does not reject. Quality in itself (blackness) is for him, as for Aristotle, the ground of a quality embodied in a substance (the stove). Peirce says explicitly: "Reference to a ground cannot be prescinded from being, but being can be prescinded from it" (W2: 53).

## *Against Descartes*

The first articles of the series "Illustrations of the logic of science" (1878) quoted above, with reference to the figures of syllogism, are aimed at Descartes. The first is a critique of methodological doubt and the second a critique of evidence by intuition.

### Critique of Methodological Doubt

In the first article, "The Fixation of Belief," Peirce objects that one cannot, as Descartes said, begin by doubting everything, that absolute doubt, even were it methodological, is impossible, for one cannot pretend to doubt. We begin with all our prejudices, all our spontaneous beliefs. Doubt is in fact a state of uneasiness and dissatisfaction from which we are always struggling to free ourselves, and to pass into the state of belief.

By *belief,* Peirce does not mean religious belief, but what the Scottish philosopher Alexander Bain defined as "that upon which a man is prepared to act" (5.12), or, in other words, as the establishment or constitution of a habit, with the result that the different sorts of belief are distinguished by the different modes of action to which they give rise.

### Critique of Evidence by Intuition

In the second article, entitled "How to Make Our Ideas Clear," which is the founding article of pragmatism, although the word "pragmatism" does not appear in it, Peirce asks how we can distinguish an idea which *is* clear from an idea which *seems* clear. Intuitive evidence, he replies, does not enable us to see the difference.

This is hardly unexpected. Already in 1868 Peirce had criticized intuition of any kind, as well that of the psychology of faculties as that of Descartes or of Kant. Ten years later he is able to reply to the question he asks in "How to Make Our Ideas Clear," thanks to "the scientific revolution that found its climax in the 'Origin of Species'" (Dewey 1910: 19). The quotation is from Dewey, who would advocate an identical method, on the base of quite another experience.

It is only *action* which can differentiate a genuinely clear and distinct idea from one which has only the appearance of clearness and distinctness. If *one* idea leads to two different actions, then there is not one idea, but two. If *two* ideas lead to the same action, then there are not two ideas, but only one. Hence the pragmatic maxim: "Consider what effects, which might conceivably have practical bearings, we conceive the object of our conception to have. Then, our conception of these effects is the whole of our conception of the object" (W3: 266).

It will be noticed that Descartes was not far removed from pragmatism when he wrote in *Discours de la méthode*:

Il me semblait que je pourrais rencontrer beaucoup plus de vérité dans *les raisonnements* que chacun fait touchant les affaires qui lui importent, et *dont l'événement le doit punir bientôt après s'il a mal jugé,* que dans ceux que fait un homme de lettres dans son cabinet, touchant des spéculations qui ne produisent aucun effet, *et qui ne lui sont d'aucune conséquence,* sinon que peut-être il en tirera d'autant plus de vanité qu'elles seront plus éloignées du sens commun. (Descartes 1952: 131, italics mine)

## THE PEIRCEAN PARADIGMS

It was only after 1885 that Peirce was able to propose a new philosophy, for he had just conceived, to replace Aristotelian logic, a logic of relatives which could do without substance. Indeed, it was with the *substantive* conception of the world and the mind that Peirce had always had difficulties. And it was the logic of relatives which enabled him to deliver a new Discourse of Method and to evolve a new phenomenology, which he called "phaneroscopy," in which substance has no place.

After saying a few words about the logic of relatives and describing briefly Peirce's new methodology, I shall examine phaneroscopy in greater detail, as without it one cannot understand and appreciate Peirce's semeiotic, which is only the application of phaneroscopy to the problem of knowledge.

### The Logic of Relatives

It is a fact that Peirce became interested in the logic of relatives long before he read De Morgan in 1866, even if he drew the epistemological implications from it after writing his "Description of a Notation for the Logic of Relatives," derived from Boole, in 1870, and the phaneroscopic implications after writing his article "On the Algebra of Logic," published in 1885 in the *American Journal of Mathematics.* Briefly, Peirce substituted, for De Morgan's "relative terms" (W2: 359), and Aristotle's inference by "substantive" inclusion, inference by "transitive" inclusion (W2: 367).

### The New Methodology

In 1903, in his sixth lecture on pragmatism, Peirce no longer divides inference into analytic and synthetic inference in the Kantian way, but describes it as a dialectical process in three stages, the order of which is: abduction (already proposed by Peirce in 1878 under the name of hypothesis), deduction, and induction. It is unfortunate that Peirce used classical terms to denote two of these stages, as empirical induction has nothing to do with the process of testing deduction which constitutes Peircean induction.

Abduction is the process of forming an explanatory hypothesis. It is the only logical operation which introduces any new idea; for induction does nothing but determine a value, and deduction merely evolves the necessary consequences of a pure hypothesis.

Deduction proves that something *must be;* Induction shows that something *actually is* operative; Abduction merely suggests that something *may be.*

Its only justification is that from its suggestion deduction can draw a prediction which can be tested by induction, and that, if we are ever to learn anything or to understand phenomena at all, it must be by abduction that this is to be brought about. (5.171)

## Phaneroscopy

Phaneroscopy replaces Kantian phenomenology. Peirce maintains, like Kant, that we can apprehend the world only by reducing the manifold of phenomena or *phanera* to unity by recourse, not to the *a priori* forms of "sensibility," and the *a priori* categories of understanding, but by recourse to those modes of being which Firstness, Secondness, and Thirdness are for him.

The substitution of "phaneron" for "phenomenon" must not be underestimated. It is not another one of Peirce's terminological "quirks" (no more than are the other neologisms he introduced), but the expression of a genuine paradigm shift. The phenomenon is no longer what *appears* to consciousness—which is the literal meaning of φαινόμενον, and which consequently has to do with psychology—but what is *apparent,* independent of the fact that we perceive it—which is the literal sense of φανερόν and which has to do with logic.

Historically, Peirce was first, from 1851 to 1867, an out-and-out nominalist: only Seconds—concrete individual existents—were real. Reality and existence were then synonymous. In 1857, he wrote: "Reality [refers] to the existence of the object itself" (W1: 18).

From 1867 onwards, more precisely during the winter of 1867–1868, in an unpublished item in which he criticized positivism, Peirce distinguished between existence and reality. What is real is "that which is independently of our belief and which could be properly inferred by the most thorough discussion of the sum of all impressions of sense whatever" (W2: 127). It will be remarked that this kind of reality, although general, is a sort of very classical Third, since it appears as the generalization of Seconds. It was not before the logic of relatives and the new methodology that Thirds were no longer abstractions, but operative rules, *a priori* empty, of the type "if *p,* then *q.*" Are they still realities?

It was not until much later, about 1890, that Peirce conceded that Firsts are also real. In 1891, he wrote: "In the beginning [ . . . ] there was a chaos of impersonalized feeling, which being without connection or regularity would properly be without existence." However, "this feeling, sporting here and there in pure arbitrariness, would have started the germ of a generalizing tendency" (6.33).

### FIRSTNESS

This Firstness is no longer the Firstness of the New List of 1867. Whereas in 1867 it could not be prescinded from being and was consequently not really first, in 1890 "the idea of the absolutely first must be entirely separated from all conception of or reference to anything else" (1.357).

The contrast is striking:

(1) 1867: "[T]he conception of *this stove* is the more immediate, that of *black* the more mediate" (W2: 52).

   1890: "The first must [ ... ] be [ ... ] immediate" (1.357).

(2) 1867: Quality is what synthesizes the manifold of sense. Thus in " 'The stove is black,' the stove is the *substance,* from which its blackness has not been differentiated, and the 'is,' while it leaves the substance just as it was seen, explains its confusedness, by the application to it of *blackness* as a predicate" (W2: 50).

   1890: The first "precedes all synthesis and all differentiation; it has no unity and no parts" (1.357).

(3) 1867: "The conception of *being* arises upon the formation of a proposition. A proposition always has, besides a term to express the substance, another to express the quality of that substance" (W2: 52).

   1890: The first "cannot be articulately thought: assert it, and it has already lost its characteristic innocence" (1.357).

(4) 1867: Quality is "a pure abstraction" (W2: 53). "The *Ground* is the self abstracted from the concreteness which implies the possibility of an other" (W2: 55).

   1890: The first is "present, immediate, fresh, new, initiative, original, spontaneous, free, vivid, conscious and evanescent" (1.357).

SECONDNESS

There is no more substance, not because Peirce has come back to his original nominalism, but because the logic of relatives has transformed his conception of the proposition. In 1867, to Secondness still belonged "those [representations] whose relation to their objects consists in a correspondence in fact, and these may be termed *indices* or *signs*" (W2: 56). In 1885, the index no longer denotes a plurality of objects (1.563); it has become, with the help of O. H. Mitchell, the existential quantifier. It was then that Peirce, in his article in the *American Journal of Mathematics* (1885), quoted above, divided the constitutive elements of the proposition into two classes, which Peirce called respectively "token" and "index." To be more precise, the token is the replica—case, instance, occurrence—of a legisign or type. It is therefore a degenerate third, and it is in this sense that "symbol" must be understood here as it is used in mathematics: a "symbol" is general by description, but always singularly inscribed within the space of its representation. On the contrary, the index is a genuine second:

Without tokens there would be no generality in the statements, for they are the only general signs; and generality is essential to reasoning. [ ... ] But tokens alone do not state what is the subject of discourse; and this can, in fact, not be described in general terms; it can only be indicated. The actual world cannot be distinguished from a world of imagination by any description. Hence the need of pronouns and indices, and the more complicated the subject the greater the need of them. (3.363)

The forefinger or index finger shows very well what an index is:

The index asserts nothing; it only says "There!" It takes hold of our eyes, as it were, and forcibly directs them to a particular object, and there it stops. Demonstrative and relative pronouns are nearly pure indices, because they denote things without describing them; so are the letters on a geometrical diagram, and the subscript numbers which in algebra distinguish one value from another without saying what those values are. (3.361)

Although logicians are satisfied with these two quantifiers, Peirce goes further in his analysis and shows that they are insufficient for reasoning; for reasoning we also need logical diagrams and sensorial—most of the time visual—"images," which are icons:

With these two kinds of signs alone [symbols and tokens] any proposition can be expressed; but it cannot be reasoned upon, for reasoning consists in the observation that where certain relations subsist certain others are found, and it accordingly requires the exhibition of the relations reasoned within an icon. (3.363)

The article of 1885 thus marks a definitive break in Peirce's philosophy of logic: the index is no longer conceptual, as it was in 1867, but, properly speaking, "existential"—a Second.

Take the proposition "This is red." I do not take the proposition "The stove is black," since Peirce has now rejected the subject as substance, although I could have done so, as we shall see. In the proposition "This is red," "this" is obviously not a substance, although it denotes an object. Of course, one could object that "This is red" is not a proposition, but is rather, as Peirce suggested in 1867, an incomplete sign. Incomplete, because, although implying the concepts of denotation and object, the object itself would never be known immediately. Would it refer to an object among other objects that another previous sign represented, but which could no longer be precisely named?

My questions are in the conditional mood for two reasons: (1) After 1885, Peirce no longer maintains this idea; and (2) Many logicians and philosophers still think, as Bertrand Russell did, that "This is red" is an incomplete sign.

What is the existential quantifier for Peirce after 1885 and what does it imply? The answer is in the description he gives of it in terms of "haecceity," a word he borrowed from Duns Scotus, but which he uses in Ockham's sense. I can say "This is red," not because "this" is a general term standing for a singular thing existing in the external world; on the contrary, if I can say "This is red," it is because the "this-ness"—haecceity—makes something exist. Haecceity is a principle of individuation and existence.

***Principle of Individuation*** This is an experience which does not consist in a "sensory perception." Of course, Peirce said in 1903: "[w]e perceive objects brought before us; but that which we especially experience—the kind of thing to which the word "experience" is more particularly applied—is an event" (1.336), something indescribable, unique, individual.

> A whistling locomotive passes at high speed close beside me. As it passes the note of the whistle is suddenly lowered from a well-understood cause. I perceive the whistle, if you will. I have, at any rate, a sensation of it. But I cannot be said to have a sensation of the change of note. I have a sensation of the lower note. But the cognition of the change is of a more intellectual kind. That I experience rather than perceive. It is [the] special field of experience to acquaint us with events, with changes of perception. Now that which particularly characterizes sudden changes of perception is a shock. [ . . . ] It is more particularly to changes and contrasts of perception that we apply the word "experience." (1.336)

***Principle of Existence*** This uniqueness of experience is thus the effect of a coupling: action–reaction, effort–resistance. Because haecceity is a principle of individuation, it is a principle of existence:

> Existence is that mode of being which lies in opposition to another. To say that a table exists is to say that it is hard, heavy, opaque, resonant, that is, produces immediate effects upon the senses, and also that it produces purely physical effects, attracts the earth (that is, is heavy), dynamically reacts against other things (that is, has inertia), resists pressure (that is, is elastic), has a definite capacity for heat, etc. To say there is a phantom table by the side of it incapable of affecting any senses or of producing any physical effects whatever, is to speak of an imaginary table. A thing without oppositions *ipso facto* does not exist. (1.457)

In short, I can say "This is red," although not because "this" stands for a substance, as, in this case, the existential quantifier would be only a constitutive element of the universal quantifier and would have no proper part or function, as was the case in Aristotle's logic. I can say "This is red," because the existential quantifier is a *sui generis* function whose nature is radically different from that of the universal quantifier and because, in addition, it constitutes the act of foundation of the world of existents without which the universal quantifier could not exercise its function of generalization.

THIRDNESS

The universal quantifier is Third. It says: "For every *x*, if *x* is *a*, then *x* is *b*." It is not an inductive generalization from particular cases. It is a rule or law of which the cases are instances. The relation of the universal and the singular is that of the type and the token. The token is a replica of the type, a replica which is an existent whose very existence was not of course necessary, but necessarily possible, according to the hierarchy of categories.

Does this conception of the universal condemn us to an aggravated form of nominalism? I do not think so, for the reason that the opposition between nominalism and realism has no longer any sense since pragmatism defined the idea as what it does. We are beyond nominalism and realism. The mind is in the world and in continuity with it. The law is a natural as well as a logical process. As a third without occurrences, the law is empty and as a second, the occurrence without law is blind. As for direct experience, a first, it is indeed "purely and simply," but it is not a cognition, because there is nothing intrinsically substantial to know beyond the triadic process which confers generality (thirdness) on the singular object (secondness) of one's direct experience (firstness).

# - 2 -

# Peirce's Philosophy of Semeiotic

Just as the Newtonian notion of Space as God cannot be separated from Newton's physics, nor Einstein's strict determinism from his physics of relativity, the following facts concerning the thought of Charles S. Peirce, the inventor of triadic semiotics, cannot and must not be neglected. Peirce is an evolutionist empiricist whose intellectual mentor was Kant and whose science of reference was chemistry and method of thinking the experimental method of the laboratory. Peirce's empiricism is not factual empiricism, "factual" in the material sense of the term. It is empiricism rescued from facts, rescued from itself: the phenomenological empiricism of Kant. Of course, Peirce is not saved from this danger by the *a priori* forms (space and time) of sensibility, but by the transformist belief in the continuity of experience in space and time. That Peirce, like Plato, has a special taste for mathematical explanations of non-mathematical (and sometimes mathematical) concepts is indubitable. I am thinking in particular of his theory of infinitesimals which are as "real" for him as the "continua," and which justify in his view the discrete uniqueness of existents. We shall see in a moment how Peirce proves mathematically that three categories are necessary to "think the world." However, mathematics is not the key to his semiotic thought, or rather, to his thought, for, as we shall see, semiotics is not a theory proposed by Peirce concerning what are nowadays called signs, but the very definition of thought. The key to Peirce's thought is chemistry. The constituent elements of the continuum, although discrete, are not "atomic" for him as they are for Wittgenstein, they have "valencies" which enable them to combine with other elements and indefinitely to constitute and reconstitute the continuum, spatially, temporally, and mentally. The continuum proceeds and extends irreversibly. How many "valencies" may an element have? In fact, we do not know, for the infinitesimal is inconceivable outside of any conception as will later be shown by the new realist Ralph Barton Perry. What is certain, according to Peirce, is that we can think only in terms of three: the monadic relation (if this expression means anything), the dyadic relation, and the triadic relation. Of the first we can say nothing: it is pure possibility; of the second we could say nothing if the third were not there to recognize it: the second can only be acknowledged, it is a "brutal shock," a pure "fact" of interaction; of the third we cannot say everything, and even if we could it would not be enough. The third is thought mediating between man and the world: a continuous construction or rather reconstruction which is logical and not psychological, experimental and not descriptive.

The three modalities of valency have engendered Peirce's three phenomenological categories: firstness, secondness, and thirdness, respectively, the mode of being as first, the mode of being as second, and the mode of being as third.

The new categories are the result of Peirce's critique of Kant's phenomenology. I shall not expatiate on that point. I shall limit myself first to describing Peirce's mathematical proof of the necessity of those three categories and then to analyze the paper of 1866/1867 in which Peirce proposed his new list.

There are three categories, no less and no more. Let us suppose that the world is a unique sheet of assertion. Let us call it "1." What can we say of "1"? Nothing—and, of course, as it is "unique," nobody is there to say anything. So to speak, "1" is not even there. It is not "something," and it is not "nothing," unless as *non-being*, in the Aristotelian sense of sheer "possibility." To conceive of "1," "1" has to have a limit and consequently we cannot have "1" without a "2" which delimits "1" on the sheet of assertion:

"1" can only *exist* in a pair. But, as Peirce points out, "it is impossible to form a genuine three by any modification of the pair without introducing something of a different nature from the unit and the pair" (1.363).

In other words, to have a pair (1, 2) one needs a "3" which mediates between "1" and "2":

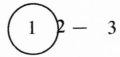

Which Peirce explains in an iconic way:

The fact that A presents B with a gift C, is a triple relation, and as such cannot possibly be resolved into any combination of dual relations. Indeed, the very idea of a combination involves that of thirdness, for a combination is something which is what it is owing to the parts which it brings into mutual relationship. But we may waive that consideration, and still we cannot build up the fact that A presents C to B by any aggregate of dual relations between A and B, B and C, and C and A. A may enrich B, B may receive C, and A may part with C, and yet A need not necessarily give C to B. For that, it would be necessary that these three dual relations should not only coexist, but be welded into one fact. Thus we see that a triad cannot be analysed into dyads. (1.363)

This is the mathematical proof of the necessity of the three categories of Peirce, and of the principle of their "hierarchization": No *three* without *two*, no *two* without *one*. Consequently, a first is monadic: it has only one element, i.e., itself; a second is dyadic: it has a dyadic relation with a first with which it forms an indecomposable dyad; a third is triadic: it has a triadic relation with a second and a first with which it forms an indecomposable triad. Thus the categories are "ordered": they are ordinal and not cardinal.

To sum up, the three categories are thus Firstness, which is sheer possibility, Secondness, which is a singular or unique existent (feeling, fact or thought, or whatever), and Thirdness, which is mediation as formal relation.

Let us remark that the above definitions are themselves formal. Now, a Third cannot be an empty mediation; it includes a Second, which is not an idea of existent, but this or that existent, and if this existent happens to be, it is because it has been a possible First.

Why do we stop at three? Peirce shows, still in an iconic way, that "a four can be analyzed into threes":

Take the quadruple fact that A sells C to B for the price D. This is a compound of two facts: first, that A makes with C a certain transaction, which we may name E; and second, that this transaction E is a sale of B for the price D. Each of these two facts is a triple fact, and their combination makes up [as] genuine [a] quadruple fact as can be found. The explanation of this striking difference is not far to seek. A dual relative term, such as "lover" or "servant," is a sort of blank form, where there are two places left blank. I mean that in building a sentence round "lover," as the principal word of the predicate, we are at liberty to make anything we see fit the subject, and then, besides that, anything we please the object of the action of loving. But a triple relative term such as "giver" has two correlates, and is thus a blank form with three places left blank. Consequently, we can take two of these triple relatives and fill up one blank place in each with the same letter, X, which has only the force of a pronoun or identifying index, and then the two taken together will form a whole having four blank places; and from that we can go on in a similar way to any higher number. But when we attempt to imitate this proceeding with dual relatives, and combine two of them by means of an X, we find we only have two blank places in the combination, just as we had in either of the relatives taken by itself. A road with only three-way forkings may have any number of termini, but no number of straight roads put end on end will give more than two termini. Thus any number, however large, can be built out of triads; and consequently no idea can be involved in such a number, radically different from the idea of three. I do not mean to deny that the higher numbers may present interesting special configurations from which notions may be derived of more or less general applicability; but these cannot rise to the height of philosophical categories so fundamental as those that have been considered. (1.363)

## A NEW LIST OF CATEGORIES (1866/1867)

The new list was born from the critique of Kant's list of categories. I should like to draw from this critique, which can be read in "A New List of Categories" which appeared in the *Proceedings of the American Academy of Arts and Sciences* in May 1867, a conception of mental distinctions which it would be very helpful, I think, to evoke when use is made of the distinctions proposed by Peirce in semiotics and elsewhere. But we must not forget that the three new categories were born in a dualistic context.

Already in the first paragraph, Peirce says that the theory of categories gives rise to "a conception of graduation" (1.546). Whence the necessity of not confusing "prescission," which Peirce applies to the three categories, with the other two distinctions, which are "discrimination" and "dissociation" (1.549). Peirce does not say that all the distinctions he will ever make in the future will be "prescissions"; he simply says that these three types of distinction must not be confused, and that "prescission" is the type of distinction which best explains the hierarchized character of categorial relations. We must, I think, take seriously this warning of Peirce's, and not "formally" apply "prescission" to "every kind of separation" (1.549). Thus some Peircean distinctions are not hierarchized and consequently cannot be assimilated to the categorial modes of being.

"Discrimination" does not imply any hierarchization of terms, it only distinguishes their meaning: "red" is not "blue," "color" is not "space" nor "space" "color," but "red" is a "color."

"Dissociation" does not imply hierarchization either. It pertains to the association of ideas. Some associations impose themselves of necessity, others do not: "red" does not necessarily evoke "blue," but "red" cannot be dissociated from "color," "color" from "space," nor "space" from "color."

"Prescission" introduces hierarchization. The word "prescission" comes from the verb "praescindere" ("prescind"). "Prescission" "is not a reciprocal process" (1.549) as are the other two distinctions. Prescission is not simply a conventional mental distinction like discrimination, and does not take into account, as dissociation does, habits or associations which are purely accidental. Prescission is a logical process which "consists in a definite conception or *supposition* of one part of an object, without any supposition of the other." Thus, if I have, by definition, only the conception or *supposition* of the "red" of an object without the conception or *supposition* of anything else, I can prescind "red" from "color" and *a fortiori* from "space." If I have the conception of "space," I cannot prescind it either from "color" or from "red" (1. 549).

We have here the principle of the hierarchization (by prescission) of the categories which we have described mathematically above.

## SEMIOSIS AND ITS COMPONENTS

Formally, the interplay of the three categories may take multiple aspects according to its sphere of activity. Whatever the latter is—the universe or communication—semiosis is always the triadic process by which a first determines a third to refer to a second to which itself refers. Semiosis, which is a process of inference, is the proper object of semiotics. The word "semiosis" was borrowed by Peirce from the Epicurean philosopher Philodemus for whom σημιοσις is an inference from signs (5.484). Semiosis is, of course, an experience which everyone has at every moment of life, but semiotics, which is the theory of this experience, is another name for logic, "the quasi-necessary, or formal, doctrine of signs" (2.227). Peirce distinguishes sign-action, which is itself another name for semiosis, from the sign-representamen, which is the point of departure of semiotic inference. This dual function led Peirce to use the word "sign" when speaking of the sign in action, and "representamen" when analyzing the constitutive elements of semiosis. But, unfortunately, this usage is not constant, and varies (which is totally justified from a semiotic point of view) according to the audience Peirce is addressing. For my part, I will abide by this distinction (in the sense of discrimination and not of prescission). The formal constituents of semiosis are thus the representamen, the interpretant, and the object, which Peirce calls the Immediate Object within semiosis in order to distinguish (discriminate) the object outside the sign, or rather outside semiosis, and which he calls the Dynamical Object. The representamen is first, the object second, and the interpretant third. These three constituents have no separate existence of their own, no more than have the *signifiant* ("signifier") and the *signifié* ("signified") in the Saussurean sign. It must always be remembered that for Peirce, semiosis as triadic sign is indecomposable. Its components are subsumed; they are that without which there would be no semiosis.

> A REPRESENTAMEN is a subject of a triadic relation TO a second, called its OBJECT, FOR a third, called its INTERPRETANT, this triadic relation being such that the REPRESENTAMEN determines its interpretant to stand in the same triadic relation to the same object for some interpretant. (1.541)

The representamen, the object, and the interpretant stand for relations or functions and not terms in relation. In other words, they can never have other relations or fulfil other functions in another semiosis. In fact, it is the other way round.

The interpretant in one semiosis will become a representamen in another. It is the "terms" whose functions change and not the reverse. In short, the three constituents of semiosis or sign-action are "sign-representamens" playing one of the three roles: "subject," "immediate object," and "interpretant," of the triadic relation (2.274).

If we develop our analysis by trichotomizing each of these components, we can distinguish (discriminate) nine types of relation or function instead of three, namely, for the representamen: the qualisign, the sinsign, and the legisign; for the object: the icon, the index, and the symbol; for the interpretant: the rhema, the dicisign, and the argument. If we make triads of these, we shall be able to distin-guish (by prescission) ten classes of possible semioses.

|                | 1 | 2 | 3 |
|----------------|---|---|---|
| Representamen  | Qualisign | Sinsign | Legisign |
| Object         | Icon | Index | Symbol |
| Interpretant   | Rhema | Dicisign | Argument |

Table 2.1.  The three trichotomies of signs

|      | R  | O  | I  |                              |
|------|----|----|----|------------------------------|
| I    | R1 | O1 | I1 | Rhematic Iconic *Qualisign*  |
| II   | R2 | O1 | I1 | Rhematic *Iconic Sinsign*    |
| III  | R2 | O2 | I1 | *Rhematic Indexical Sinsign* |
| IV   | R2 | O2 | I2 | *Dicent* Indexical *Sinsign* |
| V    | R3 | O1 | I1 | Rhematic *Iconic Legisign*   |
| VI   | R3 | O2 | I1 | *Rhematic Indexical Legisign* |
| VII  | R3 | O2 | I2 | *Dicent Indexical Legisign*  |
| VIII | R3 | O3 | I1 | *Rhematic Symbolic* Legisign |
| IX   | R3 | O3 | I2 | *Dicent Symbolic* Legisign   |
| X    | R3 | O3 | I3 | *Argument* Symbolic Legisign |

Table 2.2. The ten classes of signs. All expressions, such as R1, O2, I3,
should be read according to Peirce in the following way:
a Representamen "which is" a First, an Object "which is"
a Second, an Interpretant "which is" a Third (8.353).

We must here insist once again on the functional character of these distinc-tions: what is an index in one semiosis may be a symbol in another. Take, for instance, the symptom of an illness. As representamen it is a legisign, for both as a word and as a phenomenon it belongs to a system ruled by laws. But its relation to the object differs according to the type of interpretant functioning in the semiosis. If this symptom is referred to in a lecture on medicine as always characterizing a certain illness, the symptom is a symbol. If the doctor encounters it while he is examining a patient, the symptom is the index of an illness. Once again, nothing is in itself icon, index, or symbol. It should be pointed out here that this misapprehension is often present in the discourse of linguists and literary critics who have appropriated this part of Peirce's theory without troubling to find out in what context he uses this terminology. It is the analysis of a given semiosis (and not the formal analysis of the semiotic triad) which will tell us the "nature" of its constituents. And this analysis must respect the hierarchy of the categories. If a representamen is a sinsign, and as such singular and unique, it is a second which cannot be prescinded from a first, but can be prescinded from a third. By consequence of its relation with its object it can only be an index, and this index can in no case assume the role of a symbol, because the symbol is third. Nothing is more flexible, more open, more dynamic than Peirce's semiotic theory. To confuse the formal rigor of his definitions with a mechanical empirical description is to misunderstand the matter completely.

Which does not mean, on one hand, that Peircean semiotic analysis is easy:

> It is a nice problem to say to what class a given sign belongs; since all the circumstances of the case have to be considered. But it is seldom requisite to be very accurate; for if one does not locate the sign precisely, one will easily come near enough to its character for any ordinary purpose of logic. (2.265)

And which does not mean, on the other hand, that analysis is the ultimate aim of the Peircean analysis. Semiosis, before becoming an object of formal analysis, is an experienced inference which cannot be other than triadic, but which, because it is experienced, cannot analyze itself without destroying itself. An experienced semiosis is, as John Dewey said, a pure transaction in which the terms in relation cannot be distinguished from one another, nor from the transaction. In William James's words, it is a "transitive," not a "substantive" experience.

## SEMIOSIS, INQUIRY, AND TRUTH

To say of a semiosis that it is an inference, is thus not to make of it exclusively an object of formal analysis. Inference is a method of thought. That is why Peircean semiotics, rather than being another name for logic in the formal sense in which we use the word today, is another name for epistemology. Peircean semiotics answers the question: How do we think? Is inference the synonym of induction or of deduction? Peirce's reply is qualified. According to him, we are not doomed to suffer under the double yoke of the imperialism of facts and the imperialism of laws. To think is to "enquire," to "grope" for something, to think we have found it and act "as if" we had for a time, before recommencing that "quest" for truth which Peirce calls "fallibilist":

> Truth is that concordance of an abstract statement with the ideal limit towards which endless investigation would tend to bring scientific belief, which concor-

dance the abstract statement may possess by virtue of the confession of its inaccuracy and one-sidedness, and this confession is an essential ingredient of truth. (5.565)

Like semiosis, inference, which is its epistemological equivalent, is a triadic process; and if it is true that its three constitutive movements—abduction (introduced by Peirce), induction, and deduction—differ from one another, it would be a mistake to conceive of them as three methods of thinking which are distinct. They can certainly be distinguished, but the process is one. Abduction is first; it is "a method of forming a general prediction without any positive assurance that it will succeed either in the special case or usually, its justification being that it is the only possible hope of regulating our future conduct rationally" (2.270). Induction is second; it is founded on "past experience" and henceforth "gives us strong encouragement to hope that it will be successful in the future" (2.270). Deduction is carried out on the third level; it is "an argument whose Interpretant represents that it belongs to a general class of possible arguments precisely analogous which are such that in the long run of experience the greater part of those whose premises are true will have true conclusions" (2.267). The passage from one to another, of course, reproduces the process of semiosis: an unverifiable abduction suggests a general idea from which deduction draws various consequences which are put to the test by induction. Inference, of whatever kind— from that of pure mathematics to that of the most ordinary conversation—is, like semiosis, experimental.

## CONCLUSION

A problem raised constantly in discussions about Peircean semiotics is that of the distinction between the immediate object in a semiosis and the dynamical object outside a semiosis. What we have said should help to solve this problem. In the first place, the distinction is a discrimination, a distinction of meaning and not a de facto separation. The immediate object is a formal object. In the second place, semiosis defined as inference is an epistemological process which knows no boundaries (there is not thought on one side and the world on the other): there is only one "object" which can take the name of immediate or dynamic according to the point of view from which one is speaking, but which is what it is, and whose genuine nature appears more clearly as far as research or inquiry or the semiotic process proceeds in time and space, not toward a truth which would correspond to a pre-established reality, but toward the truth of a reality which is constructed at the same time. Reality is not making signs to us, it is we who produce the interpretants which become signs which will be tomorrow—a cumulative tomorrow to the end of time—the truth-reality eternally temporary and fallible.

Peirce's semiotics is a philosophy of lucid—that is to say, blind—hope. As Jean Wahl said:

Thus, on crutches, does Philosophy limp forward,
She has not all eternity to arrive,
Like the wisdom of God,
But knows that where she will sit,
There will she be as well
As anywhere else.
Blindfold, she sees
A long, long road
Beyond her and behind.
Her brows are horned, she weeps,
Over her tomb at the threshold
Of Chanaan.
(Wahl 1944: 6)

# - 3 -

# Peirce's First Pragmatic Papers (1877–1878)

## THE FRENCH VERSION AND THE PARIS COMMUNE

Two of Charles S. Peirce's articles—both linked to pragmatism—published in *The Popular Science Monthly:* "The Fixation of Belief" in November 1877: 1–15 and "How To Make Our Ideas Clear" in January 1878: 286–302, appeared in French in the *Revue philosophique:* "Comment se fixe la croyance" in December 1878: 553–569 and "Comment rendre nos idées claires" in January 1879: 39–57.

We know from a letter written by Peirce to Christine Ladd-Franklin in 1904 and published in *The Journal of Philosophy* in 1916, that in the course of his voyage to Europe, "between Hoboken and Plymouth," Peirce wrote "an article about pragmatism in French," "by way of practice," since he was to speak in French at a meeting of the Geodesic Association in Paris. He then translated his article "of November 1877" into French. The article which he wrote directly in French is therefore "Comment rendre nos idées claires" and that which he translated is "The Fixation of Belief."

About this pair of articles, Peirce says in a note clipped inside the volume entitled "Papers in Logic" which contained them and which he had left to the Johns Hopkins University Library: "The two French versions, which I prefer to the English of the same papers, derive their merit from the skill of M. Léo Seguin, who was killed in Tunis in 1881."

This poses two problems which are closely connected: Firstly, are the French versions of these articles better than the English versions, and secondly, what does the French of the articles published in the *Revue philosophique* owe to Léo Seguin?

It is certain that Peirce always considered the French version of "Comment rendre nos idées claires" as the authoritative text for his pragmatic thought. And it is the French version of the maxim of pragmatism that he quoted in his first lecture on pragmatism in Cambridge on March 26, 1903:

> The Maxim of Pragmatism, as I originally stated it, *Revue philosophique* VII, is as follows:
> Considérer quels sont les effets pratiques que nous pensons pouvoir être produits par l'objet de notre conception. La conception de tous ces effets est la conception complète de l'objet. Pour développer le sens d'une pensée, il faut donc simplement déterminer quelles habitudes elle produit, car le sens d'une chose consiste simplement dans les habitudes qu'elle implique. Le caractère d'une habitude dépend de la façon dont elle peut nous faire agir non pas seulement dans telle circonstance probable, mais dans toute circonstance possible, si improbable qu'elle puisse être. Ce qu'est une habitude dépend de ces deux points: quand et comment elle fait agir. Pour le premier point: quand? tout stimulant à l'action dérive d'une perception; pour le second point: comment? le but de toute action est d'amener au résultat sensible. Nous atteignons ainsi le tangible et le pratique comme base de toute différence de pensée, si subtile qu'elle puisse être. (5.18)

A detailed analysis of the French versions of the articles will, however, lead us to question the merit of "Comment se fixe la croyance" and, though to a lesser degree, those of "Comment rendre nos idées claires."

But, beforehand, we have to determine what "merit" in the French versions of these articles is actually derived from the "skill" of Léo Seguin. An active participant in the revolt of the Paris Commune, Léo Seguin was banished from France in 1871. In 1872, he fled to England where he stayed until 1876 when he went over to America. He lived in New York from 1876 to the end of 1880 at the latest. There he had several jobs, one of which was teaching French. We do not know how he came into contact with Peirce, but we do know that in the spring of 1878 Peirce recommended him for the chair of French at the University of California and that Seguin did not obtain the post. Benefiting from the amnesty which was proclaimed on May 17, 1879, Seguin returned to France. He became the military correspondent of *Le Télégraphe* and followed the French army to North Africa. He was wounded at Béja, Tunisia, on May 29, 1881, by an Algerian deserter from the French army and died the next day in Tunis. Léo Seguin was only 24 when the revolt of the Commune broke out. He was a brilliant student and intended to make the army his career, but after obtaining his baccalauréat ès-lettres and his baccalauréat ès-sciences he sat for the entrance examination to the Ecole Normale Supérieure, which he failed. His activities were many and diverse. He fenced and could read cuneiform, and was interested in Indian poetry and politics. A Republican, a patriot, and Freemason, the defeat of 1870 made him a rebel and a member of the Paris Commune. On leaving France for England, he knew not a word of English and learned the language only after his arrival in the United States, for in England he frequented mainly fellow refugees.

Such was the man from whose skill the articles published in French in the

*Revue philosophique* derive their merit. In view of the facts that, on one hand, there is no reason to doubt Peirce's statement that he wrote "Comment rendre nos idées claires" directly in French, and translated "The Fixation of Belief" into French himself, and, on the other hand, that Seguin's knowledge of English was poor, it was certainly the latter's skill as a teacher of French that Peirce was calling upon when he asked him to re-read his own French versions of the pragmatic articles of 1877–1878. Seguin must have appealed to Peirce. He was an outsider and a scientifically-trained philosopher whose independence of spirit and manners and whose brilliance were bound to impress a man like Peirce.

After a careful study of all the points in which the French versions of the articles of 1878 and 1879 differ from the English versions, we come to the following conclusions:

**1.** If we compare the French text of the articles of 1877 and 1878 with the other writings in French by Peirce in our possession—for example, the memoir "Sur la valeur de la pesanteur à Paris" (*Comptes rendus des Séances de l'Académie des Sciences,* 1880), of which we have the manuscript and the published text; the "Notes pour un traité de logique" (October 1898, Ms 339), which I edited (Peirce 1985: 3–9); and the letters to Juliette (Ms L. 340, the latter in French), A. Robert (Ms L. 378; Deledalle 1978: 192–199), and André Lalande (Ms L. 240, letter of November 22, 1905; Deledalle 1969: 37)—we can distinguish certain characteristics to be found in the French versions of the two pragmatic articles: short sentences with a minimum of conjunctive words in cases where the English sentence is far more lengthy owing to a repeated use of "but," "then," "now," "and"; a systematic use of "on" where the passive voice is used in English; and the almost total absence of the first person singular and a frequent use of the more impersonal "nous."

The vocabulary also is homogeneous. To give only a few instances, "*intellectuel*" generally corresponds to "mental," and "*intelligence*" to "mind" when knowledge is referred to, but "*esprit*" is used to translate "mind" in expressions like "dans notre esprit" ("in our minds"). "Investigation" is frequently used in French as well as in English in relation to the theory of inquiry.

But when one reads Peirce's texts which had not been corrected, one also notices his marked tendency to transpose English words into French, especially verbs, and to give French prepositions their English meanings. Thus Peirce writes, in a letter to A. Robert, that "A investe C avec B," the transposition of "A invests C with B" instead of "A met C en possession de B" (Deledalle 1978: 198); in his notes on logic, Peirce writes: "il n'y a [*sic*] le moindre avantage à gagner de [from] l'étude de la théorie du raisonnement," "la psychologie, au contraire, ne demande rien de [from] la métaphysique." Like many foreigners, Peirce commits mistakes in spelling, in gender, in agreement, in moods, and in tenses. In the same notes on logic, we read: "quelque chose de nouveaux [nouveau] à laquelle [auquel] je veux fixer la date," "comment la pensée trouve-t-elle existance [existence], c'est-à-dire comment s'exprîme-t-elle [s'exprime-t-elle]?," "la [le] mode d'être?," "cette [ce] signe," "mais la logique n'est bornée à la psychique pas plus que la métaphysique soit bornée à la physique" [la logique ne se ramène pas plus à la psychologie que la métaphysique à la physique], "mais tout cela n'intéresse point au logicien à qui il ne fait rien qu'un raisonnement fait une gratification d'un gout logique" [mais tout cela n'intéresse point le logicien pour qui il importe peu qu'un raisonnement satisfasse notre goût logique] (October 1–4 1898, Ms 339).

It is in this clearly defined field that, to my mind, Peirce was appealing to Léo Seguin's skill, when he entrusted to him the re-reading of his manuscripts.

**2.** "The Fixation of Belief" was thus translated by Peirce and corrected by Séguin: What are the respective parts of Peirce and Seguin in the text which appeared in the *Revue philosophique* under the title "Comment se fixe la croyance"?

A. By and large, and taking into account Peirce's corrections of the English text in 1893, 1903, and 1910, we can say that one may attribute to Peirce a certain number of mistakes that Seguin did not correct, the title, and an omission.

The mistakes left uncorrected by Seguin are mistranslations of words having similar forms in English and French: "deceived," "deceptive" (7) rendered by "déçu" (560) and "décevant" (561), instead of "trompé" and "trompeur"; "agreeable to *his* reason" (10) translated by "agréable à la raison" (564) instead of "ce qui est conforme à la raison" ou "ce qui convient à la raison." It will be noticed that Peirce did not make these mistakes when he wrote "Comment rendre nos idées claires" directly in French and then translated his text into English: "deception" (291 and 292) is used to translate "erreur" and "méprise" (46), although, unlike "deception" in English, "erreur" and "méprise" are not intentional, and "ce qui agréait à la raison" (40) is rendered by "agreeable to reason" (287). Other notable mistakes are "such and such" translated by "tel et tel," "such a formula" by "une semblable formule," and "rest on" by "se poser sur."

The title of the article, "Comment se fixe la croyance," is probably Peirce's own. "Comment rendre nos idées claires," having been written before the translation of "The Fixation of Belief," the rendering of the latter's title by "Comment se fixe la croyance" was more or less a matter of course.

Amongst all the modifications introduced into the French text which we are now going to examine, only one was adopted by Peirce when he corrected his pragmatic articles: the omission of the last paragraph which he probably thought too personal.

B. The changes made by Seguin in Peirce's translation had one aim: to present a version which would be more correct in style, more precise in meaning, and more easily understandable for French readers. Three sorts of modifications can be discerned: (a) improvements in style; (b) corrections of what Seguin considered to be mistakes; (c) clarifications or rather what Seguin thought to be clarifications.

(a) Improvements in style. They are undeniable, but insufficient in number, whence the unequal level of the translation which is sometimes polished and sometimes quite awkward. It is not surprising to find that awkwardness of style invariably corresponds to an incomprehension of Peirce's text.

(b) Corrections. The "twenty-two" (2) irrational hypotheses successively proposed by Kepler to explain the epicycles of Mars become "vingt et une" (554) in the translation, apparently for the reason that the twenty-second, which was the right one, could not be irrational—a "mistake" which Peirce did not correct in the later versions of his English text.

The translation of "transubstantiation of bread" (1) by "transmutation des espèces" (554) can be placed in this category. It is true that it is not only the bread which is transubstantiated, but also the wine. But why "transmutation" when the proper term is "transubstantiation"? It is the latter term that Peirce or Seguin uses in the French text of "Comment rendre nos idées claires" (47).

We may also include in the corrections the omission in the translation of the passage which says that "no religion has been without one" (i.e., priesthood) (9), because this is not true, Islam having no priests.

In another passage (568), it is the example of Islam which has been retained ("reformed Mussulman") and the allusion to Protestantism omitted ("or to a reformed Catholic who should still shrink from reading the Bible" [14]).

We can also include in this category the correction of a detail which had become out of date: Pius IX is replaced by Leo XIII (562) in the translation of "from the days of Numa Pompilius to those of Pius Nonus" (9), because between the date of writing of the English text and that of the revision of Peirce's translation, Pius IX had died and been succeeded by Leo XIII (1878). This has no implications concerning the date of Peirce's translation, as he did not modify the aforesaid detail in his later revision of the text and might well have kept the name of Pius IX in his French translation after the latter's death.

Was it also out of concern for accuracy that Seguin did not translate, on 565, "In Lord Bacon's phrase" (11), because he did not know himself whether Lord Bacon was Roger Bacon (553) or "l'autre Bacon, le plus célèbre" (554), the author of the *Novum Organum,* or else did he think that Peirce had made a mistake, or more probably that the French reader would not understand the allusion?

(c) Clarifications. Few, if any, of these clarifications can be considered improvements on the English text, even when they appear to make the translation more comprehensible. Peirce writes: "But it so happens that there exists a division among facts such that one class [ . . . ], while the others [ . . . ]" (4). The translation says: "mais les faits se trouveront etre divisés en deux classes" (557), which is stylistically clearer, but less accurate, as the classes are not limited to two.

For those today who are more familiar with Peirce's thought, the so-called clarifications for which Seguin is responsible are more of a hindrance than a help. Let us examine three main points: the theory of inquiry, realism, and the criticism of the method of authority.

## The Theory of Inquiry

Seguin does not seem to have understood the part played by doubt in inquiry. He appears to think that the aim of inquiry is the elimination of doubt which is to be replaced by belief, without seeing that doubt is a necessary condition for arriving at a true belief, i.e., a belief capable of directing our actions, and that one cannot reject a belief "which does not seem to have been so formed as to insure this result" only "by creating a doubt in the place of that belief" (6). The omission of this last sentence in the translation proves that Seguin does not see why doubt should be created in order to fix belief, since the aim of inquiry is precisely to eliminate doubt. For Seguin, inquiry means the discovery of what is already there, not the creation of something new. Seguin shared the pre-scientific conception of science of most of the French scholars of his time.

Neither did Seguin understand that inquiry is a social, cooperative, and cumulative process. He conceives of it as a private, non-public affair, which is the contrary of Peirce's conception. Thus he does not understand why Peirce says that no one "can really doubt that there are realities," for this is a hypothesis that "every mind admits" "so that the social impulse does not cause me [or 'men,' as he says later] to doubt it" (12). That is why Seguin did not translate the last sentence.

It is also to an erroneous interpretation of Peirce's theory of inquiry that we can impute the translation of "the most that can be maintained is that we seek for a belief that we *shall* think to be true" (6, my italics) by "ce qu'on peut tout au plus soutenir, c'est que nous cherchons une croyance que *nous pensons vraie*" (599), and that of "The feeling which gives rise to any method of fixing belief is a dissatisfaction of two repugnant propositions. But here already is a vague concession that there is some one thing to which a proposition *should* conform" (12, my italics) by "Le sentiment d'où naissent toutes les méthodes de fixer la croyance est une sorte de mécontentement de ne pouvoir faire accorder deux propositions. Mais alors on admet déjà vaguement qu'il existe quelque chose à quoi puisse être conforme une proposition" (566). The translation of "we shall think" by "nous pensons" in the first sentence, and of "should" by "puisse" in the second one transforms a dynamic conception of inquiry into a static and stereotyped pattern.

## Realism

It is the social character of the process of inquiry which links the theory of inquiry to the theory of reality. Now the use of the word "réalité" to translate "fact" (2 and 11), as well as "real thing" (11) and "reality" (12), obscures the fact that what Peirce is defending here is the reality of universals ("generals") whose characteristics are completely independent of what we feel, believe, or think. This translation makes an ontological theory of universals into an epistemological theory of the reality of the external world. It is true that the word "reality" used by Peirce at that time was confusing, and that he was soon to replace it by the word "Real," used as a substantive (5.384) to express the nature of universals, but he never thought that the latter could be "realities" in the sense of "facts."

## Criticism of the Method of Authority

Seguin's mistrust of the "instinct social," which is probably at least partly responsible for his incomprehension of the preceding theories, explains perfectly why, on the other hand, as a strong individualist, he enthusiastically adopts Peirce's theses on the method of authority, at the same time distorting the latter, for Peirce rejects arbitrary authority, but not that of the "communauté des chercheurs." The French text of these pages is characterized by a polished style and a resonance quite different from that of the English text, and inevitably evokes echoes of the voice of the Paris Commune.

Finally, it must be pointed out that at least two mistranslations are not to be attributed either to Peirce or to Seguin, since they are printer's errors: "who originated" (10) is translated by "les créatures" (564) instead of "les créateurs," and "Men who pursue it are distinguished for their decision of character, which becomes very easy with such a mental rule" (13) is translated by "Ceux qui en font usage sont remarquables par leur caractère décidé, la décision devenant très faible avec une pareille règle intellectuelle" (568), a sentence which makes sense only if one replaces "faible" (weak) by "facile" (easy).

**3.** With "Comment rendre nos idées claires," our work is simplified: it is a text written directly in French and not a translation. The only problems here are to identify the modifications of the corrector by comparing the text with its English translation written by the author himself, and to ascertain whether the original French version is in fact superior to the English translation, as Peirce claims.

My answer is threefold.

A. The French text of "Comment rendre nos idées claires" is unquestionably superior to that of "Comment se fixe la croyance." It is homogeneous and it never distorts Peirce's doctrines.

B. The English translation, which is more explicit, helps to clarify several points of the French version.

C. The modifications of the corrector are fewer, or at least less apparent, than in "Comment se fixe la croyance."

A. I shall be brief about the first point. There is none of the imprecision of vocabulary which often distorts the meaning in "Comment se fixe la croyance." "Epreuve" (40 and 48) exactly expresses the idea of "test" (287 and 294), which is translated by "criterium" in "Comment se fixe la croyance" (567). A word like "engendrement" (43), of which the equivalent in the English translation is "production" (290) and which might appear somewhat clumsy, in fact aptly expresses the process of inquiry. There is nothing ambiguous here in the description of belief, of habit, and of the part played by doubt (45), nor in Peirce's idea of "reality": "L'opinion prédestinée à réunir finalement tous les chercheurs est ce que nous appelons le vrai, et l'objet de cette opinion est le réel. C'est ainsi que j'expliquerai la réalité [ . . . ]. Mais la réalité du réel ne dépend pas de ce fait que l'investigation, poursuivie assez longtemps, doit enfin conduire à y croire" (56).

B. The English translation is, however, superior to the French original which it clarifies. Whereas in the French text of "Comment se fixe la croyance," there were modifications and omissions which obscured the meaning, we have here mainly additions which complete and explain the French text. A few examples will suffice. The expression: "Les premiers principes" (41) becomes the more explicit "The first principles of science" (286); "Accordingly in adopting the distinction of *clear* and *distinct,* he described the latter quality as the clear apprehension of everything contained in the definition" (288) is clearer than "C'est pourquoi en discernant entre les idées claires et les idées distinctes, il décrivit ces dernières comme les idées dont la définition ne contient rien qu'on ne saisisse clairement" (41); in the sentence: "Le résultat final de pensée est l'exercice de la volonté, fait auquel n'appartient plus la pensée" (45), the reader does not know what the word "fait" refers to, but the English translation is unambiguous: "The final upshot of thinking is the exercise of volition, and of this thought no longer forms a part" (291); the modification of the sentence: "Cependant on peut concevoir que cela apparaisse au premier abord et qu'un homme de deux propositions présentées d'une façon analogue, puisse accepter l'une et rejeter l'autre" (46) which becomes "Yet it is conceivable that a man should assert one proposition and deny the other" (291), is an improvement and so is the transformation of "une qualité essentiellement mystérieuse de l'objet" (46) into "a quality of the object which is essentially mysterious" (292); "we deceive ourselves and mistake a mere sensation accompanying the thought for a part of the thought itself" (293) is clearer than "c'est s'abaisser et prendre une simple sensation accompagnant la pensée pour une partie de la pensée elle-même" (48); again, the sentence: "Il est absurde de dire que la pensée contient quelque élément qui soit sans rapport avec son unique fonction" (48) is rendered clearer by the use of "meaning" instead of "élément": "It is absurd to say that thought has any meaning unrelated to its only function" (293); even the expression of the maxim of pragmatism is better in English than in French: "effects [having] practical bearings" (293) being more precise than "effets pratiques" (48).

C. The modifications of Seguin are difficult to identify. Thus if we compare: "Lorsqu'on a mis en face de l'absurdité d'une telle vue certains philosophes, ils ont imaginé une vaine distinction entre des conceptions positives et des conceptions négatives, dans un effort pour donner à leur idée une forme moins manifestement saugrenue" (52) with "The truth is, there is some vague notion afloat that a question may mean something which the mind cannot conceive; and when some hair-splitting philosophers have been confronted with the absurdity of such a view, they have invented an empty distinction between positive and negative conceptions in the attempt to give their non-idea a form not obviously nonsensical" (297), we shall find that the English text is more downright: "some hair-splitting philosophers" translates "certains philosophes"; "non-idea," "idée vide"; "nonsensical," "idée saugrenue." Was it Peirce who exaggerated the antiphilosophical tone of this paragraph, or was it Seguin who watered down Peirce's French text in order to avoid offending French philosophers?

Is it to Peirce or to Seguin that we must attribute the style of the following French sentence: "un trajet est déterminé par la direction que prend et par la distance que franchit un point qui le parcourt depuis son origine" (51) which is better than the English: "a path is determined by the varying direction and distance of the point which moves over it from the starting-point" (296)?

It was certainly Peirce who wrote that the Cartesian theory, "ce joyau de la logique," is "assez jolie," but that "il est grand temps de reléguer au musée des curiosités cet antique bijou" (41), if we may judge from the English translation in which "ornament of logic" is in inverted commas and *bijou* in italics, not to speak of the expression "our cabinet of curiosities" (288).

In the same way, we can be fairly sure that Peirce was responsible for the transposition of a situation concerning the payment in French money (piece d'argent, billon), of an "emplette" in the French text (43) and the payment in American money (nickel, copper) of a "fare" in the English text (288).

Can one be as certain that the expression "dans tous les genres de culture intellectuelle" (42), translated in the English version by "in every branch of mental acquirement" is Peirce's? And who is responsible for the rendering of "microscope moral" (43) as "mental microscope" in English (289)?

When we have in the French version "arrangements d'idées" (49) and in the English version "arrangements of facts" (294), is this a mistake made by Peirce or one of Seguin's corrections? For here it is in actual effect a question of "faits" and not of "idées," and this is confirmed by the French version which, a few lines further on, also uses the expression "arrangements de faits."

Did Peirce use the term "certitude" to express the idea of "infallibility" (287)? He might have done so in order not to offend his Catholic readers. But Seguin might have done just the same.

As for the parenthetical clause, typical of Peirce's writing, which figures in the English version, but not in the French: "but if mathematics are unsupportable to him, pray let him skip three paragraphs rather than we should part company here" (295), is this a case of an addition made by Peirce for the English text or of an omission by Seguin?

Finally, it is highly improbable that Peirce should have written in French and afterwards omitted the end of the article in which he announces the other articles of this series, the publication of which was not scheduled for the *Revue philosophique.*

One last point on which the French version is authoritative: after alluding to the ideas to which some men dedicate their lives and which, one fine day, vanish like "Mélusine, la belle fée," Peirce says: "J'ai connu moi-même un de ces hommes [this man was himself and "Mélusine, la belle *fée,*" who, one day, disappeared, was his first wife Harriet *Melusina Fay,* who left him in 1876], and goes on: "Qui pourrait compter tous les quadrateurs de cercle, métaphysiciens, astrologues, que sais-je encore, dont les annales de la vieille Allemagne pourraient nous redire l'histoire?" (42-43). The shorter English version: "Who can tell how many histories [ ... ] may not be told in the old German story" (289) misled the editors of the *Collected Papers,* who thought Peirce was referring to the story of Melusina which was French and not German, and who placed after the word "German" the comment "French" in brackets with an exclamation mark: [French!] (5.393).

What conclusion can we draw from this analysis? Peirce loved France, its language, its wines, its liberalism, and its culture. There can be no other reason than this blind love to account for the fact that Peirce preferred the French versions of his articles on pragmatism to the English versions, for the French version of "Comment se fixe la croyance," apart from several well-written passages and a few elegantly turned phrases is positively bad, and that of "Comment rendre nos idées claires," although unquestionably superior to "Comment se fixe la croyance," lacks the clarity and precision of the English translation.

## THE POSTCRIPTUM OF 1893:
## FROM LIBERTARIANISM TO
## DEMOCRATIC COLLECTIVITY

In a postscriptum of 1893 published in the *Collected Papers* (5.402, n. 2), which he intended to include in his *Search for a Method,* Peirce recognizes that, in his first version of the papers of 1877 and 1878, pragmatism could be "said to be a sceptical and materialistic principle, [although] it is only an application of the sole principle of logic which was recommended by Jesus: 'Ye may know them by their fruits,'" for the reason that "this rule" was then understood in too individualistic a sense. It was so, on one hand, because of Seguin's reading of Peirce: There were two kinds of "anarchism" in the 1870s in France: a "libertarian" and a "collective." And Seguin belonged to the first tribe. On the other hand, Peirce was inclined to "non-authoritarianism" which is the main characteristic of "libertarian anarchism."

Anyhow, it is not a reason why we should understand "the practical in any low and sordid sense. Individual action is a means and not our end. Individual pleasure is not our end; we are putting our shoulders to the wheel for an end that none of us can catch more than a glimpse at—that which the generations are working out. But we can see that the development of embodied ideas is what it will consist in" (5.402, n. 2).

Ten years earlier, in "Some Consequences of Four Incapacities," Peirce had shown that "the real" is independent of what we think:

> The real [ . . . ] is that which, sooner or later, information and reasoning would finally result in, and which is therefore independent of the vagaries of me and you. (5.311)

Consequently, "the very origin of the conception of reality shows that this conception essentially involves the notion of a COMMUNITY, without definite limits, and capable of a definite increase of knowledge" (5.311). Is this community of knowers and reasoners the only possible community which pragmaticism can produce? Before the Paris Commune, it was certainly the case, for Peirce's pragmatism was a theory of action, but not of any action; it was a theory which "makes thought ultimately *apply* to action exclusively—to *conceived* action" (5.402, n. 3). After the Commune, "collective anarchism" had its say: Their fruit is, therefore, collective; it is the achievement of the whole people.

When we come to study the great principle of continuity and see how all is fluid and every point directly partakes the being of every other, it will appear that individualism and falsity are one and the same. Meantime, we know that man is not whole as long as he is single, that he is essentially a possible member of society. Especially, one man's experience is nothing, if it stands alone. If he sees what others cannot, we call it hallucination. It is not "my" experience, but "our" experience that has to be thought of; and this "us" has indefinite possibilities. (5.402, n. 2)

The nature of this society, as described here, is closer to Dewey's idea of democracy than to Peirce's idea of the "community of inquirers." It is no longer a "club" for the *élite,* but the whole people's democracy.

# PART TWO

# *Semeiotic as Semiotics*

> Logic, in its general sense, is, [ ... ] only another name for
> *semiotic* (σημειωτική), the quasi-necessary, or formal, doc-
> trine of signs.
> —Peirce (2.227)

> Know that from the day when at the age of 12 or 13 I took
> up, in my elder brother's room a copy of Whately's *Logic,*
> [ ... ] it has never been in my power to study anything,—
> mathematics, ethics, metaphysics, gravitation, thermo-dy-
> namics, optics, chemistry, comparative anatomy, astronomy,
> psychology, phonetics, economic, the history of science,
> whist, men and women, wine, metrology, except as a study
> of semeiotic.
> —Peirce (Letter to Lady Welby,
> 1908, Dec. 23 in Hardwick 1977: 85–86)

The present part will be devoted to Peirce's theory of signs. In the first chapter
(ch. 4), I shall describe semeiotic as semiotic, that is to say as a method for analyzing anything which appears as a "sign" and, in the second chapter (ch. 5), I
shall approach the question of interpreting Peirce or the way of understanding
or translating Peirce in another language, yours or mine, English, French, or in
any other context: linguistic, private, or ideological.

# - 4 -

# Sign

## SEMIOSIS AND REPRESENTAMEN

For Peirce, as already noted above (p. 18), the word "sign" has two acceptations: sign-action and sign-object. He calls the first *semiosis*, the second *representamen*.

Semiosis is the action of the sign, the sign in action, that is to say: in process. For there to be a semiosis, an event A (the sign-object or representamen: e.g., the order given by an officer to his troops) must produce a second event B (the interpretant: the *signified* result of the sign-object or representamen) *as a means of* producing a third event C (the object as such: here, the execution by the soldiers of the order given by the officer—the execution or object being for the officer the *cause* of the sign-object or representamen (encoding) and for the soldiers its *effect* (decoding) (cf. 5.473).

The representamen is an "object serving to represent something to the mind" (*Century Dictionary*, 1887). Peirce borrowed the idea of the representamen as sign-object from Hamilton, to whom Peirce refers in the *Century Dictionary*. Hamilton wrote:

> The Leibnitio-Wolfians [ . . . ] distinguished three acts in the process of representative cognition: 1° the act of representing a (mediate) object to the mind; 2° the representation, or, more properly speaking, *representamen,* itself as an (immediate or vicarious) object exhibited to the mind; 3° the act by which the mind is conscious immediately of the representative object, and, through it, mediately of the remote object represented. (Reid 1863: 877 note)

Peirce himself explicitly makes the distinction in the context of representation where 'sign' is given as a synonym of 'representation' defined as 'semiosis' and opposed to 'representamen'. "I confine the word *representation* to the operation of a sign or its *relation* to the object *for* the interpreter of the representation. The concrete subject that represents I call a sign or representamen" (1.540). The sign, the concrete subject of the representation, or representamen, is the sign-object which must not be confused with the common idea of the sign defined as "anything which conveys any definite notion of an object in any way" (1.540).

This latter definition refers to semiosis, which is the object of semiotic analysis. By virtue of this, the sign-action or semiosis is the point of departure of the analysis and the sign-object or representamen "whatever that analysis applies to" (1.540), i.e., the repertory of representamens. Consequently, the representamen of the semiosis is, like the latter, triadic: it comprises the sign-representamen, the object-representamen, and the interpretant-representamen.

> A Representamen can be considered from three formal points of view, namely, first, as the substance of the representation, or the *Vehicle* of the *Meaning*, which is common to the three representamens of the triad, second, as the quasiagent in the representation, that is as the *Natural Object*, and third as the quasi-patient in the representation, or that modification in the representation makes its *Intelligence*, and this may be called the *Interpretant*. Thus, in looking at a map, the map itself is the *Vehicle*, the country represented is the *Natural Object*, and the idea excited in the mind is the *Interpretant*. (Ms 717)

And, in fact, Peirce always defines the sign-object, the object, and the interpretant as representamens.

> A *Sign*, or *Representamen*, is a First which stands in such a genuine triadic relation to a Second, called its *Object*, as "to be capable of determining a Third, called its *Interpretant*, to assume the same triadic relation to its Object in which it stands to itself to the same Object." (2.274)
>
> *A REPRESENTAMEN is a subject of a triadic relation to a Second, called its OBJECT, FOR a Third, called its INTERPRETANT, this triadic relation being such that the REPRESENTAMEN determines its interpretant to stand in the same triadic relation to the same object for some interpretant.* (1.541)

These two passages describe the process of sign-action or semiosis, set off by the presentation of the sign-object or representamen. "Representamens are of three kinds, *icons* (or *likenesses*), *indices*, and *symbols* (or general signs)" ("Logic (Exact)" in Baldwin's *Dictionary*, 1902). Thus "an *Icon* is a Representamen whose Representative Quality is a Firstness of it as a First. That is, a quality that it has *qua* thing renders it fit to be a representamen" (2.276).

> A representamen, or sign, is anything which stands at once in a relation of correspondence to a second thing (not necessarily real), its object and to *another possible representamen*, its *interpretant*, which it determines to correspondence with the same object. ("Logic [Exact]" in Baldwin's *Dictionary*, 1902)

Another consequence of the distinction between sign-action or semiosis and sign-object or representamen: every sign is a representamen (1.540), but

> possibly there may be Representamens which are not Signs. Thus, if a sunflower, in turning towards the sun, becomes, by this very act, fully capable, without further condition, of reproducing a sunflower which turns in precisely corresponding ways toward the sun, and of doing so with the same reproductive power, the sunflower would become a Representamen of the sun. (2.274)

In other words, "all signs convey notions to human minds; but I know no reason why every representamen should do so" (1.540), although it must be conceded that "*thought* is the chief, if not the only, mode of representation" (2.274). It will accordingly be granted that one may "call a thing considered as having a signification, a representamen" (Ms 796), and that a representamen is a third:

> A 'representamen', like a word,—indeed, most words are representamens,—is of a single thing, but is of the nature of a mental habit, it consists in the fact that something *would be.* (Ms 695)

However, the representamen can exist only as materialized in some singular thing, a replica.

## The Representamen and the Object of the Sign

### Representamen and Representative

The representamen is not the sensory image, the sensorial reproduction of the object which it represents (although it may be). It stands for something, just as an ambassador stands for his country, represents it in a foreign country; just as a deputy represents his electors in an assembly (Hardwick 1977: 193).

### Semiosis and Representative

The simile must not lead us to confuse semiosis or sign-action with representamen or sign-object. The representamen represents its object, and the action of the sign as such (i.e., as representamen) does not affect the object represented. Which is not the case of "a legislative representative" who "is, on the contrary, expected in his functions to improve the condition of his constituents" (ibid.).

This does not mean that the sign-action does not affect the world in which it functions. On the contrary, semiosis, which can come into existence only by means of a sign-object, takes place in the world of things: it is a process immanent to the things of which signs are a part—thought-signs and man-signs—and which it in-forms and trans-forms (principle of pragmaticism). The representamen may indeed be considered "as the quasi-agent in the representation" (in other words, the sign-action or semiosis) which, as far as the representation conforms to it, constitutes its truth (Ms 717)—a conformity which is not given once and for all, but is the "ideal limit" (5.565) which semiosis "is fated" to attain

(407). Properly speaking, semiosis starts because a representamen is opaque, but, when the representamen is transparent, semiosis becomes a blind process.

## The Object in Semiosis and the Object Outside Semiosis

The representamen is the quasi-agent of the natural object in sign-action or semiosis (Ms 717). We must distinguish between the natural object outside semiosis which Peirce calls the dynamical or mediate object, and the immediate object in semiosis and of which the representamen is the quasi-agent (Hardwick 1977: 83). The representamen refers immediately to the immediate object and mediately to the natural object. But this distinction is a methodological or functional one, or, properly speaking, a semiotic one.

## Object and Representamen

Every sign-representamen has an object which it represents. Every sign has a single object, but this object may be a single set or continuum of objects (5.448). "In order that anything should be a Sign it must 'represent,' as we say, something else, called its *Object,* although the condition that a Sign must be other than its Object is perhaps arbitrary, since, if we insist upon it, we must at least make an exception in the case of a sign which is part of a sign" (2.230). But, even in this case, the one becomes the object of the other, for "on the map of an island laid down upon the soil of that island, there must, under all ordinary circumstances, be some position, some point, marked or not, that represents *qua* place on the map, the very same point *qua* place on the island" (2.230).

Every object is not represented by a sign-representamen. The whole universe "is perfused with signs, if it is not composed exclusively of signs" (5.448). The universe of firstness being the universe of possibles, only those objects that come "before thought and the mind in any usual sense" are represented by signs, whether they be "perceptible, imaginable and even unimaginable" (2.230).

Only objects already known in the universe of secondness, that of existence, objects known by collateral acquaintance (Hardwick 1977: 72) can signify. "The Sign can only represent the Object and tell about it. It cannot furnish acquaintance with or recognition of that Object" (2.231). To the reader who might question this idea, Peirce gives an answer which explicits its meaning:

> If there be anything which conveys information and yet has absolutely no relation nor reference to anything with which the person to whom it conveys the information has, when he comprehends that information, the slightest acquaintance, direct or indirect—and a very strange sort of information that would be—the vehicle of that sort of information is not, in this volume, called a Sign. (2.231)

Elsewhere, Peirce explicits this still further:

> A person who says Napoleon was a lethargic creature has evidently his mind determined by Napoleon. For otherwise he could not attend to him at all. But

[ ... ] the person who interprets that sentence (or any other Sign whatsoever) must be determined by the Object of it through collateral observation quite independently of the action of the Sign. Otherwise he will not be determined to thought of that object. If he never heard of Napoleon before, the sentence will mean no more to him than that some person or thing to which the name "Napoleon" has been attached was a lethargic creature. For Napoleon cannot determine his mind unless the word in the sentence calls his attention to the right man and that can only be if, independently, [a] habit has been established by him by which that word calls up a variety of attributes of Napoleon the man. (8.178)

Much the same thing is true of every sign. In the sentence quoted, Napoleon is the immediate object of a semiosis, an object known in other respects outside this semiosis as a "natural object" possessing many other attributes than lethargy. And lethargy is also an immediate object that "collateral experience had taught its interpreter" is a "natural object" whose attribution is not limited to Napoleon (8.178).

Consequently, an object may determine "a lying or erroneous sign" and an object may be "brought into existence by the sign": "The object of 'Napoleon' is the Universe of Existence so far as it is determined by the fact of Napoleon being a member of it," just as "the Object of the sentence 'Hamlet was insane' is the Universe of Shakespeare's Creation so far as it is determined by Hamlet being a part of it" (8.178).

All the objects of the Universe of Thirdness, which is that of mediating thought, are by definition represented by signs: "All thought [ ... ] must necessarily be in signs" (5.251).

### From the Sign to the Object

In a letter to Lady Welby of December 14, 1908, Peirce writes:

I do not make any contrast between Subject and Object, far less talk about "subjective and objective" in any of the varieties of the German senses, which I think have led to a lot of bad philosophy, but I use "subject" as the correlative of "predicate", and speak only of the "subjects" of those signs which have a part which separately indicates what the object of the sign is. A subject of such a sign is that kind of object of the sign which is so separately indicated. (Hardwick 1977: 69)

A first and fundamental clarification is given here: "object" is not opposed to "subject." We are not in a dualistic universe where the "subject"—a human being—refers a "subjective" sign to an "object"—the "objective" world—outside itself.

"Object" says nothing more than the Latin word *objectum*. The object is "thrown" (*jectum*) "in front of" (*ob*). This calls forth two interrogative remarks: (1) Could not "ob-jectum" (what is thrown in front of) be rather the definition

*ob-ject = thrown in front of*

of the object? (2) Does it not imply that there is an obstacle, and consequently that the sign—since it is the sign which is in question here—should not normally encounter an obstacle, not have an object? But the sign has an object. Peirce writes:

> I use the term "object" in the sense in which *objectum* was first made a substantive early in the XIIIth century; and when I use the word without adding "of" what I am speaking of the object, I mean anything that comes before thought or the mind in any usual sense. (ibid.)

The preceding remarks must therefore be more precisely formulated. On one hand, there is an object because there is a thought. On the other hand, it is when the object constitutes an obstacle for the thought that the thought gives itself a sign, not in order to know the object, but to try to get round the obstacle, or rather, to set up a screen in front of it. Which is why the sign is not transparent, but opaque. If the sign were transparent, the thought would not have to *designate* the object; it would not have to propose a sign to represent it. Now Peirce says explicitly: "The sign can only represent the Object and tell about it. It cannot furnish acquaintance with or recognition of that Object" (2.231).

These preliminary remarks lead us to ask in what conditions one can say something about the object. First, there is an "object" only for a thought which "sees" it on the sole condition that it represents in its own right this object in a sign. Is idealism the only other solution? Yes, unless we distinguish between an object in the sign and an object outside the sign. Which is what Peirce does: "It is usual and proper to distinguish between two Objects of a Sign, the Mediate without, and the Immediate within the Sign" (Hardwick 1977: 83). He usually calls the first "dynamical." Elsewhere he refines this distinction:

> we have to distinguish the Immediate Object which is the Object as the Sign itself represents it, and whose being is thus dependent upon the Representation of it in the Sign, from the Dynamical Object, which is the Reality which by some means contrives to determine the Sign to its Representation. (4.536)

As it is clear that it is either the thought or the mind which "determines" the sign to represent the object, the dynamical object appears as the projection out of the sign of the immediate object which is the only one produced by thought, unless thought be the Thought which created the Universe.

If Peirce thus appears to define the sign by this distinction between object in the sign and the object outside the sign, he is in fact only displacing the difficulties: the "outside" is in itself a problem if one rejects dualism. We shall examine this question later on. But the real difficulty resides in the nature of the sign itself as subordinate to thought. What is a sign? What is thought?

I do not want to deal thoroughly with these questions here, but they cannot be eluded if one wishes to understand what constitutes the object so defined. Despite Peirce's terminological laxity, which must, paradoxically, be condemned in the name of the strict terminological ethics which he himself defended, it is possible, and even relatively easy, to answer these questions.

What is a sign? Taking into account only the texts quoted above, the written, gestural, or spoken sign, which is a determinable physical token, is usually confused with the "mental" sign in thought. In order to avoid this confusion, Peirce proposes to substitute two other terms, without always respecting his own rule of substitution: the sign, representing (by means of thought) the object, is called the "representamen"; the sign, as an act of attribution of an (immediate) object to a sign-representamen, is called sign-action, or usually semiosis or more rarely "semeiosy" (5.473). Semiosis is thus the production and attribution by a thought of the sign-interpretant, or more simply interpretant, of a sign-representamen to an immediate object, i.e., the sort of object that the thought takes for the object, given the action or semiosis it has accomplished. What is thought? It is what it does: a semiosis, thought in action, obviously. Thought in itself, if it can be distinguished from its actions, is the possibility of drawing up plans of action: a mind or quasi-mind, as Peirce termed it. But that is another story.

## The Object in the Sign

At this point we can say that the object produced by the interpretant is in the semiosis or sign-action. The immediate object is thus closely connected with and, to be exact, is determined by, the nature of the interpretant. We have seen that Peirce used the word "interpretant" with various meanings. I shall distinguish three types of meanings of the word. A formal one and two others I shall call temporal: one which is more social and public and the other one which is more individual and private, or, let us say "subjective," not by opposition to "objective," but to "social." It is not at all certain that the latter two are the formal interpretant incarnate, nor that the "subjective" interpretant is the same as the "social" interpretant seen from the point of view of the subject. I shall endeavor to be as clear as possible concerning the type of interpretants I am discussing.

1. Formally speaking, the interpretant is another sign or representamen that is occasioned but not "determined," properly speaking (although Peirce does sometimes use the word), by the representamen which sets off the semiosis. A sign (or representamen) is "anything which determines something else (its *interpretant*) to refer to an object to which itself refers (its *object*) in the same way, the interpretant becoming in turn a sign, and so on *ad infinitum*" (2.303). In this formal context, the word "determine" obviously cannot have the same meaning as in a spatio-temporal context, which is the scene of action for the interpretants which I shall now examine.

2. This *regressus ad infinitum* makes any definite grasp of the object theoretically impossible. But the sign as an act, the sign-action, a semiosis, is not formal and intemporal. It is *in time*. It starts, goes on, and stops. The play of signs and objects is thus possible, providing the interpretant is defined, not formally, but in space and time. Whence the well-known Peircean trichotomy of the interpretant: immediate, dynamical, and final. Of course, there are not three interpretants, but

only one interpretant which assumes different roles distinguished by the words: immediate, dynamical, and final. This distinction of roles is itself no more than a convenient means of expression, and not a distinction between roles that could be assumed independently of one another.

The immediate interpretant could be called the sign of interpretability. It is "familiarity with a sign and readiness in using it or interpreting it" (8.185).

The dynamical interpretant is interpretation in action *hic et nunc*. It is the "actual effect" of the sign-representamen on the *interpreter* (8.314). Here we must insist on the terms used by Peirce. "Actual effect" must be understood as the expression is used in physics: the result produced in certain conditions which obtain at the moment at which it is produced. "Interpreter" is not a "sop to Cerberus" thrown to the reader in order to appease his or her incomprehension of the real nature of the interpretant. It means here the interpreter in possession of the immediate interpretants he or she has acquired and with which he or she is familiar to the point of interpreting certain signs in certain ways in a given situation.

3. The final interpretant I shall call "interpretantation." It is not a given "final interpretant," no more than the immediate interpretant is a given "immediate interpretant." The latter is a disposition, the former a set of rules for interpreting which have become the interpreter's habits of interpreting signs as representamens.

This is so true that Peirce sometimes insists on a trichotomy which is the private (conscious) obverse of the trichotomy I have just described and which is, so to speak, its public (institutional) reverse. This trichotomy has three types of interpretants, respectively emotional, energetic, and logical. The emotional interpretant is "a feeling produced by it (the sign). . . . Thus the performance of a piece of concerted music . . . conveys, and is intended to convey, the composer's musical ideas; but these usually consist merely in a series of feelings" (5.475). The energetic interpretant "will always involve an effort. . . . The effort may be a muscular one . . . but it is much more usually an exertion upon the inner world, a mental effort" (5.475). But, Peirce specifies, "it never can be the meaning of an intellectual concept, since it is a single act [while] such a concept is of a general nature" (5.475). May this meaning be the distinctive feature of the logical interpretant? May the latter be this "general effect"? Peirce wonders. It may well be a "thought, that is to say, a mental sign," but then "it must have itself a logical interpretant; so that it cannot be the *ultimate* logical interpretant of the concept." In consequence, "the only mental effect that can be produced and that is not a sign but is of a general application is a *habit-change;* meaning by habit-change a modification of a person's tendencies toward action, resulting from previous experiences or from previous exertions of his will or acts, or from a complexus of both kinds of cause" (5.476).

Are these trichotomies homologous? Or does one of them overlap the other? It is certain, in any case, that the final logical interpretant includes both the logical and the final interpretants, since, according to Peirce, the final logical interpretant which concludes a semiosis is not a sign-representamen but a habit of acting in a certain way (5.491). As to the others, if they overlap—which they do—it is not surprising, being indecomposable aspects of one formally defined sign-interpretant.

All these precautionary considerations are not unnecessary and are not leading us away from the subject. On one hand, they situate rigorously the interpretant in its relation to the object. On the other hand, they shed light on the nature of the immediate object, whose unity and diversity in spatio-temporal contexts, which are by definition in continual transaction and reconstruction, they both determine and justify.

## *From the Immediate Object to the Dynamical Object*

The question which may now be legitimately asked is the following: since the play of interpretants in a given society at a given moment can be reduced to a geo-social habit which is the final logical interpretant of which Peirce says that it is—"that which *would finally* be decided to be the true interpretation if consideration of the matter were carried so far that an ultimate opinion were reached" (8.184)—how can we distinguish the dynamical object outside the sign from the immediate object in the sign?

Admittedly, Peirce was alluding to a scientific truth "fated to be ultimately agreed to by all who investigate" (5.407), and which would transcend the geo-social, and, *a fortiori,* the geo-political. However, he was here displaying a utopian attitude which would be thought very naïve today—when we know how easily ultimate truths can force themselves upon the community of scientific investigators as well as on the community of nations. But, fortunately, Peirce foresaw "habit-changes" that investigation cannot fail, in the long run, to produce, in order to negotiate the obstacles along the path towards truth, which we are now convinced can never be ultimate.

Is it investigation as method, i.e., semiosis, or the dynamical object which denies the immediate object its claim to be an ultimate one?

Let us first look back to semiosis. The sign-representamen (of an object) "determines" a sign-interpretant to designate its object (the object of the sign-representamen). This designation is rarely pure designation: it spans a long process from the modification of a previously designated object to the production of a new object. But Peirce does specify, as we have already noted, that the representamen "can only represent the Object and tell about it. It cannot furnish acquaintance with or recognition of that Object ... namely, that with which it presupposes an acquaintance in order to convey some further information concerning it" (2.231). Where does this previous knowledge come from and what is the object concerned?

By "knowledge," Peirce means here what William James, following Grote, called "knowledge-by-acquaintance" and not "knowledge-about." The latter, which is indirect, is the knowledge by sign-representamens in the continuous process of sign-action or semiosis. And the object known in the latter case is the immediate object.

"Knowledge-by-acquaintance" thus concerns another kind of object: the dynamical object. How can it be known? Peirce replies: by "collateral experience" (8.514), which is precisely a "collateral acquaintance" (8.144). This experience gives us knowledge of the existence of the dynamical object, but not of its nature in itself, its substantial nature. In any case, Peirce remarks, "it must be borne in mind" that the "substantive . . . is not an indispensable part of speech" (8.184), whether it be grammatical or metaphysical.

If neither knowledge-by-acquaintance nor knowledge-about is knowledge, properly speaking, i.e., direct knowledge of the dynamical object—their object being the immediate object—can we dispense with the dynamical object? Peirce does not think so, because the immediate object is the object "cognized in the Sign and therefore an Idea" (8.183). We must therefore, unless we fall back into idealism, admit the *existence* of an "external" object: the dynamical object, which is "as it is regardless of any particular aspect of it, the Object in such relations as unlimited and final study would show it to be" (8.183). What is known is thus the relations of an *existing* object independent of ourselves in the course of the semioses in which we are, it and ourselves, engaged.

The ultimate object is consequently neither the dynamical object nor the immediate object. It is that unique object cloaked by methodologically necessary mental distinctions, which dualistic metaphysics consigns to "external" reality. As the distinction between the dynamical object and the immediate object is also methodological, a distinction of reason, it does not require an external reality. External to what, in any case, if one rejects idealism? There is only one continuous reality in which each of the two objects plays a particular part according to how it is defined in terms of one or the other of the categories of being, the dynamical object belonging essentially to secondness, the immediate object to firstness and thirdness. This is confirmed by Peirce in the following passage, in which the corresponding categories are designated in square brackets.

> [T]he Dynamical Object . . . is the Object that Dynamical Science (or what at this day would be called "Objective Science") can investigate. Take, for example, the sentence "the Sun is blue". Its Objects are "the Sun" and "blueness". If by "blueness" be meant the Immediate Object, which is the quality of the sensation, it can only be known by Feeling [firstness]. But if it means that "Real", existential condition, which causes the emitted light to have short mean wavelength . . . the proposition is true. So the "Sun" may mean the occasion [secondness] of sundry sensations [firstness] and so is the Immediate Object, or it may mean our usual interpretation of such sensations in terms of place, of mass, etc. [thirdness] when it is the Dynamical Object. It is true of both Immediate Object and Dynamical Object that acquaintance cannot be given by a Picture or a Description, nor by any other sign which has the Sun for its Object. If a person points to it and says, See there! *That* is what we call the "Sun", the Sun is *not*

the Object of that sign. It is the *Sign* of the sun, the *word* "sun" that his decla-
ration is about; and that *word* we must become acquainted with by collateral
experience. (8.183)

### *From the Dynamical Object to the Representamen*

To complete the cycle, we must examine the relation between the representamen
and the dynamical object. This will be a semiotic cycle, formal and descriptive,
for semiosis never comes back to the same point. It is not a "vicious circle," as
Lady Welby said, but a "virtuous spiral." When Peirce says that

> the Dynamoïd Object determines the Immediate Object
> which determines the Sign itself,
> which determines the Destinate Interpretant,
> which determines the Effective Interpretant,
> which determines the Explicit Interpretant, (Hardwick 1977: 84)

he is alluding to the circle. The spiral follows another path.

We are no longer at the beginning of time; we were born into a world which
was already constituted, a world, it is true, and fortunately so, which is being continually reconstructed. Here we do not start from the dynamical object. We start
from signs. Not formal sign-representamens, but signs already constituted with
their final logical interpretants and their objects. Our distinctions shed light on
the processes of their constitution and reveal their functions. They do not describe states of things.

But these distinctions are technically necessary. The representamen is really
what sets the process in motion. However, it also is constituted by and for a given
society at a given moment. And it appears as if "determined" by the dynamical
object. In fact, matters are more complex, as we have seen. If one has a weakness
for diagrams, the semiotic triangle

O

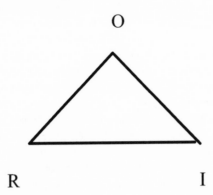

R                                               I

can be represented by a point where R, I, and O merge into one: a representamen
determines an interpretant to designate an object of which the representamen is
the complete and finished expression, closed and fixed in a society of robots like

that described by Aldous Huxley in *This Brave New World*. It is a geographical map on a world scale: it is the world . . . and supererogatory. At best, in a closed and fixed world where humans are not yet robots, programmed computers, we can think "our" world. In this case, there would be two points in relation—a homothetic relation, of course—a fixed point (O–R together): the world, corresponding to each and every point of another point (R–I together): thought. It is in this way that we can understand the dualism of Western philosophy from Plato to Descartes.

If, in an open world, we are not satisfied with the formal triangle which is an analytical and didactic abstraction, it must be developed in spirals, but with stops when the sign-interpretant becomes a habit, fortunately always liable to be broken, as Peirce reminds us. Let us stay put at one of these stops.

Let us suppose that this stop interrupts our progression—the process of a given semiosis—in front of a painting. We would have the following diagram:

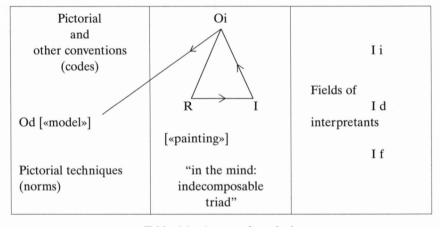

| Pictorial and other conventions (codes) | Oi | I i |
|---|---|---|
| Od [«model»] | R → I [«painting»] | Fields of interpretants I d |
| Pictorial techniques (norms) | "in the mind: indecomposable triad" | I f |

Table 4.1.  A case of semiosis

The painting (R) calls forth an interpretant (I) which is part of the fields of interpretants on three levels: that of the immediate interpretant (Ii), which is the interpretability of the painting; that of the final interpretant (If), which is the acquired habit of interpreting a painting according to the rules proper to a given group in a given society, and even to one member of this society; and that of the dynamical interpretant (Id), which is the interpretation of this painting at this moment in such an art gallery by a given visitor. The interpretant, always multiple, of course, will refer to an immediate object (Oi) in the mind of the viewer. But the latter will not think for one second that there is no painting in front of him. He will think spontaneously that the representamen (R) is in his "mind" and it is also there at the same time in front of him, that what he is looking at is a dynamical object (Od). However, the analysis does not stop here, because the representamen (R)—this painting: image (Oi) and thing (Od)—has not been created *ex nihilo*. The subject of the painting, whatever it may be, is with and by this painting rooted in a world we can call dynamical, whose constituents correspond very exactly to the levels of interpretants already described, the latter being "instantiated" in the manner in which a painter, with his pictorial and other conventions (codes) and the techniques (norms) at his disposal (left column in table 1), has revealed them to the eye.

## SEMIOSIS AND TIME

According to modern physicists, time is not a function nor an operator nor a factor without the things which it can measure, nor is it a psychological result of a physical movement. "Time is real" (1905: 5.458). It is a *continuous arrowed process.*

Peirce's semiotics is triadic, not only because it is tri-relational (Representamen → Interpretant → Object), but because a semiosis is a temporal process. It unites the three universes of possibility, existence, and discourse. That is to say that Peirce's semiotics can be considered either as a formal theory of signs or as a pragmatical theory of signs.

*Formally,* of course, time is not taken into account in the definition of a sign, not even the elements which are formally subsumed in a phenomenon or rather a *phaneron.*

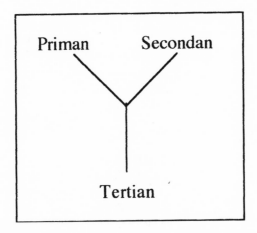

No proper place can be given to the three constitutive formal elements: the sign is indecomposable and its constitutive elements do not stand phaneroscopically for something which could be concretely described. The three phaneroscopical categories described respectively as Firstness, the category of quality or possibility, Secondness, the category of existence, and Thirdness, the category of mediation are possible illustrations rather than descriptions, properly speaking, and the same thing may be said of the Representamen (First), Object (Second), and Interpretant (Third).

Given the trichotomization of the Representamen (as R1, R2, R3), of the

Object (as O1, O2, O3), and of the Interpretant (as I1, I2, I3), and the rule of the hierarchization of the categories, there can be only ten classes of signs:

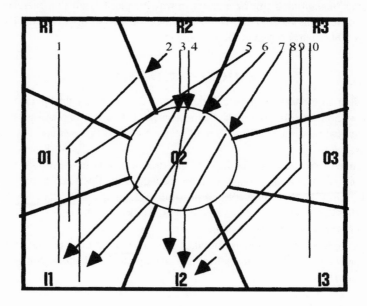

The classes of signs can be either only possible (1) or partially "realized" (2, 9), "existential" (3, 4, 6, 7) or "thought," without any reference to their "realization" (5, 8, 10). The directly or indirectly existential classes are in bold type in the table below.

| Possibility | Existence | Thought |
|---|---|---|
| 1 (R1, O1, I1)<br>2 **(R2, O1, I1)** | | |
| | 3 **(R2, O2, I1)**<br>4 **(R2, O2, I2)** | |
| | | 5 (R3, O1, I1) |
| | 6 **(R3, O2, I1)**<br>7 **(R3, O2, I2)** | |
| 9 **(R3, O3, I2)** | | 8 (R3, O3, I1) |
| | | 10 (R3, O3, I3) |

Table 4.2. The ten classes of signs. See also Table 2.2 on p. 19.

It should be stressed that the non-existential classes are also real: the class of possibility as well as the classes of thought which state the rules to be applied in the existential world, even when they are actually enacted. Peirce says:

(1) Concerning possibility:

Some years ago [1903], [ . . . ] when in consequence of an invitation to deliver a course of lectures in Harvard University upon Pragmatism, I was led to revise that doctrine, in which I had already found difficulties, I soon discovered, upon a critical analysis, that it was absolutely necessary to insist upon and bring to the front, the truth that a mere possibility may be quite real. That admitted, it can no longer be granted that every conditional proposition whose antecedent does not happen to be realized is true, and the whole reasoning just given breaks down. (4.580)

(2) Concerning thought as law:

The real, then, is that which, sooner or later, information and reasoning would finally result in, and which is therefore independent of the vagaries of me and you. (1868: 5.311)

This conception of the real is closely connected to the definition of thought as a continuous *temporal process,* with all that this definition implies, to wit that this process is self-correcting (i.e., includes "absolute chance") and subject to public or communal testing.

Thus, the very origin of the conception of reality shows that this conception essentially involves the notion of a COMMUNITY, without definite limits, and capable of a definite increase of knowledge. And so those two series of cognition—the real and the unreal—consist of those which, at a time sufficiently future, the community will always continue to re-affirm; and of those which, under the same conditions, will ever after be denied. Now, a proposition whose falsity can never be discovered, and the error of which therefore is absolutely incognizable, contains upon our principle, absolutely no error. Consequently, that which is thought in these cognitions is the real, as it really is. There is nothing, then, to prevent our knowing outward things as they really are, and it is most likely that we do thus know them in numberless cases, although we can never be absolutely certain of doing so in any special case. (ibid.)

*Pragmatically,* semiosis is then a continuous process from a representamen (R) to an immediate object (Oi) (an actual event, or a sense or meaning) through an interpretant (I) which is also a sign, as long as the object is not found. When it is found, the interpretant is no longer a sign but a final interpretant, that is to say, a *habit*—either a new habit or the reinforcement of a previous habit.

Od (the dynamic object) belongs to the world of existence as such. Oi (the immediate object) belongs to the world of discourse, i.e., of thought as a rule or law which organizes the world of existence according to its intrinsic possibilities. Both objects change along with time: *t, t',* until the *ultimate t,* when semiosis ends at the end of "time" either for an individual being or the whole world.

Let us remark that Frege distinguishes two universes: the universe of discourse (*Zeichen-Sinn*) and the universe of reference (*Zeichen-Bedeutung*) which is in fact the universe of the objects of discourse (astronomical, grammatical)—and that Wittgenstein confounds them (*Zeichen-Sinn*): "*The limits of my lan-*

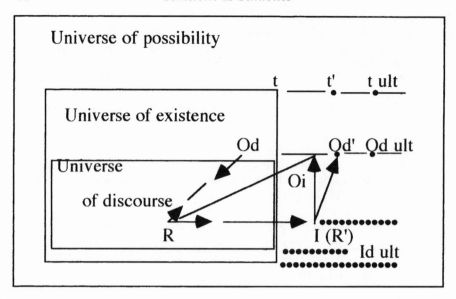

guage means the limits of my world." As there is no interpretant in either theory, there can be no time.

Without time, the relation between a sign as representamen and the dynamic object is a "vicious circle"; with time, it is a "virtuous spiral" as shown in the graph below:

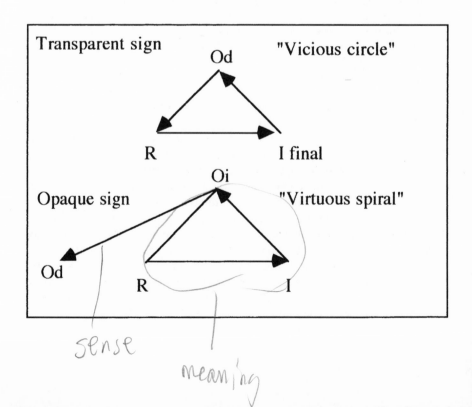

The relation $R-Od$ is called "sense," the relation $I(R')-Oi$ is called "meaning."

> The Immediate Interpretant is an abstraction, consisting in a Possibility. The Dynamical Interpretant is a single actual event. The Final Interpretant is that toward which the actual tends. (Hardwick 1977: 111)

Sense, meaning, and significance are *relations*. Meaning is the triadic relation proper. Sense (or rather "acceptation" [8.184]) is a first degree degenerate triadic relation (1.364). Significance is "the effect the sign *would* produce upon any mind upon which circumstances should permit it to work out its full effect" ( Hardwick, 110). It is the "interpretative result to which every interpreter is destined to come if the sign is sufficiently considered" (ibid., 111).

# - 5 -

# Sign

## THE CONCEPT AND ITS USE

Peirce's theory of signs is by description mostly concerned with translation. No sign can be understood without being interpreted. That is why I shall mainly deal here with Peirce's terminology and its translation or interpretation. It will not be a question of languages proper, but of conceptual expressions of the signs used by Peirce to convey his ideas, although we cannot do that without also touching upon the question of the languages used: English, French, Italian, etcetera.

It is a fact that Peirce tried out many neologisms to express his thought right until the end of his life. To give an instance, in a letter of 1911, he wonders whether *logon* (the Greek word λόγον) would not be a better word than "sign," or even "representamen" to convey what he means by "sign."

Nobody was ever more concerned than he was by what he calls the ethics of terminology.

> [...] our first rule [...] will certainly be that every technical term of philosophy ought to be used in that sense in which it first became a technical term of philosophy. (Peirce 1979: C053)

If we want to understand Peirce, we have to be as careful as he was when we translate him.

As I have just said, the problem of translation is not a question of using one word instead of another one; it is to ask the pragmatic question Peirce was the first to raise: What does this word do? If both words do the same thing, one word is enough; but if one word induces two (or more) trends of actions or rather, in the present case, *mental* actions, the differences ought to be expressed by different words.

I shall start with common mistranslations in present-day theories of signs. Everybody knows that Peirce defines a sign as a triad made of three indecomposable elements: a representamen, an object, and an interpretant.

For Saussure, a sign is an indissoluble pair or couple composed of a signifier and a signified.

Can we translate Peirce's definition into Saussure's? There is at least one point in common in both definitions: a sign is an indecomposable or indissoluble unit. But which element is which? Is the representamen a signifier? Let us concede this translation. Now which, of the "object" and the "interpretant," is the signified? I should not dare to answer the question. Some semioticians do, and translate "interpretant" by "signified," and manage to find something to translate "object" into Saussurean terminology—"referent"—which makes Saussure's sign a *mariage à trois*. My opinion is that the two theories are untranslatable into one another, because their underlying philosophies and logics are incompatible. Saussure's are dualistic, Peirce's dialectic.

Another question may help us to be more cautious. How are we going to translate "sign" into their respective terminologies, since they both use the same word? Let us be more precise: when does a sign stop being a sign in Saussure's semiology and in Peirce's semiotics or rather semeiotic? Saussure's sign is *linguistic*; Peirce's sign can be linguistic too, but it is not linguistic as such. A sign can be three things: a qualisign, a sinsign, or a legisign—and the linguistic sign is only one type of legisign.

Another difference should be stressed here. Saussure's definition is *formalistic*; Peirce's is formalistic too, if one considers what Peirce calls the "sign-object," but it is also a process which he calls the "sign-action" or *semiosis*.

The three formalistic elements of a sign-object become functions in a sign-action. And I agree that it is not always easy to be sure of which sign (sign-object or sign-action) Peirce speaks. That is why I prefer to use the word "representamen" for the sign-object, and the word "semiosis" for the sign-action—and leave "sign" as a technical term to Saussure's semiology.

A third argument can be used to show how far both theories are from one another. I already used this argument implicitly when I said that Peirce's sign can be a qualisign, a sinsign, or a legisign. Peirce's theory of signs rests on a phenomenology or, to use Peirce's term, a phaneroscopy, the categories of which are ordinal. There are three phaneroscopical categories: 1, 2, and 3, which are not cardinal but ordinal numbers. That is to say that 3 does not mean the single number 3, but a "Third," which presupposes a "Second," which presupposes a "First." Peirce's phaneroscopy is hierarchical. A Third is the law which "facts" or Seconds obey, but which no fact or Second can provide. A fact or Second exists because it was possible or First, but a First or a sheer possible cannot produce a fact or Second.

We cannot translate and understand Peirce, if we do not have all that in our minds; that and many other things.

Above I was concerned with the problem of whether it is possible to explain one theory in the terminology of another theory. I showed, I think, that this is not the best way to understand Peirce.

Would it be better to translate Peirce into his own terms? Perhaps. But we have to be very cautious and ask ourselves two questions before using this way for understanding: (1) When was the text used as a translation; published or written? (2) To whom was it addressed?

1. Let us take a first example to answer the first question—the word to be understood being "representamen" as used by Peirce between 1895 and 1903.

Peirce wrote in 1867 "On a New List of Categories" (see ch. 1) of which I am quoting two passages:

> The five conceptions [ . . . ] obtained [by precision] [ . . . ], may be termed *categories.*
> *Being*
> Quality (reference to a ground)
> Relation (reference to a correlate)
> Representation (reference to an interpretant)
> *Substance*
> The three intermediate conceptions may be termed accidents. (1.555)

> Since no one of the categories can be prescinded from those above it, the list of supposable objects which they afford is,
> *What is,*
> Quale (that which refers to a ground)
> Relate (that which refers to ground and correlate)
> Representamen (that which refers to ground, correlate, and interpretant)
> *It.* (1.557)

Can these passages be quoted to understand the meaning of "representamen" as used from 1895 to 1903, or rather, according to me, until the end of Peirce's life, although after 1903, it is as if in disguise, as I shall show later?

It is true that this test is very important (and can be used in more ways than I am ready to discuss here). It is important because it is the foundation stone of the theory of the hierarchy of categories, which is obtained by "precision." "Precision" is one of the three kinds of distinction which Peirce relies upon in all his writings, together with "discrimination" or "mental distinction," and "dissociation" or "physical distinction." Peirce borrows "precision" *(praecisio* from *praescindere)* from John Duns Scotus. Precision introduces an ordinal order in the categories: a representation (the object of which is the *representamen*) implies a relation (the object of which is a *relate*) which implies itself a quality (the object of which is a *quale*).

However, this article is confusing when one tries to refer to it to explain what a representamen is in semeiotic. It is a fact—which one can accept easily enough—that the three intermediary conceptions will become the fundamental categories of phaneroscopy. It is not so easy to use the definitions of the terms in this paper and especially of the word "representamen" in another context.

When Peirce wrote "On a New List of Categories," he was still a Kantian of Aristotelian obedience. When he proposed his phaneroscopical semeiotic, perhaps he was still a Kantian, but with a new logic, the logic of (triadic) relations.

Is the representamen of 1867 (which is an intermediary Third) the same as the representamen of the semeiotic theory which is a first? From 1895 on, the representamen is a First and trichotomizable into a representamen which is a possible, a representamen which is an existent, and a representamen which is a law or rather a rule. If the representamen is a First, can it still be understood in terms of "representation" as in the paper of 1867? If the "quality" of 1867 is merely possible, can it be referred to a ground? We are in another world, a "pre-Peircean" world, so to speak, a world which is Aristotelico-scholastic and even Thomistic. Peirce writes in a paper of 1868:

> [A]s far as the sensation is a mere feeling of a particular sort, it is determined only by an inexplicable, occult power; and so far, it is not a representation, but only the material quality of a representation [ ... ]. A feeling, therefore, as a feeling, is merely the *material quality* of a mental sign. (5.291)

Material quality, the ground of which is "pure abstraction" to which one refers, Peirce said, as to "a quality or general attribute" (1.551).

Peirce's Thomism is, however, revised by Kant. Being and Knowing are continuous, although Being is incognizable and Knowing is a transcendental construct. The material quality of Being is the *species impressa: "species coloris est in aere: per aerem ad pupillam defertur"* (Color is in the air: by means of the air it enters the eye); the mental quality is the *species expressa: "ista actione (scilicet visu rei exterioris) visus non videt se videre. Visus enim non videt se, sed colorem"* (By this action [that is to say, by seeing the exterior thing] sight does not see itself seeing. Thus sight does not see itself, but the color).

In the semeiotic theory of the nineties, there will be no ground, except inside the sign-action, far away from Being and without any relation to Being. If there is something which could be taken for the ground it is the *qualisign,* a pure possible, the possibility of which is known only after becoming an existent in a *sinsign* and the meaning of which a *legisign* alone, within a semeiotic process, will enable us not to know, but to guess.

There will no longer be any substance, but only relations, productive of objects within a system of signs in process. A proposition will no longer consist of a substantive term and of a predicative term which expresses the quality of the substance. A proposition will consist of a predicate (or verb—Peirce says a *rhema*) and of an index which will give an existence (or substance) to a predicate (or quality).

Therefore the answer to the first question is that it is possible to translate

Peirce into his own terms, provided the context of the writings is also taken into account. As I pointed out in the general introduction of the present book, it is an aspect of the method I used to write on Peirce. I shall deal now with the other aspect of the method discussed in the general introduction: the chronological reading.

2. I am going to keep the same example, the meaning of the word "sign" or most of the time its equivalent, "representamen," to try to answer the other question: To whom were the writings proposed as an argument, addressed? For the difficulty of a historical translation is complicated when the author tries to convince a reader or an audience by using the very terms to which he himself gives another meaning than that of the people he wants to convince. I am not at all sure that "throwing sops to Cerberus" is the best way to clarify a theory.

The history of the use by Peirce of the word "representamen" to denote the formal element constitutive of the semeiotic triad, can be divided into four periods:

1. Up to 1873, Peirce uses *representamen* to mean the object of representation.

2. From 1873 to 1895, he does not use the word "representamen" at all—and when he uses the word "sign," it is in a non-technical way.

3. From 1895 to 1903, he again makes use of the word "representamen."

4. From 1904 to 1911, he abandons it again and uses instead "sign" except in four cases, which we will examine briefly.

With the first period (1866–1873), we have dealt sufficiently. Peirce's writings are very clear. They belong to a dualistic world and a time when everybody agrees that words must have objects with which to correspond. The only point of contention is the "how" of the correspondence.

When Peirce stops using the word in the second period (1873–1895), it is not because he thinks that the word is unsuitable for one reason or another. It is merely because he is occupied with other things. He travels extensively and especially in Europe for the Geodesic Survey, for one thing. And, at the same time, as he is no longer satisfied with Aristotelian logic, he is busy searching for another way of reasoning. The solution struck him on board ship on his way to Europe in 1877, when he wrote the French original of: "How to Make Our Ideas Clear." It was the foundation stone of pragmatism:

> There is no distinction of meaning so fine as to consist in anything but a possible difference of practice. (5.400)

But a new theory of inference was not enough. It had to be supplemented by a new logic to replace the Aristotelian logic of predicates: it was the logic of relatives (or relations) which Peirce elaborated in the eighties. A new conception of signs was then possible.

The reintroduction of the word "representamen" in the third period (1895–1903) corresponds to the now-rendered possible, logical, and phaneroscopical elaboration of a new semeiotic which distinguishes clearly a sign-representamen, a formal definition of each element of the triad and of its formal trichotomies, and a sign-action, which is the semeiotic process proper or semiosis, in which an interpretant-representamen refers a sign-representamen to an object-representamen.

The representamen is no longer the object of a representation, nor a psychical phenomenon. It is there in the sign-action as representing—in the sense in which a "deputy," a "representative," an "ambassador" represents—a dynamic object.

> A sign, or *representamen,* is something which stands to somebody for something in some respect or capacity. (2.228)

Representation is thus restricted to "the operation of a sign or its *relation to* the object *for* the interpreter of the representamen" (1.540).

Every sign is a representamen.

By a sign I mean anything which conveys any definite notion of an object in any way, as such conveyers of thought are familiarly known to us. Now I start with this familiar idea and make the best analysis I can of what is essential to a sign, and I define a representamen as being whatever that analysis applies to. (1.540)

Whence the formal definition of a representamen:

A Representamen is a subject of a triadic relation to a second, called its object, for a third, called its interpretant, this triadic relation being such that the Representamen determines its interpretant to stand in the same triadic relation to the same object for some interpretant. (1.541)

Therefore, every representamen is not a sign. If a representamen has no mental interpretant, it is not a sign.

If a sunflower, in turning towards the sun, becomes by that very act fully capable, without further condition, of reproducing a sunflower which turns in precisely corresponding ways toward the sun, and of doing so with the same reproductive power, the sunflower would become a Representamen of the sun. (2.274)

"But," Peirce goes on, as if regretfully, "*thought* is the chief, if not the only mode, of representation" (2.274); that is to say, the only mode which man has ever experienced.

The fourth period (1904–1911), which coincides with the vogue of pragmatism, starts with the review Peirce wrote of Lady Welby's *What is Meaning?* For the first time, Peirce has a public. In his letters to Lady Welby, he first sums up his semeiotic theory and then develops it to a point where it is not easy to say whether he is experimenting with ideas as he used to do in his *Logic Notebook* or whether he really thinks that Lady Welby is ready to accept his semeiotic. On the other hand, he is invited to write articles in various journals to defend his own brand of pragmatism or rather Pragmaticism. Apart from the very technical letters to Lady Welby, some of which were not sent, Peirce is eager to please her or his readers, so that when he writes to her he uses a terminology which is hers and not his own, and when he publishes articles he uses a terminology meant rather not to offend the readers of the journals than to expose his technical views on the topic.

Therefore, it is not at all surprising to see Peirce, for instance, adopt Lady Welby's distinctions between sense, meaning, and significance and equate them with his trichotomies of interpretants: immediate, dynamic, and final. Although I agree that this trichotomy is very useful when one analyzes a sign, let us say a literary text or a painting, I am not quite sure that this trichotomy has anything to do with the interpretant of the formal definition of the sign.

And, among the reasons I could give, there is at least one which is difficult to reject: the formal interpretant requires an interpretant to be a sign and so on *ad infinitum.* That is what one can read in the definition of a sign in Baldwin's *Dictionary:* A sign is

> anything which determines something else (its *interpretant*) to refer to an object to which itself refers (its *object*) in the same way, the interpretant becoming in turn a sign, and so on *ad infinitum.* (2.303)

The word defined is "sign," but it stands unquestionably for "representamen," like nearly all the definitions of a sign in this period. Another quotation may be enough. It belongs to a manuscript of 1910, entitled *Meaning.*

> The sign can only represent the Object and tell about it. It cannot furnish acquaintance with or recognition of that Object; for that is what is meant in this volume by the Object of a Sign; namely, that with which it presupposes an acquaintance in order to convey some further information concerning it. (2.231)

When Peirce uses the word "representamen" in this period, it is not, as one would think, to explain why he rejects it, but to show how necessary it is from a formal point of view. I cannot argue my contention at length, but a few hints may suffice.

Peirce discusses the question four times. The first time, in a draft of a letter to Lady Welby written in July 1905, Peirce speaks as if he had stopped using the word "representamen," because "there was no need of this horrid long word" (Hardwick 1977: 193). However, he goes on, "I admit still that it aids the comprehension of the definition" (ibid.). A sign represents as a legislative representative does, so that "representamen" is the right word for such a sign, except that a "representative" has a duty towards his constituents and that there is nothing of the sort in the idea of a sign. In other words, "representamen" is not formal enough. Is "sign" more formal? Peirce wanted it to be so, if we believe his own definition in the same draft:

A "Sign" is anything, A, which (1) in addition to other characters of its own, (2) stands in a dyadic relation, R, for a purely active correlate, B, (3) and is also in a triadic relation to B for a purely passive correlate, C, this triadic relation being such as to determine C to be a dyadic relation, S, to B, the relation S corresponding in a recognised way to the relation R. (ibid.: 192)

It seems to me that the whole draft suggests that, if "representamen" were to be deprived of its private and psychological connotations, it would be the right term for a sign as a formal entity.

The second time he mentions the word "representamen," the next year, on January 8, 1906, Peirce says that logically "representamen" is preferable to "sign":

Truth is the conformity of a representamen to its object, its object, ITS object, mind you. (5.554)

Although a representamen cannot be true without "an action of the object upon the sign to render the latter true" (5.554).

"Sign" stands here for a sign-action of which a "representamen" is the formal element.

In another letter to Cousin Jo, three years later, on June 26, 1909, Peirce comes back to the problem and defines a sign as the "concrete representamen" of a representation, such as a diagram in mathematics. By "concrete," he means of course a replica, and by "representation," a sign-action. His definition of a sign here again is that of a representamen:

I define a sign as anything—be it an existent thing or actual factual fact, or be it, like what we call a "word," a mere possible form to which an audible sound, visible shape, or other sensible object may conform to [sic], or be it a property or habit of behaviour of something either experienced or imagined,—which is on the one hand so determined (i.e. affected either by causation or through the medium of a mind) by an object other than itself and on the other hand, in its turn so affects some mind, or is capable of doing so, that this mind is thereby itself mediately determined by the same object. (*The New Elements of Mathematics,* 3:233)

The last time Peirce mentions "representamen," in 1911, it is in a manuscript full of corrections and rewritings. This would deserve a thorough commentary, the conclusion of which would be that logic is not a psychological science, nor the science of signs, as sign-actions (which is semeiotic proper), but the science of representamens or rather of legisigns, which he proposes to call for the present (three years before he died) "by the provisional appellation of 'logons'" (Ms 675).

In brief, the logic of inference which is the logic of the signs in action or semiosis rests on the formal logic of the triadic relations of the representamen.

If I were permitted to give some advice to the readers of Peirce, I would say:

if you want to understand Peirce's theory of signs, never read "sign" when you see the word, but translate it either by "representamen" or by "semiosis." And leave the word "sign" to Saussure's semiology.

To conclude, I shall quote a commentator on Peirce, George A. Benedict, who wrote at some length on the "representamen":

> [ ... ] semioticians ought to put this term to use because (1) the described role is still without an unambiguous name to denote it, (2) it provides a plausible solution for the nearly vicious ambiguity that plagues the term "sign," (3) it would make it harder for those working in the theory of signs to lapse into forgetfulness about *a sign's triadic nature* and (4) Peirce's contributions to the field qualify him to be honored in this way. (Benedict 1979: 3)

## READING AS TRANSLATION

I should like, in conclusion, to return to the problem of translation in general. Obviously, the way in which I have dealt with the "translation" of Peirce's terminology, both from the interpretative as well as the linguistic point of view, should be much further elaborated. My suggestions, in brief, are as follows. There are three types of translation in the classical sense of the transposition of one language into another (the question of interpretation depending in this case on the translator and not on the reader):

1. Translation of the representamen: in other words, the text of the source-language is transferred literally into the target-language. This is the procedure adopted by André Chouraqui for the translation of the Bible into French, and by Charles Mopsik and his collaborators for that of the Talmud in the collection *Les Dix paroles* (Editions Verdier). This classical procedure (which was commonly used for Greek and Latin when these languages were still on the syllabus) either requires to be complemented by a great many notes, or else implies, on the reader's part, such a perfect knowledge of the source-language that the translation might seem to serve no useful purpose.

2. Translation of the objects of discourse: in this case the reader must also be familiar with the culture of the source-language readers. This method, which was sometimes used in translations from Greek and Latin, especially in dictionaries, is not very satisfactory. It also requires supplementary information such as photographs or drawings, with explanatory notes since images do not speak.

3. Translation of the interpretants of the representamens (or shall we say *representamina*?) of the source-language: English workmen having a cup of tea during their break could be rendered in a French text by workmen drinking a glass of wine at a bar counter. Marcel Duhamel's collection, *Série Noire* greatly appreciated by its readers, has specialized in this type of translation which also sometimes resorts to literal renderings of the type noted above, in order to give the text a certain air of authenticity. A curious example of the influence exerted by this kind of translation should be noted here: French authors writing novels

*in French,* which supposedly take place in the United States, and are published in the same collection, tend to adopt the same Americanisms as those used by the translators.

The ideal would be to combine the three methods. Philosophical writings are fairly easy to deal with in this way. It is with this in mind that I have translated Peirce, trying not to distort the "text"-representamen of the source-language, nor the concept-objects expressed by the representamens, nor the representamens-interpretants of the target-language. But a knowledge of philosophy and its history remains indispensable.

# PART THREE

# *Comparative Semiotics*

[O]ne's point of reference should not be to the great model
of language and signs, but to that of war and battle. The history which bears and determines us has the form of a war
rather than that of a language: relations of power, not relations of meaning. [ . . . ] [Semiotics] is a way of avoiding
[history's] violent, bloody and lethal character by reducing
it to the calm Platonic form of language and dialogue.
—Foucault (1972: 114)

# - 6 -

## Semiotics and Logic

### A REPLY TO JERZY PELC

As William James put it, in his picturesque manner, if at the
last day all creation was shouting hallelujah and there re-
mained one cockroach with an unrequited love, *that* would
spoil the universal harmony.

—Santayana (1920: 107)

I am one of those logicians and consequently (according to Peirce) semioticians
who "believe" in Peirce's theory of signs. That is why I venture to answer Jerzy
Pelc's questions to Peircean semioticians,* although I have to confess that my
reading of Peirce is biased by my previous travels in the field of philosophy,
through Aristotle, Thomas Aquinas (by way of Jacques Maritain), Kant, and
John Dewey.

## INTRODUCTION

Is the following quotation from Peirce "vague" and "incomprehensible," or, to
put it in other words, is it "a kind of poetry" [64]?

The idea of the absolutely first must be entirely separated from all conception
of or reference to anything else; for what involves a second is itself a second to
that second. The first must therefore be present and immediate, so as not to be
second to a representation. It must be fresh and new, for if old it is second to its
former state. It must be initiative, original, spontaneous and free; otherwise it is
second to a determining cause. It is also something vivid and conscious; so only
it avoids being the object of some sensation. It precedes all synthesis and all
differentiation; it has no unity and no parts. It cannot be articulately thought:
assert it, and it has already lost its characteristic innocence; for assertion always
implies a denial of something else. Stop to think of it, and it has flown! What the

* Jerzy Pelc, "Several Questions to Experts in Peirce's Theory of Signs" in *Peirce in Italia,* eds.
M. A. Bonfantini and A. Martone (Napoli: Liguori Editore, 1993), 63–84. References to J. Pelc's article will be given by page between brackets.

world was to Adam on the day he opened his eyes to it, before he had drawn any distinctions, or had become conscious of his own existence—that is first, present, immediate. (1.357)

The first part may seem "incomprehensible" and particularly Peirce's argument to prove that the idea of absolutely First "must be separated from all conception of or reference to anything else." Peirce writes: "for what involves a second is itself a second to that second." It is of course incomprehensible if the definitions of First, Second, and Third are not given:

The first is that whose being is simply in itself, not referring to anything nor lying behind anything. The second is that which is what it is by force of something to which it is second. The third is that which is what it is owing to things between which it mediates and which it brings into relation to each other. (1.356)

Otherwise, it is perfectly clear: a First with a reference is no longer a First, but "second to that second," for what involves a second (any dyadic relation which, by definition, as such is reciprocal) is second to what (another dyadic relation) determines it to be a second. For example, there is effort on the part of a term if, and only if, effort involves resistance on the part of another term and *reciprocally*. Is this way of describing a concept "a kind of poetry"?
Paul Valéry said:

La poésie la plus élevée essaye de balbutier ces choses [intellectuellement inexprimables]. (Valéry 1973, 1:415)

La poésie n'a pas à exposer des idées. [ ... ] Elle doit donc former ou communiquer l'état sub-intellectuel. (Valéry 1974, 2:1091)

As a First cannot be "expressed" symbolically, it has to be "mumbled" poetically or, rather, iconically. That is what Peirce did in the last two sentences (of the first extract in this chapter): "Stop to think of it, and it has flown! What the world was to Adam on the day he opened his eyes to it, before he had drawn any distinctions, or had become conscious of his own existence—that is first, present, immediate."
This iconic "expression" of a First is not just the result of a rhetorical technique, it is the rigorous conclusion of a logically defined phenomenology or rather phaneroscopy, not in the sense of Husserl or Ingarden, but in the sense of Kant and in reaction to him. Far from being influenced by German philosophy, as Jerzy Pelc suggests [64], Peirce was always very critical of the German way of thinking. Peirce's phaneroscopic categories are hierarchical. A Third (category of mediation or thought or logical implication as law) includes a Second (category of instances or existing occurrences: events or any kind of individual) which includes a First (category of potentiality or quality in the Aristotelian sense). But not the reverse: A possible First cannot give birth by itself to an existing

Second, and an existing Second (or any number of Seconds, even an infinity) cannot produce an organizing Third. (This is, by the way, the reason why Peirce proposed to substitute an abductive logic of invention for the inductive logic of discovery.)

Peirce's "triadomania" is grounded not in his own peculiar personality, but in the logical and phaneroscopical definition of relation. Any relation proper is triadic.

> Every genuine triadic relation involves thought or *meaning*. Take, for example, the relation of *giving*. A *gives* B to C. This does not consist in A's throwing *B* away and its accidentally hitting C [ ... ] If that were all, it would not be a genuine relation, but merely one dyadic relation followed by another [ ... ] Giving is a transfer of the right of property. Now right is a matter of law. And law is a matter of thought and meaning. (1.345)

The hierarchy of Peirce's categories, the fact that they are "ordinal" and not "cardinal," i.e., that they are First, Second (including First), and Third (including Second and First) and not just One, Two, and Three is clearly stated in the following quotation:

> The other premiss of the argument that genuine triadic relations can never be built of dyadic relations and of qualities is easily shown. In existential graphs, a spot with one tail—X represents a quality, a spot with two tails—R—a dyadic relation. Joining the ends of two tails is also a dyadic relation. But you can never by such joining make a graph with three tails. You may think that a node connecting three lines of identity Y is not a triadic idea. But analysis will show that it is so. I see a man on Monday. On Tuesday I see a man, and I exclaim, "Why, that is the *very* man I saw on Monday." We may say, with sufficient accuracy, that I directly experienced the identity. On Wednesday I see a man and I say, "That is the same man I saw on Tuesday, and consequently is the same I saw on Monday." There is a recognition of triadic identity; but it is only brought about as a conclusion from two premisses, which is itself a triadic relation. If I see two men at once, I cannot by any such direct experience identify both of them with a man I saw before. I can only identify them if I regard them, not as the *very* same, but as two different manifestations of the same man. But the idea of *manifestation* is the idea of a sign. Now a sign is something, A, which denotes some fact or object, B, to some interpretant thought, C. (1.346)

## ONTOLOGICAL AND GNOSEOLOGICAL CATEGORIES

As a philosopher, I shall dare to go on with the topic, because I agree that the problems of "being and cognition" [65-70] encountered in Peirce's theory of signs have to be solved in order to understand it. I would add that I had myself, and sometimes still have, the same problems, when or if inadvertently I try to interpret Peirce within the context of the classical Aristotelian and Kantian way of thinking which was also Peirce's at one time and very often accidentally so. That is why it is very important to date the quotations in the first case and notice the context in the second, for instance, when he writes to Lady Welby. I shall thus focus mostly here on the "ontological and gnoseological" questions, because the answers to the semiotic questions will only be corollaries of my answers to the ontological and gnoseological questions.

The word "gnoseology" was invented by Theodore Flournoy (whom, by the way, Peirce read when he prepared his B.A. at Harvard). Flournoy distinguished "gnoseology" from "epistemology": The latter is the theory of knowledge in general and the former is "the systematic analysis of the concepts used by thought to interpret the world" (Lalande 1947: 374).

As to "ontology," it is, according to J. Clauberg (*Metaphysica,* 1646),

quaedam scientia quae contemplatur ens quatenus ens est, hoc est, in quantum communem quamdam intelligitur habere naturam [ . . . ] [quae] omnibus et singulis entibus suo modo inest. (Lalande 1947: 697)

D'Alembert stated more precisely what "communis natura" meant: "Beings, spiritual as well as material, having some properties like existence, possibility and duration" (D'Alembert 1751: §71).

Is there anything like "ontological and gnoseological categories" in Peirce's phaneroscopy? Peirce's theory may be summed up in the following way. In the course of natural evolution an animal found a special means of adapting itself to its environment. This "means" was called "intelligence." "Intelligence" is thus a tool which is not supernatural, but an extension or rather a continuation of nature. Thus nature has become intelligent, but no more nor less "intelligible" than before the appearance of the human mode of adaptation. As John Dewey put it later in his *Experience and Nature:*

[E]xperience is *of* as well as *in* nature. It is not experience which is experienced, but nature—stones, plants, animals, diseases, health, temperature, electricity, and so on. Things interacting in certain ways *are* experience; they are what is experienced. Linked in certain other ways with another natural object—the human organism—they are *how* things are experienced as well. Experience thus reaches down into nature; it has depth. It also has breadth and to an indefinitely elastic extent. It stretches. That stretch constitutes inference. (Dewey 1929: 4a-1)

We have here the scholastic distinction between *an sit* and *quid sit.* The *an sit* is Dewey's "experience" and Peirce's "collateral experience," the *quid sit* is Dewey's "*how* things are experienced" and Peirce's "semiosis."

For Peirce, gnoseology and ontology are one and the same thing: the ontological categories are the gnoseological modes of adaptation. Dewey's way of saying the same thing is more likely not to resist Pelc's objections. We cannot discuss Dewey's position here. It is as "realistic" as Peirce's, not in a Platonistic and aristocratic way, but rather in a social and democratic way. Peirce writes:

My view is that there are three modes of being. I hold we can directly observe them in elements of whatever is at any time before the mind in any way. They are the being of positive qualitative possibility [Firstness], the being of actual fact [Secondness], and the being of law that will govern facts in the future [Thirdness]. (1.23)

Peirce's categories cannot be conceived *separately;* neither from nature, for they are material and spiritual or, in other words, physical and mental, nor from one another, for they are logical and not psychological, relational and not grammatico-ontological, and, as already stated, ordinal and not cardinal. That is why, as modes of being, the categories can be "directly observed"; not "known," properly speaking, but *collaterally* "experienced." A collateral experience is always Second, but as a Second (token), it is a *replica* of a law (type).

The only problem is that a token—any occurrence or Second—must have been possible—a First—before happening. Thus a Second must presuppose a First. How is it then that Peirce says that a First is "that which is such as it is, positively and without reference to anything else"? Because his categories are logically defined as ordinal: A First is, by definition, without reference whatsoever, a Second by reference to a First, and a Third by reference to a Second and a First.

Does this lead to circularity? No, because the categories are ordinal, that is to say, non-reciprocal. Let us take the relations of A, B, and C in that order: A (1st), B (2nd), C (3rd). If, through prescission, we take A (1st) without B (2nd) and B (2nd) without C (3rd), we can prescind A (1st) from B (2nd) and C (3rd), and B (2nd) from C (3rd). But we cannot prescind C (3rd) from B (2nd), nor B (2nd) from A (1st) (see W1: 519). Hence the following table:

| C (3rd) without B (2nd) | B (2nd) without A (1st) | A (1st) without B (2nd) | B (2nd) without C (3rd) |
|---|---|---|---|
| 0 | 0 | 1 | 1 |

Table 6.1. The non-reciprocal order of Peirce's categories

Is there a "vicious circle" in the following quotation?

Existence [ . . . ] is a special mode of reality [ . . . ] Reality in its turn is a special mode of being, the characteristic of which is that things that are real are whatever they really are, independently of any assertion of them. (6.349)

No, because reality is independent of what we think of it and, as there are three kinds of reality according to the categories to which they belong—Possibility (Firstness), Existence (Secondness), and Mediation or law (Thirdness)—if each of them is independent of what we think of it, there cannot be any vicious circle:

> [T]he first, the second, and the third are all three of the nature of thirds, or thought, while in respect to one another they are first, second and third. The first is thought in its capacity as mere possibility; that is mere *mind* capable of thinking, or a mere vague idea. The *second* is thought playing the role of a Secondness, or event. That is, it is of the general nature of *experience* or *information.* The third is thought in its role as governing secondness. It brings the information into the mind, or determines the idea and gives it body. It is informing thought, or *cognition.* But take away a psychological or accidental human element, and in this genuine Thirdness see the operation of a sign. (1.537)

Is there any parallelism between the gnoseological categories or categories of consciousness and the ontological categories? The ontological categories are logical, the gnoseological categories are psychological, just as the objects of physics, although non-psychological, are conscious when a physicist theorizes or experiments with them. Which explains the distinction between phaneron and phenomenon, not because they are two different things, but because there are two different approaches: one logical (phaneron), the other psychological (phenomenon).

Is it contradictory to assert that the gnoseological categories are Third and the ontological categories First, Second, and Third? On the contrary, as thought gnoseologically they are conscious and then Third, as ontological they are real, that is to say, according to Peirce's definition of reality, either a possibility, or a fact, or a law. A logician as a human being deals, like a physicist, with objects completely different from the consciousness he may have of them. But he *cannot* think them without "instances," or "occurrences," or, to use the Peircean neologism, *replicas* of which he is aware and of which he has "in his mind" an image or icon: the being of positive qualitative possibility [Firstness], the being of actual fact [Secondness], and "the being of law that will govern facts in the future [Thirdness]" (1.23) are only examples, they are neither synonymous nor equivalent.

## PEIRCE'S SEMIOTIC CONCEPTS
### *Representamen [70–71]*

> A sign, or representamen, is something which stands to somebody for something in some respect or capacity. (2.228)

Peirce distinguishes the "sign-representamen" from the "sign-action." The latter is semiosis, the former is the first element of the triad as revealed by logical analysis. The triad itself can be described formally: Y. (I must confess that, in spite of his own "ethics of terminology," Peirce uses the word "sign" with one or the other meaning, sometimes in the same sentence—a practice which is of course very confusing. I try to avoid the word "sign" when the meaning of the word is not clear.) "Stands for" is a perfect definition of the representamen which "stands for" something which we do not know yet but that semiosis will possibly indicate in the course of the interpretative process. An ambassador "represents," stands for his country, exactly like the word "cake," but, of course, neither does the ambassador resemble nor is he a copy of his country, nor can the word "cake" be eaten. They are both representamens, but not interpretants. An interpretant is another sign-representamen "in the mind" of "somebody" and depends upon the experience and the context in which an ambassador or a cake was seen or the word "ambassador" or "cake" was read or heard.

## Ground [71–72]

When he was still a Kantian, Peirce thought that there were five categories: Substance, Quality, Relation, Representation, and Being. Quality was then "reference to a ground" (1.555). When he reduced the categories to three, he used the term only once in 1897 in reference to his first theory of signs of 1867:

> The sign stands for something, its object. It stands for that object, not in all respects, but in reference to a sort of idea, which we have sometimes called the ground of the representamen. (2.228)

In 1867, the *ground* was what will become later the *qualisign* which is the representamen as First. It is described in the first quotation (1890: 1.357). Its description cannot but be poetical, because as an "absolutely First," it cannot be grounded in anything on which it would rest. In other words, there is no place for a ground of a ground. The word does not belong to Peirce's mature semiotic terminology (Deledalle 1984/1985: 101–105).

## Object [72–75]

Does the object of a sign determine this sign and its interpretant? There are two ways of understanding Peirce's theory of signs: formally or semiotically. Formally, "the Dynamoid Object determines the Immediate Object which determines the Sign itself, which determines the Destinate Interpretant, which determines the Effective Interpretant, which determines the Explicit Interpretant" (Hardwick 1977: 84). Or, to quote a passage from the *Minute Logic* of 1902:

> A *Sign* is anything which is related to a Second thing, its *Object,* in respect to a Quality, in such a way as to bring a Third thing, its *Interpretant,* into relation to the same Object, and that in such a way as to bring a Fourth into relation to that Object in the same form, *ad infinitum.* (2.92)

Both quotations refer to the logical and formal analysis of semiosis, not to a semiosis *in actu.* The Fourth thing mentioned in the last quotation is not another Peircean concept, it is the beginning—a representamen—of a new formal semiosis which will have no end. Logically and formally there is no room for a dynamical object in this *ad infinitum* semiosis.

It is only in a temporal and pragmatical semiosis that a dynamical object can appear. What is a dynamical object? The accumulative result of semioses whose interpretants as social and/or private habits have produced immediate objects in as many singular semioses as the time and the circumstances have allowed:

> We must distinguish between the Immediate Object,—i.e. the Object as represented in the sign,—and the Real (no, because perhaps the Object is altogether fictive, I must choose a different term, therefore), say rather the Dynamical Object, which, from the nature of things, the Sign *cannot* express, which it can only *indicate* and leave the interpreter to find out by *collateral experience.* For instance, I point my finger to what I mean, but I can't make my companion know what I mean, if he can't see it, or if seeing it, it does not, to his mind, separate itself from the surrounding objects in the field of vision. (Letter to James, 8.314)

Is it possible to retain the concept of immediate object of a sign in which the object is "that which so determines a sign that the latter determines an idea in a person's mind" (8.343)? Yes, provided "determines" be understood as "gives birth to" and "idea" as the interpretant sign producing the immediate object.

## *Interpretant [75–81]*

The interpretant has two meanings according to whether it is considered *in* the process of semiosis or as *putting an end to* the process. In the process, it is a sign-representamen; at the end, it is a habit reinforced or modified. In the last case, it is not a sign, but a habit or disposition to react to sign-representamens in such a way that an immediate object is produced with or without semiosis. Here and only here does the division of interpretant between immediate, dynamic, and final obtain, and they are not *signs.* The final interpretant is a rule, the dynamical interpretant a case, and the immediate interpretant is the spontaneous application of the rule to the case:

> For instance, suppose I awake in the morning before my wife, and that afterwards she wakes up and inquires, "What sort of a day is it?" *This is* a sign, whose Object, as expressed, is the weather at that time, but whose Dynamical Object is the *impression which I have presumably derived from peeping between the window-curtains.* Whose Interpretant, as expressed, is the quality of the weather, but whose Dynamical Interpretant, is *my answering her question.* But, beyond that, there is a third Interpretant. The *Immediate Interpretant is* what the Question expresses, *all* that it immediately expresses, which I have imperfectly restated above. The *Dynamical Interpretant is* the actual effect that it has upon me, its interpreter. But the Significance of it, the *Ultimate,* or *Final, Interpretant is* her *purpose* in asking it, what effect its answer will have as to her plans for the ensuing day. I reply, let us suppose: "It is a stormy day." Here is another sign. Its

*Immediate Object is* the notion of the present weather so far as this is common to her mind and mine—not the *character* of it, but the *identity* of it. The *Dynamical Object is* the *identity* of the actual or Real meteorological conditions at the moment. The *Immediate Interpretant is* the *schema* in her imagination, i.e. the vague Image or what there is in common to the different Images of a stormy day. The *Dynamical Interpretant is* the disappointment or whatever actual effect it at once has upon her. The *Final Interpretant is* the sum of the *Lessons* of the reply, Moral, Scientific, etc. (Letter to James, 8.314)

### *Interpreter [72-73]*

The interpretant is a sign in an *ad infinitum* formal semiotic process—a semiosis; it is not an interpreter. In this case, Peirce defines an interpretant as "being that which the Sign produces in the Quasi-mind that is the Interpreter by determining the latter to a feeling, to an exertion, or to a Sign, which determination is the Interpretant" (4.536).

When a process comes to a stop, the interpretant is no longer a sign, but a habit, as we have already said. Whose habit? The habit of an interpreter, of course—an interpreter who is a conscious being, perfectly aware of *what* he feels, does, and thinks, but who is not the author or creator of this "what" as such. He is the seat of the signs which are "welded" (4.551) in himself by himself.

Feeling unable to convey what he meant by "interpretant" in both senses, Peirce often uses the word "interpreter" as "a sop to Cerberus" (Hardwick 1977: 81), but prefers to speak of Quasi-mind, Quasi-utterer, or Quasi-interpreter (4.551). Why? This is Peirce's explanation:

The reader probably wonders what is meant by a "quasi-mind." This conception is best reached through the system of Existential Graphs, which affords the truest representation of logical relations. (Ms 283: 111. Systems of Representation, Logical, 1905/1906)

Was it a kind of "psychophobia" [73] which led Peirce to prefer logic to psychology as a philosophical method? Not at all; it is the logic of relatives which convinces him to reject the psychological method, used from Aristotle to Kant, without denying the fact that man has feeling, awareness, and reflective conscience.

## CONCLUSION

All those semiotic distinctions are neither ontological nor gnoseological; they only apply to semiotics as "a method of inference from signs through signs," to quote Philodemus. What is at stake, in fact, is not Peirce's theory of signs, but his experimental metaphysics, as Professor Pelc confesses at the end of his paper [81-83]:

I would embrace [Peirce's] interpretation if permission was granted for ideal objects, timeless by nature, to occur as phases in the process of semiosis, developing in time, with this process being one of sign interpretation by an interpreter; not by a Quasi-mind but by a human being who, using a certain object, property, phenomenon or event—according to a specific rule defined in a given system—resorts to inference to refer to some other object, property, phenomenon or event, indicates or cognizes them, moving through successive stages of semiosis consisting in mental activities which the great Peirce deprived of their psychic character—the good Lord only knows why—labelled them interpretants and, inspired by Hegel and moved by his own peculiar penchant, bundled them together in threes, and arranged the bundles in three rows. [27]

Neither the ideal objects, nor the omnipotent interpreter with his psychic character can be granted. It is not denied that there are ideal objects and human interpreters, but they are not substantial, just quasi-objects and quasi-minds, i.e., events among events, signs among signs. Let us quote Dewey again at some length:

[O]ne can hardly use the term "experience" in philosophical discourse, but a critic rises to inquire "Whose experience?" The question is asked in adverse criticism. Its implication is that experience by its very nature is owned by some one; and that the ownership is such in kind that everything about experience is affected by a private and exclusive quality. The implication is as absurd as it would be to infer from the fact that houses are usually owned, are mine and yours and his, that possessive reference so permeates the properties of being a house that nothing intelligible can be said about the latter. It is obvious, however, that a house can be owned only when it has existence and properties independent of being owned. The quality of belonging to some one is not an all-absorbing maw in which independent properties and relations disappear to be digested into egohood. It is additive; it marks the assumption of a new relationship, in consequence of which the house, the common, ordinary, house, acquires new properties. It is subject to taxes; the owner has the right to exclude others from entering it; he enjoys certain privileges and immunities with respect to it and is also exposed to certain burdens and liabilities. (Dewey 1929: 231–232)

Substitute "experience" for "house," and no other word need be changed. Experience when it happens has the same dependence upon objective natural events, physical and social, as has the occurrence of a house. It has its own objective and definitive traits; these can be described without reference to a self, precisely as a house is of brick, has eight rooms, etc., irrespective of whom it belongs to. Nevertheless, just as for some purposes and with respect to some consequences, it is all-important to note the added qualification of personal ownership of real property, so with "experience." In first instance and intent, it is not exact nor relevant to say "I experience" or "I think." "It" experiences or is experienced, "it" thinks or is thought, is a juster phrase. Experience, a serial course of affairs with their own characteristic properties and relationships, occurs, happens, and is what it is. Among and within these occurrences, not outside of them nor underlying them, are those events which are denominated selves. In some specifiable respects and for some specifiable consequences, these selves, capable of objective denotation just as are sticks, stones, and stars, assume the care and administration of certain objects and acts in experience. Just as in the case of the house, this assumption of ownership brings with it further liabilities and assets, burdens and enjoyments. (Dewey 1929: 232–233)

# - 7 -

## Semeiotic and Greek Logic

### PEIRCE AND PHILODEMUS

Men do not know how what is at variance agrees with itself.
It is an attunement of opposite tensions, like that of the bow
and the lyre.
—Herakleitos of Ephesos (frag. 45)

Now logic, being for Peirce "only another name for *semiotic* [σημειοτική], the quasi-necessary, or formal doctrine of signs" (2.227), it is difficult to see how one can distinguish philosophy as metaphysics from semiotic as logic. I would like to try to answer this question, and while doing so, to answer another question: Is Peirce's pragmaticism an idealism or an empiricism, a realism or a nominalism?

I shall not begin by quoting Peirce, as, whatever answer be given, there will be no lack of Peirce's own texts to support it. Peirce himself suggests a way of circumventing the problem: "If there be a reader who cannot understand my writings, let me tell him that no straining of his mind will help him: his whole difficulty is that he has no personal experience of the world of problems of which we are talking" (3.419). Now, in order to share, however, one must read the works he read, and in the case of problems of logic, read the logicians of Antiquity. This is what we shall try to do as briefly as possible.

When one reads Aristotle, the Stoics, the Epicureans, and the Sceptics, one is first of all struck by the fact that they do not separate logic from semiotics. For all of them, as for Peirce, semiotics is another name for logic. The same applies to the whole school of Scholastics; and also to Locke, who, having divided the sciences in a quasi-phaneroscopic manner into three branches—"Physica, Practica and σημιοτική, or the 'doctrine of signs,' the most usual whereof being words"—says of σημιοτική that "it is aptly enough termed also λογική 'logic'" (Locke 1690: IV, ch. XXI).

Aristotle explicitly defines the sign (σημεῖον) as "a demonstrative proposition [ἀποδεικτικὴ πρότασις], either necessary or probable" and the enthymeme, not as an incomplete syllogism, as is often done, but as "a syllogism which starts from plausible premises or from signs [ἐξ εἰκότων ἢ σημείων]." A plausible premise is a proposition which is simply probable, whereas the sign is a demonstrative proposition, as we have just seen. "Ἐὰν μὲν ὧν ἡ μία λεχθῇ πρότασις σημεῖον γίνεται μόνον, ἐὰν δὲ καὶ ἡ ἑτέρα προσληφθῇ, συλλογισμός" (If then only one premiss [πρότασις] is stated, only one sign [σημεῖον] is obtained. But if the other premiss is used, a syllogism [συλλογισμός] is obtained) (Aristotle 1831: II, 27, 70a).

For the Stoics, "a sign is an antecedent judgment in a valid hypothetical syllogism, which serves to reveal the consequent" (Sextus Empiricus Vol. 1: II, 104).

There are, of course, important differences between the Aristotelian logic and that of the Stoics, if only because the latter is propositional and the former predicative. The only rule of Stoic logic is that "syllogism begins with the true and ends with the true" (ibid.: II, 219). "And they say that of [all syllogisms] only that which begins with truth and ends in falsehood is invalid, and the rest is valid" (ibid.).

For Aristotle, the demonstrative force resides in the "sense" of the sign according to the place occupied by the middle term in the figures. "Οἷον τὸ μὲν δεῖξαι κύωσαν διὰ τὸ γάλα ἔχειν ἐκ τοῦ πρώτου σχήματος· μέσον γὰρ τὸ γάλα ἔχειν ἔφ ᾧ τὸ Α κύειν, τὸ Β γάλα ἔχειν, γυνὴ ἐφ' ᾧ Γ" (For instance, the proof that a woman has conceived, because she has milk, belongs to the first figure [ἐκ τοῦ πρώτου σχώματος]. For *to have milk* [τὸ γάλα ἔχειν] is the middle term. One can represent *has conceived* by **A**, *to have milk* by **B**, and *woman* [γυνή] by **Γ**) (Aristotle 1831: II, 27, 70a).

Hence the syllogism:

Every woman who has milk (B) has conceived (A)
This woman (Γ) has milk (B),
Thus this woman (Γ) has conceived (A).

In his *Outlines of Pyrrhonism*, Sextus Empiricus uses the same example to explain the hypothetical syllogism or implication (συνημμένον) of the Stoics: " 'Antecedent', they say, is 'the precedent clause in a hypothetical syllogism which begins in truth and ends in truth'. And it 'serves to reveal the consequent', since in the syllogism 'If this woman has milk, she has conceived', the clause 'If this woman has milk' seems to be evidential of the clause 'she has conceived' " (Sextus Empiricus Vol. 1: II, 106).

When it is a question of dividing the sign, whereas Aristotle is able to distinguish the classes of signs just according to the place occupied by the middle term in the figures of the syllogism, the Stoics are obliged to have recourse to something outside the implicative reasoning—and they distinguish between the sign which is suggestive (ὑπὸ μνηστικόν) (either natural like the smoke, which is the sign of fire [ibid.: II, 100], or conventional [ibid.: II, 193, 200, 202]), and the sign which is "indicative" (ἐνδεικτικόν), like the movements of the body which are the signs of the soul (ibid.: II, 101).

But these differences are negligible compared to what Aristotle and the Stoics have in common and which opposes them to the Epicureans and the Sceptics. For them all, logic or semiotics is the study of inference from signs, but while for the former, the dogmatists, the inference is analytical and the signs are signs of the ideas we have of things, for the latter, the empiricists, inference is inductive and signs are signs of things.

The empiricists are not more in total agreement than the dogmatists, but it will be more easily understood what they have in common and what opposes them if one situates their respective conceptions both of the sign and of inference from signs in the controversy between the Stoics and the Epicureans as it appears in one of the most well-preserved Greek papyri discovered in Herculanum. It is entitled Περὶ σημείων καί σημειώσεων ("On signs and inferences from signs"), and was written by a Greek from Syria, Philodemus, who, having studied Epicureanism in Athens, founded an Epicurean school in Naples (Philodemus [79 AD] 1978).

Of course, Philodemus is only the spokesman of a school, and in order to interpret Epicurean logic, one must take into account the other available sources, in particular the letters of Epicurus quoted by Diogenes Laertius, and the expositions and discussions by Sextus Empiricus who defends the Sceptic point of view as much against the Stoics as against the Epicureans.

The particular interest for us of Philodemus's text is that Peirce was sufficiently interested in it to accept that one of his students, Allan Marquand, should make its translation the subject of his doctoral dissertation. Peirce studied Philodemus with Marquand, and it may be supposed that he approved of the interpretation which Marquand gave in the introduction to his translation ("The Logic of the Epicureans" [cf. Fisch 1986: "Peirce's Arisbe: The Greek Influence on His Later Philosophy" [1971]: 190–192]). Moreover, we know that it was from Philodemus that Peirce borrowed the term "semiosis," that inference from signs, of which semiotics is the theory (5.484), "the doctrine of the essential nature and fundamental varieties of possible semiosis" (5.488). "On Signs and Semioses" would be a perfect Peircean translation of Philodemus's title. In any case, with or without Marquand, Peirce could have also borrowed the word and the idea of "semiosis" from Sextus Empiricus (Sextus Empiricus Vol. 2: II, 269).

According to Marquand, for the Epicureans "The function of logic consists in inference from the observed to the unobserved" (Marquand 1883: 4). "The Epicureans," Marquand further notes, "looked upon a sign as a phenomenon, from whose characters we might infer the characters of other phenomena under conditions of existence sufficiently similar. The sign was to them an object of sense" (Marquand 1883: 6).

Following tradition, they distinguished the general (or common: κοινόν) sign from the particular sign (σημεῖον):

A general sign is described as a phenomenon which can exist whether the thing signified exists or not, or has a particular character or not. A particular sign is a phenomenon which can exist only on the condition that the thing signified actually exists. The relation between sign and thing signified in the former case is resemblance; in the latter, it is invariable sequence or causality. (1883: 6)

One cannot fail to recall Peirce's description of the icon and the index (2.304) and all the more so as we know that the Epicureans distinguished three sorts of sign, although Philodemus describes only two.

It is obvious that a Sceptic like Sextus Empiricus could no more admit the Epicurean division of the sign than he could the Stoic division, not that he totally rejected the particular sign or sign of indication—there is, he says, an "apparent equivalence of the arguments adduced for its reality and for its unreality" (Sextus Empiricus Vol. 1: II, 103)—but the only thing empirically sure or at least plausible is the "suggestive sign" (τὸ ὑπομνηστικὸν): "For the suggestive sign is relied on by living experience, since when a man sees smoke fire is signified, and when he beholds a scar he says that there has been a wound" (Sextus Empiricus Vol. 1: II, 102).

Sextus Empiricus, like Philodemus, criticizes the way in which the Stoics pass from the antecedent to the consequent in a conditional proposition, by contraposition or *modus tollens,* in other words by showing "that from the negative of the consequent the negative of the antecedent follows" (Marquand 1883: 6). On one hand, for the empiricists, the sign is an object of direct apprehension by the senses and not an object of thought. On the other hand, says Philodemus:

When a person makes an inference from men among us and concludes about men everywhere that they are mortal, from the fact that those whose lives are known through history and those who have fallen under our observation are all mortal (θνητοὺς), there is no evidence of the contrary, he makes his inference by analogy; and the statement that men among us, insofar as they are men, are mortal, which is equivalent to the statement that men with this property are men, is confirmed by this very fact. None of those who pursue philosophy by the method and procedure of contraposition provides such a confirmation. (Philodemus 1978: 108, §24)

One can only arrive at propositions—far from beginning by them—neither by contraposition nor by syllogism, but by *induction.* In fact, contraposition rests upon induction. To refute the method by analogy, Philodemus says:

The arguments that they devise [ . . . ] they present to us as confirmations of it. Thus when for example [ . . . ] they oppose the inference "If living creatures among us are destructible, those in unperceived places are also," and in making their case they say that some living creatures, though similar in kind, exhibit differences from one another according to atmosphere and food and all the other things, however many they may be, they are starting from appearances in our experience and proceed by making like judgments about things elsewhere. [ . . . ] It is the same with the rest of their arguments, so that they bring with them the complete reversal of their position. (1978: 121–122, §46)

Sextus Empiricus agrees with Philodemus in defending the empirical argument against contraposition or any other argument:

> Thus [ ... ] a certain philosopher [Diogenes the Cynic] when the argument against motion was put to him, without a word, started to walk about; and people who follow the usual way of life proceed on journeys by land and sea and build ships and houses and beget children without paying attention to the arguments of motion and becoming. (Sextus Empiricus Vol. 1: II, 244–245)

But on condition that the empirical argument is limited only to things observed. He contests the idea that one may establish the proof (ἐπιμαρτύρησις) of what is not observed, like causality (Sextus Empiricus Vol. 1: I, 185), and rejects induction, whether it be Aristotelian or Epicurean.

> For, when they propose to establish the universal from the particulars by means of induction, they will effect this by a review either of all or of some of the particular instances. But if they review some, the induction will be insecure, since some of the particulars omitted in the induction may contravene the universal; while if they are to review all, they will be toiling at the impossible, since the particulars are infinite and indefinite. Thus on both grounds, as I think, the consequence of that induction is invalidated. (Sextus Empiricus Vol. 1: II, 204)

What is the position of the Epicureans on the subject of whether we must examine all the cases of a phenomena or only a certain number of cases? Philodemus replies by quoting his Athenian master, Zeno of Sidon:

> [ ... ] it is not necessary to make the rounds of all appearances accessible to us or merely to encounter chance appearances, but to encounter many homogeneous and varied ones, so that from our acquaintance with them we may establish the property inseparable from each of the particulars, and from these pass to all the others. For example, if men are found to differ from one another in all other respects, but in this respect [mortality] they have been observed to have no difference, why should we not say confidently on the basis of men we have met with and those of whom we have historical knowledge, that all men are liable to old age and disease? When this is established and there is no evidence to the contrary, we shall say that they are mistaken who say, "And men were invulnerable." (Philodemus 1978: 112–113, §35)

Marquand summarizes Zeno's theory in two rules or canons in which, starting from the idea that Nature is, according to the Epicureans, already divided into classes and sub-classes, inductive inference proceeds from one class to another, not haphazardly, but from one class to that which it most resembles.

> Canon I.—If we examine many and various instances of a phenomenon, and find some character common to them all, and no instance appears to the contrary, this character may be transferred to other unexamined individuals of the same class, and even to other closely related classes.

Canon II.—If in our experience a given character is found to vary, a corresponding amount of variation may be inferred to exist beyond our experience. (Marquand 1883: 9)

That Marquand (1883: 1) and Peirce (8.379) should have established a comparison between Philodemus and John Stuart Mill is hardly surprising. There are differences, obviously, but they do not concern the nature of signs nor the inductive nature of inference. For Mill, names are signs of things and not signs of our conceptions of things: "When I say: 'The sun is the cause of day,' I do not mean that my idea of the sun causes or excites in me the idea of day; but that the physical object, the sun itself, is the cause from which the outward phenomenon, day, follows as an effect" (Mill 1843: I, ch. 2). Mill's inductive inference is based on the principle of the uniformity of nature—a principle which allows of the inference from the particular to the general, which is justified by the well-known rules or canons of concordance, difference, residues, and concomitant variations (1843: III).

It is clear to anyone who has read Peirce, however little, that Peirce's logic is closer to the empirical logic of the Epicureans than to the other logics of Greek antiquity, including the formal logic of the Stoics, which he was, however, one of the first to revive. Referring to the Epicurean philosophy of logic, Peirce said: "This philosophy is my particular pet, or one of my pets" (Ms 1604, quoted by Fisch 1971: 208 n. 14).

Peirce refuses to think, to infer, or to reason from *ideas*. Let us say, to give a partial answer to one of the questions we asked at the beginning, that Peirce contests all the logicians—Aristotle and Descartes among them—who base logic on metaphysics, which is, just because it is not based on the "science of logic," "of all branches of scientific inquiry the most shaky and insecure" (2.36).

We shall come back to this question when we have seen how the reading of Philodemus can enable one to understand more clearly some of the problems with which Peirce was faced and the solutions he proposed—particularly in semiotics.

We shall begin with a problem which has not yet been broached, that of the categories and the part they play in the physical world. In *A Guess at the Riddle*, Peirce writes: "One bold saltus landed me in a garden of fruitful and beautiful suggestions" (1.364). What was this garden? "The garden of Epicurus," replies Max Fisch. And what was this "bold saltus"? That which enabled Peirce to pass from the conception of chance as "that diversity in the universe which laws leave room for," and not as "a violation of law" (6.602), to the conception of chance as absolute chance of which the Epicurean *clinamen* is the model, or at least the emblem. "[ . . . ] we establish through appearances," says Philodemus, "that nothing conflicts [with this view]. It is not enough to accept the minimal swerves of the atoms on account of chance and free will; one must also show that no other clear perception conflicts with this view" (1978: 126–127, §54). It is thus, through the garden of Epicurus, that chance—"that diversity in the universe which laws

leave room for, instead of a violation of law, or lawlessness" (6.602)—enters the
Peircean cosmos, a cosmos whose continuity, the physical paradigm of thirdness,
is no more affected than the Epicurean cosmos, nor brute reaction, the physical
paradigm of secondness (6.202). We can call chance the "physical paradigm,"
though only on condition that we make it clear that, as for the Epicureans, it
[chance] is synonymous for Peirce with "freedom or spontaneity" (6.201).

Semiotics is for Peirce, as for the Epicureans, the theory of semiosis or inference from signs. What is a sign? Peirce gives it the technical name of "representamen" in order to show that it is not a mental representation, but an object
which does affect the senses, but is not defined by its apprehension by the senses.
As such, the representamen represents the thing, exactly as the sign does for the
Epicurean logician. What is true of the sign or representamen in a semiosis will
be true of the thing outside the semiosis, although this does not allow the
semiosis to infer about the nature of the thing or the whole of the thing or of
the sign. As representamen, the sign is not an idea, it is not even an object of
direct knowledge, it is only a simple "material quality" (5.290), without which,
however, there could be no knowledge through signs. At the utmost, we can call
it direct experience: "Direct experience is neither certain or uncertain [ . . . ] it
just *is* [ . . . ] direct experience means simply the appearance. It involves no error,
because it testifies to nothing but its own appearance" (1.145).

I refer the reader to the articles of 1868 in which Peirce denies even the possibility of direct knowledge, be it called "intuition," "introspection," or even
"perception." In the case of perception, which is particularly enlightening for
our understanding of the nature of the sign, "percept" must be distinguished
from "perceptive judgment." The representamen is, as such, a "percept."

> The direct percept, as it first appears, appears as forced upon us brutally. It has
> no generality; and without generality there can be no psychicality. [ . . . ] The
> percept brutally forces itself upon us; thus it appears under a physical guise. It
> is quite ungeneral, even antigeneral—in its character as a percept; and thus it
> does not appear as psychical. The psychical, then, is not contained in the per-
> cept. (1.253)

"The percept," says Peirce elsewhere, "is a single event happening *hic et
nunc*. It cannot be generalized without losing its essential character" (1.146).
Consequently, "a percept contains only two kinds of elements, those of firstness
and those of secondness" (7.630).

With perceptive judgment the representamen enters the semiosis and becomes representation and third. "This is a very important difference," remarks
Peirce, "since the idea of representation is essentially what may be termed an
element of 'Thirdness', that is, involves the idea of determining one thing [the
representamen] to refer to another [the object]" (7.630).

Semiosis is inference through signs. A sign-representamen determines a
sign-interpretant to refer to its object (2.228). Peirce distinguishes between two

sorts of object, the object in the semiosis, and the object outside the semiosis (Hardwick 1977: 83–84). The sign or representamen can only represent the object outside the semiosis; "It cannot furnish acquaintance with or recognition of that Object" (2.231). Of the object outside the semiosis one can thus have only either a "direct experience," like that we have of the percept, or a "collateral knowledge," the result of former semioses, personal or "historical," in the words of the Epicureans (Philodemus 1978: 24, 35).

Semiosis is an inductive process. We will not here discuss the nature of induction. It is enough to say that Peirce understood it in the sense in which he read Philodemus with Marquand. *"The inference that a previously designated character has nearly the same frequency of occurrence in the whole of a class that it has in a sample drawn at random out of that class is induction"* (6.409). Unless it is specified—which certainly makes a considerable difference—the Epicureans refuse to introduce any sort of calculation. This does not change the fact that, contrary to the procedure of sceptical empiricism, which is nominalistic, Epicurean inference and Peircean induction or semiosis are realistic. By "realistic" is meant that for the Epicureans, as for Peirce, however empiristic they may be, "universals" exist, although they are not separate from things. And even in one sense it could be said that, no more than Peirce, do the Epicureans reject the formal logic of the Stoics as such since what they reproach the Stoics with is not having seen that contraposition presupposed implication and with not having, properly speaking, reasoned by contraposition.

This is true of the science which is formal in the highest sense of the word, mathematics, which is for Peirce, as for the Epicureans, an "implicative science." Philodemus says:

And the fact that the square of four is the only square having its perimeter equal to its area does not hinder us from inferring some things by analogy. The square numbers themselves, when all have been tested by trial, have shown that this very distinction exists among them, so that the person who makes an inference from such numbers in our experience to those in the infinite universes, that every square of four has its perimeter equal to its area, will be inferring well. (Philodemus 1978: 107, §21)

Which Peirce echoes in 1895:

No doubt demonstrations are more important in mathematics, than in most sciences; but, for all that, mathematics advances, just as the physical sciences do, by observation and generalization. Its observations are, it is true, only observations of the mind's own constructions, but they often have that *startling* quality which indicates that they *are* observations. (Peirce 1978: II, 102)

Peirce's pragmaticism is thus really an empiricism and a realism. Is his semiotic theory derived from it, or is it its foundation? We can now give a fairly sure reply to this question. If it is true, as De Lacy has shown, that Epicurean empiricism is not limited to sensory experience, but forms the basis of an empirical metaphysics (De Lacy 1964: 377–401), it is equally true that Peirce's semiotic method is the body and soul of his pragmaticist metaphysics. If today metaphysics demands another logic of experience, more complex and formalized than the Epicurean empirical metaphysics, which required only observation, this by no means implies that its object is different. Peirce says:

> Metaphysics consists in the results of the absolute acceptance of logical principles not merely as regulatively valid, but as truths of being. Accordingly, it is to be assumed that the universe has an explanation, the function of which, like that of every logical explanation, is to unify its observed variety. It follows that the root of all being is One; and so far as different subjects have a common character they partake of an identical being. This, or something like this, is the monadic clause of the law. Second, drawing a general induction from all observed facts, we find all realization of existence lies in opposition, such as attractions, repulsions, visibilities, and centres of potentiality generally. [ ... ] This is, or is part of, a dyadic clause of the law. Under the third clause, we have, as a deduction from the principle that thought is the mirror of being, the law that the end of being and highest reality is the living impersonation of the idea that evolution generates. (1.487)

If the object is the same, the method which is still semiotic, empirical, and inductive, has more and more recourse to formal logic, so that the metaphysical concepts, which are the adaptation of it, require the mastery of a "minutely accurate and thoroughgoing system of formal logic" (1.625). Thus the metaphysician of today must be a semiotician "prepared to grapple with all the difficulties of modern exact logic," otherwise "he is not the genuine, honest, earnest, resolute, energetic, industrious, and accomplished doubter that it is his duty to be." In this case, Peirce concludes, he "had better put up his shutters and go out of the trade" (1.624).

# - 8 -

# Semeiotic and Significs

## PEIRCE AND LADY WELBY

Never confound, and never divide.
— Lady Welby (Hardwick 1977: 21)

Never block the path of inquiry.
— Peirce

Lady Welby's correspondence and writings span a period of more than sixty years. She corresponded altogether only nine years with Peirce, from 1903 to 1911. It was Lady Welby who took the initiative of the correspondence after reading some entries written by Peirce in Baldwin's *Dictionary of Philosophy and Psychology* (1902). She had her publisher send her book *What is Meaning?* to Peirce. She was convinced that she could convert Peirce to the new science she had invented: *Significs,* also called *Sensifics.* Peirce responded with delight for he himself saw the opportunity of converting a responsive reader to his *Semeiotic.* Neither surrendered, although Lady Welby never lost hope for her pet science while encouraging Peirce not to despair of his *Semeiotic*—for the worst reason she could think of:

> Of course I am fully aware that Semeiotic may be considered the scientific and philosophic form of that study which I hope may become generally known as Significs. Though I don't think you need despair of the acceptance of your own more abstract, logically abstruse, philosophically profound conception of Semeiotic. (Hardwick 1977: 91)

Lady Welby is famous for the part she played in promoting ideas, and especially Peirce's ideas, among the English and Continental intelligentsia by sending copies of Peirce's most important letters to people like Bertrand Russell, C. K. Ogden, and Giovanni Vailati. Ogden's reaction was decisive and it is mostly through him that Peirce became known, thanks to *The Meaning of Meaning,* written with I. A. Richards (Ogden and Richards 1923), and through him and

F. P. Ramsey that Wittgenstein knew of Peirce (Deledalle 1964, 1972, 1981; Hardwick 1977; Schmitz 1985; Thayer 1968; Wittgenstein 1969).

What Wittgenstein owed to Peirce is not easy to say, because he could apparently think for himself, and had read James, and had many talks with Ramsey who had a great esteem for Peirce's logic and philosophy (Ramsey 1924, 1931) and used Peirce's distinction between Type (Legisign) and Token (Replica) to explain Wittgenstein's thought in his thorough review of the *Tractatus Logico-Philosophicus* (Ramsey 1923)—which review Wittgenstein read and discussed with Ramsey.

However, Lady Welby seemed to have won here, for it is the question of meaning which became central in the current discussions instead of the question of sign, which was the crucial question for Peirce.

One of Lady Welby's mottoes was "Never confound, and never divide" (Hardwick 1977: 21). If we had to sum up her philosophy, we would say that she inclined more toward the therapeutic turn of Wittgenstein's philosophy than the semeiotic turn of Peirce's. She would have been delighted with Wittgenstein's idea that the purpose of philosophy was to cure language of its diseases: "Philosophy is a battle against the bewitchment of our intelligence by means of language" (Wittgenstein 1953, 1909); "A main cause of philosophical disease—a one-sided diet: one nourishes one's thinking with one kind of example" (Wittgenstein 1953: 593); "What is your aim in philosophy? Shew the fly the way out of the fly bottle" (Wittgenstein 1953: 309). But of course the remedy is the same for her as for Peirce and Wittgenstein, as testified by the motto: "Philosophy does not result in 'philosophical propositions', but rather in the clarification of propositions" (Wittgenstein 1961: 4.112). This is a remedy that Peirce was the first to prescribe in *How to Make our Ideas Clear,* founding at the same time a new school of philosophy: pragmatism. "Consider what effects, that might conceivably have practical bearings, we conceive the object of our conception to have. Then, our conception of these effects is the whole of our conception of the object" (5.402). We must not let ourselves be deceived by language. We have to be careful not "to mistake a mere difference in the grammatical construction of two words for a distinction between the ideas they express" (5.399).

## ETHICS OF TERMINOLOGY: MEANING AND METAPHOR

Peirce's ethics of terminology was bound to please Lady Welby.

> I welcome with gratitude your "profession of faith" on the ethics of terminology—a sadly neglected subject. It will be of the greatest value to me and I hope I may use it in a second edition of *What is Meaning?* (Hardwick 1977: 21)

Lady Welby was more explicit on the subject than Peirce. (On the part of Peirce, it was more a matter of literary property or, let us say, word copyright, than anything else.) It is probably in her struggle against the misuses of language that her philosophy is closer to Peirce's than in her theory of *Significs* with which we will deal later. She shares, for instance, Peirce's anti-dualism all the way, when she denounces the use of "metaphors."

In her essay of 1893 on *Meaning and Metaphor* (Welby 1893: 510, 525), Lady Welby describes the way language works through metaphors. She had already anonymously published the previous year a collection of reflections on the subject presented to the International Congress of Experimental Psychology, entitled *The Use of 'Inner' and 'Outer' in Psychology: Does the Metaphor Help or Hinder?* (Welby 1892). By "metaphor," Lady Welby means "symbolism," unlike Peirce for whom metaphor is a hypoicon, and, more precisely, an icon as third. Theoretically the difference is important, because, according to Peirce, we cannot think without some kind of iconicity. For Lady Welby, however, although she also agrees that we need some kind of "imagery" to think, metaphors as symbols, far from helping to think, are a hindrance:

> Imagery runs in and out, so to speak, from the symbolic to the real world and back again. As matters stand, we never know where we are because we know so little where our phrases or our words are; indeed, perhaps they and we are "neither here nor there"! (Welby 1893: 511)

Between "symbols" and "real existences," there may be a "third value." Lady Welby does not give it a name. For a Peircean, it can only be of the nature of an interpretant. This is suggested by Lady Welby herself: "We need a 'Critique of Plain Meaning'" (Welby 1893: 513).

> The fact is that we have been postulating an absolute Plain Meaning to be thought of, as it were, in capital letters. We have been virtually *assuming that our hearers and readers all share the same mental background and atmosphere.* (Welby 1893: 512, italics mine)

Two things are thus neglected: the changes time introduces into our language and the context in which language—the very same language—is used:

> To 'signify' is the one test of the important. The significant is alone worth notice. We inherit a mode of thinking which we are at last becoming able to criticise in the light of knowledge gained by observation and experiment. But if we persist in using, without warning hearer or reader, imagery which has no longer either sense or relevance, or which tends to call up a false mental picture or to perpetuate an else decaying error, we shall to that extent forfeit the very gifts which science brings us, and must not complain of the obstinate persistence of ideas which needlessly divide us. (Wittgenstein 1953: 525)

On the other hand, we must take account of the context in which words are used. One can pride oneself "on a carefully sharp distinction between 'image' and 'thing' or 'object'" (Wittgenstein 1953: 511), as if distinction *is* self-sufficient.

It is so easy to confound distinction and separation. "'And I had gathered, I hope not quite mistakenly,' Lady Welby writes to Peirce, 'that you also saw the disastrous result of digging gulfs to *separate* when it was really a question of *distinction*,—as sharp and clear as you like'" (Hardwick 1977: 21). Of course, the context can help to see where we are, because nothing *is* more ambiguous than a *literal* meaning:

> One is tempted to say that there is only one term more figurative as well as more ambiguous than "metaphorical," and that is "literal." Most certainly much that is called "literal" is tinged with the figurative in varying degrees, not always easy to distinguish even with the help of context. (Welby 1893: 512)

The list of verbal distinctions erroneously solidified into real partitions is long and does not apply only to ordinary speech, but even to the most elaborate philosophical discourse. Lady Welby in her paper of 1893 quotes Jowett at length:

> The famous dispute between Nominalists and Realists would never have been heard of, if, instead of transferring the Platonic ideas into a crude Latin phraseology, the spirit of Plato had been truly understood and appreciated. Upon the term substance at least two celebrated controversies appear to hinge, which would not have existed, or at least not in their present form, if we had 'interrogated' the word substance, as Plato has the notions of Unity and Being. Those weeds of philosophy have struck their roots deep into the soil, and are always tending to reappear, sometimes in new-fangled forms; while similar words, such as development, evolution, law, and the like, are constantly put in the place of facts, even by writers who profess to base truth entirely upon facts. (Welby 1893: 522 note)

Any separation of things which we cannot see or exactly define, though it may be necessary, is "a fertile source of errors," says Jowett: the division of the mind into faculties, or powers or virtues (Welby 1893: 522 note), the distinctions between "Inner and Outer" (Welby 1893: 525 note) "as metaphorical expressions *of* the mental and the physical" (Welby 1911: 22), between mind as "internal" ("*inside* some nonentity not specified") and matter ("*outside* this nonentity") (Welby 1911: 16).

Lady Welby writes, in an essay entitled "Primal Sense and Significs," written April 15, 1907, and only recently published:

> We talk of the inner and the underlying where there is no question of either: we talk of he and she where there is nothing corresponding to sex: we talk of beginning and end as complementary and then of "both ends"; but never of both beginnings. We talk of truth when we mean accuracy or fact: we talk of the literal ("it is written") when we mean the actual ("it is done"). We talk of natural "law," reducing its sphere to that of the "lawcourt" with its imposed decisions, forgetting that a law is a rule deliberately decreed and enforced or "passed" by

consent and liable to abrogation: we talk of mind or consciousness as the analogue of a bag or box, or of a piece of stuff in various "states": we talk of the
unknowable when what that is and whether it exists is precisely what we cannot
know—the idea presupposes what it denies: we talk of immortality, ignoring its
correlative innatality [ . . . ]. (Welby 1985: ccxl)

We should in the same way speak of "the spatial as 'upward' while using
'downward' for the non-spatial" (Welby 1911: 16).

Lady Welby's tracking of misused metaphors is second nature to her and in
her correspondence with Peirce she cannot help pointing them out when they
occur in Peirce's letters: the use of "brute" (Hardwick 1977: 63), "proof" applied
to religion (Hardwick 1977: 63–64), "growth" (Hardwick 1977: 64), "attractive
fancy" (Hardwick 1977: 64–65), "certain" and "certainty" (Hardwick 1977: 90).

She goes even further than Peirce when she deals with the "laws of nature":

Among the many defeating absurdities of current imagery perhaps that of "laws
of nature" is one of the worst. One would really think sometimes that nature
had primordially summoned councils and decreed laws, or even brought in a bill
in some National Assembly, discussed it, passed it, clause by clause, carefully de-
fining its regulations and penalties! And one would think that nature's lawyers
and judges expounded or laid down her laws and enforced her decrees, imposing
the statutory penalties for their infringement. For, of course, we are supposed to
"break" nature's "laws"—though the idea is [ . . . ] grotesque [ . . . ]. (Welby
1911: 24)

Of course, there is a solution to the problem, according to Lady Welby: it is
the extensive use of her Significs. Lady Welby's solution is close to William
James's "pure experience" prior to the mental distinction of mind and matter:

It might be useful (and there may be more warrant for it than we know) if we
were to regard the physical world as a complex acted metaphor of the mental
world, and both as essentially expressive of a common nature. (Welby 1911: 45)

Supposing that we personified Nature in a scientific sense, postulating her as a
unified series of impressions, would she now be found speaking of us in a metaphor as we of her, only with speech reversed? That is, would her every "word"
be taken metaphorically from the action or process of consciousness, reason, reflection, judgment? Thus might we not say that motion, and mass, and the so-
called "matter" assumed as behind them, are as full of mind-metaphor as mind
is of matter-metaphor; the mind-metaphor arising in the conscious world, and
reaching us through intelligence, and intellect, as matter-metaphor arises in the
unconscious world, and reaches us through sense? (Welby 1911: 46)

## SIGNIFICS AND PRAGMATICISM

Significs is mostly concerned with *practice*. In *What is Meaning?*, Lady Welby
opposes the Significian mind to the logician mind:

Significs concerns the practical mind, e.g. in business or political life, more closely and inevitably than it does the speculative mind. For the thinker may go on through all his life turning over his own and others' thoughts and working them logically out. But the man of action must translate thought into deed as fast as ideas come to him; and he may ruin the cause he would serve by missing the significance of things. (Welby 1903: 8)

Significance is linked to action, as meaning is in Peirce's pragmatism. In "Primal Sense and Significs," already quoted, Lady Welby compares her work on significs with pragmatism. Action is the key word, as we have already seen: "The sense of a word is our sense of its special use, of what it signifies," Lady Welby says in another essay ("The Social Value of Expression" 1908, in Welby 1985: ccliii). However, Significs goes further than pragmatism, because it is concerned with action as creation. It is in "the work of the significian" that "the Pragmatist will find the prolific germ of his own thought," without rejecting anything and certainly not intellectualism. Of course, it is James's and Schiller's pragmatism which is meant here. What Lady Welby says of her significs applies to Peirce's pragmatism or rather pragmaticism compared to James's and Schiller's pragmatism:

[ ... ] Significs can never become a denial of any opposite. It can never be controversial. Nobody will seriously champion insignificance or defend the senseless and the unmeaning from the significial onslaught! Intellectualism, for significs, has its work no less than pragmatism; though as a fact and in the sense of a return to a too widely neglected and ignored standpoint, it is prior to Pragmatism and absorbs the controversial element. Absorbs? Yes: if we add—energises, vitalises, transmutes and transfigures all this [ ... ]. For it recognises—and this for the first time—the full significance and the full meaning and sense of Value itself, in all expression of "energy" in the widest sense of that great word, and in the expressive nucleus which we call articulate speech, the supreme link between mind and mind. (Welby 1985: ccxlv)

Peirce is less optimistic than Lady Welby. He thinks that "perfect accuracy of thought is unattainable, *theoretically unattainable.*" Undue striving for it has the opposite result. *"It positively renders thought unclear"* (Hardwick 1977: 11, italics mine).

This very summer I rejected over a hundred consecutive pages of my MS, most painfully and slowly made, simply because it was too elaborated. After all, we want to get our thought expressed in short meter somehow. (Hardwick 1977: 11)

Peirce's letter is dated December 1, 1903. Four years later, F. C. S. Schiller also questioned "what can practically be done to remedy the defects of language" (Welby 1985: ccxlv). His answer is worth comparing with Peirce's. Schiller does not think that

Language is such an imperfect instrument and that we are so dominated by its tricks. On the whole, we think it reflects pretty accurately the mental condition of its users. If it is confused and fragmentary and perverse, it is because the mind of its users are this. [ ... ] If you provided such minds with a perfect instrument they would at once proceed to ruin it. But [ ... ] we don't think that in actual use language is so imperfect. In their context, words get and convey meanings which they do not seem to bear per se. (Welby 1985: ccxlviii)

Peirce would agree with that: the solution to the question of meaning is pragmatic. He is not as sanguine as Schiller is, but it is not enough to denounce the misuse of language and appeal for action. Pragmatism at large is only a banner. What is needed is a set of rules of action to apply to each and every part of the body of language which is infected. Significs, says Schiller, does "not suggest anything positive or specific to remedy the evil" (Welby 1985: ccxlviii).

## SIGNIFICS AND SEMEIOTIC

Lady Welby's thought can be expressed in a nutshell as the theory of sense, meaning, and significance. She dealt with this trilogy all her life and especially in "Sense, Meaning and Interpretation" *(Mind), What is Meaning?*, "Significs" *(The Encyclopaedia Britannica), Significs and Language,* and in her correspondence with Peirce.

Perhaps owing to goodwill on the part of both, there is a fundamental misunderstanding between Peirce and Lady Welby. *Significs* would be better called, as Lady Welby sometimes does call it, *Sensifics,* for its subject matter is sense, while *Semeiotic* is, properly speaking, the theory of the action of signs. Pragmaticism is the link, if any, between the two "sciences." That is why any attempt to explain the concepts of significs in semeiotic terms and *vice versa,* is bound to confuse the issues.

What does Lady Welby say? In "Sense, Meaning, and Interpretation," she starts by distinguishing five terms: Signification, Import, Sense, Significance, and Meaning, as meaning-terms in different lines of thought, classified as follows:

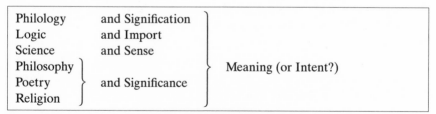

Table 8.1. From Welby 1896: 25

*Signification* "represents the value of language itself"; *Import* "marks the intellectual character of the logical process," it implies "more than bare linguistic value"; *Sense* coupled with "physical science" is to be understood in its three current "senses": "sense" as meaning free from "any speculative taint," as opposed to "senseless," "sense" as "the inevitable starting-point and ultimate test of scientific generalisation," "sense" as a faculty. "Here we may perhaps note that the word seems to give the link between the sensory, the sensible, and the significant," Lady Welby remarks: "there is apparently a real connection between the 'sense'—say of sight—in which we react to stimulus, and the 'sense' in which we speak or act"; *Significance,* in fact, "stands on a different footing from the other meaning-terms" (Welby 1896: 26–27).

> We naturally lay stress on the significance of some fact or event like the French Revolution or the Chino-Japanese [*sic*] war, when we feel that its "import," its "sense"—even its "meaning"—are quite inadequate to express its effect on our minds, while it would not occur to any one to speak of its "signification." It has "significance," it is "significant," because it indicates, implies, involves, (or may entail) great changes or momentous issues: because it demands serious attention and, it may be, decisive action: or because it must modify more or less profoundly our mental attitude towards the nations or races affected by it, and towards the problems called social. (Welby 1896: 27)

What about *meaning?* It differs from *sense,* because when we "mean," we intend to do something. In "meaning" are linked the ideas of intention and end, and, consequently, sense and significance, and also import which is "the secondary sense of the word Meaning" (Welby 1896: 28). Only "signification" seems excluded. Lady Welby does not give us the reason, but we can guess that it is for her "a merely linguistic question," which has only "a logical or psychological value" (Welby 1896: 29).

Sense, meaning, and significance are the only terms retained in *What is Meaning?* and in "Significs" where they are defined as "terms of expression-value."

> 1. Sense. Associated "with the organic response to environment, and with the essentially expressive element in an experience."
>
> 2. Meaning. Sense not being purposive, meaning is "reserved for the specific sense which it is intended to convey."
>
> 3. Significance. "As including sense and meaning but transcending them in range, and covering the far-reaching consequence, implication, ultimate result or outcome of some event or experience, the term 'Significance' is usefully applied." (Hardwick 1977: 169)

In *What is Meaning?* Lady Welby says that this triad is found in many forms of which she quotes "the most striking" from *The Vedanta Sara:*

> The meaning (that may belong to a word) is held threefold, namely, Express, Indicated, and Suggested. The Express meaning is that conveyed to the under-

standing by the (word's) Denotation; the (meaning) Indicated is held to be conveyed by the (word's) Suggestion. Let these be the three powers of a word.
(Welby 1903: 46)

This triadic standpoint, respectively "expressive, descriptive, and interpretative," which appeared already in the previous writings as hierarchical, is defined
as such in *Significs and Language,* Lady Welby's last work: "Significance [ . . . ] is
reached through sense and meaning" (Welby 1911: 83).

In spite of the misunderstanding concerning the respective subject matter of
significs and semeiotic, the general attitude behind the theories was similar
enough to explain both the attempt by Peirce and Lady Welby to read their own
theory in each other's writings, and the misunderstanding.

Peirce, in his review of *What is Meaning?,* says that the "authoress" has rendered a great service in bringing home the fundamental question of the "three
kinds of meaning" and by doing this in pointing out indirectly "three orders of
signification," and "she has wisely abstained from any attempt at formal definitions of these three modes of significance," because all this is not new: "Her
three kinds of meaning correspond roughly to Hegel's three stages of thought,"
and her "three orders of signification" were described by Peirce fifteen years before (in 1878: 5.388–410) and summed up as follows in a letter to Lady Welby:

To understand a word or formula may, in the first place, consist in such familiarity with it as will enable one to apply it correctly; or secondly, may consist in
an abstract analysis of the conception or understanding of its intellectual relations to other concepts; or, thirdly, may consist in a knowledge of the possible
phenomenal and practical upshot of the concept. (Hardwick 1977: 159)

"We might point out other interesting applications of her thought," Peirce
concludes, "sufficient to show that she must be upon the right track" (Hardwick
1977: 159). Lady Welby thanked Peirce for his review and confirmed that she had
"made no attempt at formal definition of the 'triad of signification'" (Hardwick
1977: 6). Her significs is, so to speak, a "practical extension" of logic proper which
is not confined to rational order alone, but gives "its human value to life,—that
is (1) its 'sense' and sense-power in every sense from the biological to the logical,
(2) its intention, conscious and increasingly definite and rational, which we call
'Meaning' and (profess to) use language to express, (3) its Significance, its bear-
ing upon, its place among, its interpretation of, all other cosmical facts" (Hardwick 1977: 6).

In the second longest theoretical letter (Dec. 1908) that Peirce wrote to
Lady Welby, Peirce tells Lady Welby that Significs is only a part of Semeiotic,
that part "which inquires into the relation of signs to their 'interpretants'" and
"assuming this to be your meaning, we should hardly think it possible, in the
present state of the subject, to make much headway in a truly scientific investigation of significs in general without devoting a very large share of one's work
to inquiries into other questions of semeiotic" (Hardwick 1977: 80).

In a letter to J. W. Slaughter, dated September 2, 1909, Peirce justifies his enterprise:

> [ . . . ] I have determined that for Lady Welby's sake I will write briefly and without argument what I conceive to be the real nature of her aspiration, beginning with considering what a sign is and what its signification as opposed to its denotation really is, and what is the nature of the process of performing a logical analysis of it. Possibly I may add some thoughts on the question of how new needful terms of logic had best be framed in the present condition of the subject. I believe that my process for performing logical analysis will be found very valuable when it is well illustrated and explained. (Welby 1985: clviii)

In a third long letter in 1909, Peirce comes back to the subject of Lady Welby's trichotomy and wonders whether he was influenced by it in "settling" his own trichotomy of interpretants, only to conclude that he does "not believe this did happen." "But as far as the public goes, we can only point out the agreement, and confess to having read your book" (Hardwick 1977: 109).

How well do the two trichotomies coincide? Peirce's final interpretant "is exactly the same as" Lady Welby's "Significance," "namely the effect the sign would produce upon any mind upon which circumstances should permit it to work out its full effect" (Hardwick 1977: 110). The immediate interpretant does not differ much from "sense," provided, as seems to be the case, that it be "sensal," "of the nature of an 'impression'," i.e., without any "volitional element" (Hardwick 1977: 110). If there is some discrepancy, it concerns the possible equivalence of the dynamical interpretant and meaning. Lady Welby's meaning "consists in the effect upon the mind of the Interpreter that the utterer (whether vocally or by writing) of the sign intends to produce," while Peirce's dynamical interpretant only "consists in direct effect actually produced by a sign upon an interpreter of it," with or without intention to do so. However, as Peirce says elsewhere, although "I do not think we can properly say that God *utters* any sign when He is the Creator of all things [ . . . ] when (Lady Welby) says, as she does, that this is connected with volition, we at once note that the volitional element of Interpretation is the *Dynamical interpretant*" (8.185). The main difference in the two trichotomies is to be found elsewhere, in the way the trichotomies were produced: Lady Welby's trichotomy rests on "a prodigious sensitiveness of Perception"; Peirce's own "reasoning from the definition of a sign," derived from the description of the three possible structures of the phaneron: monadic, dyadic, and triadic. "The immediate Interpretant is an abstraction, consisting in a Possibility. The Dynamical Interpretant is a single actual event. The Final Interpretant is that toward which the actual tends" (Hardwick 1977: 111).

Was Lady Welby convinced that her significs was a section of the larger science of semeiotic? Was Peirce right in reading his trichotomy of interpretants in Lady Welby's trichotomy of meaning? Can we equate "interpretant" with "meaning"? I share Peirce's doubt which, to Lady Welby's relief, would lead us to consider significs and semeiotic as two different although complementary "sciences."

A last question before leaving the subject of the relation between significs and semeiotic: What did Lady Welby understand of Peirce's semeiotic through the letters which Peirce wrote her? Her comments are surprisingly and generally misleading. She indirectly gives the reason why she does not elaborate on Peirce's theory. Upon receiving from Peirce the first long theoretical letter on semeiotic, she writes a month later: "I have not yet really begun to frame a comment upon it from my own embryonic point of view" (Hardwick 1977: 37). In another letter, she confesses to writing on the subject "in pauper (why not pauperate?) form," "since I claim nothing but what I could describe as the conscious Primal Sense or reaction to the gist or essential point of things" (Hardwick 1977: 87).

She confuses, for instance, Peirce's categories with Cook Wilson's "oneness, twoness, and threeness" (Hardwick 1977: 36), for the reason that she does not understand the ordinal nature of Peirce's categories. Once she ventures in a comment on time to write: "[ . . . ] I start from and in and with and as Motion. For me, in the 'spiritual' as well the physical world, there is of course no Rest as the ultimate goal or as the antithesis of Motion. The changeless is less than dead, it is the non-existent. The secret here again for me lies in the unexplored conception of Order" (Hardwick 1977: 39). Peirce comments in the margin of the letter: "What you call Order I conceived not to be mere serial arrangement. What you mean is Law looked upon from the point of view of its effects. So understood, it is, as you say, precisely parallel to the question What is meaning" (Hardwick 1977: 39 n. 3)—which cannot be settled with this notion of Order.

The only category Lady Welby understands very well is Firstness. "In my humble way I claim to be a Muser, though I see that entrance into the world of Musement needs [ . . . ] an ungrudging study of the conditions of a healthy exploration" (Hardwick 1977: 65). She is for "the new, the young, the fresh, the possible" (Hardwick 1977: 40). But when she comes to semeiotic, her use of the terms are far from accurate:

> I may also claim to be conscious of the unique value of Sign (and Icon) in all its forms, including Indices and Symbols; and of the necessity of the 'corrolarial'. Of course (as you write) "all thinking is performed in signs" and a concept is intentional,—has meaning. (Hardwick 1977: 65)

Most of the time, Lady Welby's comments are polite questions or irrelevant remarks:

> Your illustration of "Cain killed Abel," with its wealth of implication, applies here. And the rule you suggest, though it belongs to a complicative world beyond my limit, is obviously of great interest. (Hardwick 1977: 89)

Your exposition of the "possible" Sign is profoundly interesting; but I am not equal to the effort of discussing beyond saying that I should prefer *tone* to mark for the homely reason that we often have occasion to say "I do not object to his words, but to his *tone.*" Could the word *Suggestant* be used for Possible Sign? (Hardwick 1977: 91)

Meanwhile may I venture to suggest that logic in graphic form as you give it, is as it were an "immuniser," and enemy and destructive absorbent of rational *toxins,* and also that it weds the pictorial and the abstract. (Hardwick 1977: 93)

## THE PHILOSOPHY BEHIND SIGNIFICS AND SEMEIOTIC

Lady Welby is probably right here, as she is very often when she expresses her philosophy of the critique of language, which philosophy does not differ fundamentally from Peirce's. We have already insisted on the anti-dualism of both philosophies, on their pragmatic and contextualistic turns. Like Peirce's, Lady Welby's philosophy is continuous: not only does it leave room for novelty, firstness of the new, but also for "uncertainty," "possible deception," and "the vagaries of natural hazard" which are presupposed, Peirce would say, by "order and consistency" (Welby 1911: 78). Like Peirce's, Lady Welby's philosophy is social:

> That we are already essentially social, that our very humanity is that, needs here no proving. We are indeed social first in the animal sense of mutual dependence and in the power and need of consciously and rationally concerted action. But we are social next and pre-eminently in virtue of that power of expression for the development of which I plead. And we are social because only thus can we be truly individual: because we are bound to work for a future "collective" intelligence and "collective" conscience [ . . . ]. (Welby 1985: cclxi)

Even the main difference between the two philosophies can be explained away. Unlike Peirce, Lady Welby advocates "intuition" and "psychology." But for a reason which has nothing to do with Peirce's promotion of "inference from and by signs" and "logic." Lady Welby had asked Schiller: "Why then is it that the world in general has rejected [the] guidance [of Mother Sense] and preferred that of [masculine] logic, thin, arid, and miserably one-sided and inadequate as that has often been? *That is the question which you Pragmatists have to answer*" (Welby 1985: ccxlix, italics hers).

Lady Welby's attitude is certainly that of a feminist: "As to the majority of women, the dominant Man with his imperious intellect has for uncounted ages stamped down their original gift: all their activities beyond the nursery (and, alas, there also, now) are masculinised: language, originally the woman's as custodian of the camp, creator of its industries and first trainer of the next generation, is now wholly 'male': the whole social order is laid down, prescribed for the woman on masculine lines only" (Welby 1985: ccxlix–ccl).

Thanks to the Pragmatists however, she said, mother-sense is bound to become for all "common sense"—which it is:

> It is sheer mother-sense—instinct of intellectual danger,—which in you, as in Dewey, Peirce and James, calls out the pragmatic reaction! It is the direct descendant of the keen awareness of the signs of primitive danger to the babes of the pair or the tribe, left in relatively weak hands. But let the pragmatists beware of exchanging one fallacy or one overworked method for another, perhaps the opposite. (Welby 1985: ccxlix)

## CONCLUSION: PHILOSOPHY AND LANGUAGE—A NEVER-ENDING BATTLE?

"And your real master of language always manages to find words wherewithal to express himself," Schiller says in his letter to Lady Welby (Welby 1985: ccxlviii).

And what language says contradicts very often what people think. In the battle for the clarification of language, language managed to cheat Peirce and Lady Welby. They did their best to help language express a new philosophy in which Platonic ideas would leave the Intelligible World to be active in the Sensible World, but they were unaware of Plato's guardians who were on duty at the entrance of the Cave and let them in to do what they thought they could do, but with the wrong password: Reality. For Peirce, although Reality is not for him a category, it is the Ultimate Aim of the Community of Inquirers looking for Truth, which, when reached, will do exactly the contrary of its *raison d'être:* block the path of inquiry. Lady Welby says:

> We need not inflate Reality with our empty bladders of used-up thoughts, or shrink her into the wrinkled skin of decay, [but] to say "we know not," and for an unnecessary moment to rest content with that, is a crime against the Real around us and within us which calls in the most pleading, as the most commanding, of all voices. *Live in Me; learn and know Me,* saith all that is Real [ . . . ]. (Welby 1985: 93)

> The true word, let us realise, is not merely a conventional noise or scrawl or stamp, it is the Logos, it is Reason. It is more than that. It is that which Can truly say "I am": it is the revelation of the way through truth to life. (Welby 1985: 85)

It is of course, for Plato, a great victory. But all this does not seem to be the logical conclusion of the signific or semeiotic argument; it would rather appear to be the symptom of the last disease of language, doomed to be fatal. Let us call it *dementia realitatis* and let us hope that Plato's victory is a Pyrrhic one. Peirce and Lady Welby deserve it.

# - 9 -

## Semeiotic and Semiology

### PEIRCE AND SAUSSURE

Let us not precide our conclusions beyond what our pre-
misses definitely warrant.

—Peirce (8.244)

## PEIRCE OR SAUSSURE

Contemporary research on the sign proceeds from two sources: Charles S. Peirce
(1839–1914) who is at the origin of the semiotic trend, and Ferdinand de Saussure (1857–1913) who is at the origin of the semiological trend. That there are
two trends is simply that Peirce's and Saussure's *a priori* conditions for thinking
are different. I am going to explain why I have preferred to follow Peirce rather
than Saussure. This will entail some repetition, but some things are better said
twice than once; I shall also appear sometimes to be stating what is perhaps obvious, but is better said than left unsaid.

First some preliminary remarks. The standard Saussurean theory of signs
was publicized by the *Course of General Linguistics* which is a posthumous reconstruction based on lecture notes taken by students. Although the publication
of Peirce's writings is also partly posthumous, and although we do not know
what Peirce would have retained or rejected, all the texts of the *Collected Papers*
are by Peirce himself.

A pioneer in many fields, Peirce continued all his life to elaborate his theory
of signs, even when he seemed to be giving his attention to other subjects.
He gave a first version of it in 1867 and 1868, developed the "pragmatic" aspect
of it in 1877 and 1878, provided it with a new logical foundation between 1880
and 1885, and developed it on this new basis from 1894 to the end of his life.
Saussure did not mention the subject before giving his second course of general
linguistics in 1908–1909, even if he did, as it would seem, have the idea before
1901 (according to Adrien Naville). Historically, Peirce's priority to Saussure is
unquestionable.

Saussure was essentially a linguist, more inclined to study languages than to elaborate theories about language. Thus his linguistics is based on the analyses of languages, and semiology only comes later as a general theory of linguistic signs. And even this was not his main interest, as he was at the same time (1909–1911) carrying out research on Saturnian verse, and this took much more of his time than the preparation of his lectures on general linguistics. After his death, nothing or practically nothing about linguistics and semiology was found in his papers, which, however, contained a hundred and fifty books of notes on Saturnian verse.

The first problem—and it is to this that I shall confine myself here—encountered by the reader of Peirce or Saussure is that of the context in which Peircean semiotics and Saussurean semiology originated and developed. Of Saussure, Georges Mounin says that he was "a man of his time" (Mounin 1968: 21). Which means that the Saussurean theory finds its *a priori* conditions for thinking within the framework of the associationistic psychology which was still very much alive, and Durkheim's sociology which came into fashion around the turn of the century. Now, as Mounin remarks, to say, as Saussure said, that "the linguistic sign unites not a thing and a name, but a concept and a sound-image" (66) is to base "linguistic facts" on mental facts "considered as well-known and accepted" and about which the linguist "knows probably less than he does about language" (Mounin 1968: 21).

Nonetheless, the linguistic fact is for Saussure a "psychological entity" (66). From Durkheim he borrows the idea that "language is a social fact" (6) without realizing perhaps that it is contradictory to assert that "language is the social side of speech, outside the individual who can never create nor modify it by himself," and, at the same time, that "it exists only by virtue of a sort of contract signed by the members of a community" (14). But is this not to dodge the question at the risk of complicating the system without resolving the contradiction of the impossible union of psychologism and sociologism? For what are these members? Individual or social beings? Saussure's answer lies in the famous distinction between language which is social and speech which is individual (13). But how can an individual who can never create nor modify language be "its master," the "executive side" of language (13)? Peirce, Saussure's contemporary, is in advance of his time. He denounces psychologism—which enables him, as we shall see, to adopt a coherent sociological position. His antipsychologism is constant and can be found in the 1868 articles as well as in the letters to Lady Welby which he wrote at the end of his life. "To explain the proposition in terms of the 'judgment'," he wrote in 1902, "is to explain the self—intelligible in terms of a psychical act, which is the most obscure of phenomena or facts" (2.309 note). In an article of 1868, he made the following remark which one of the most daring ideas of Michel Foucault seems to echo: "Just as we say that a body is in motion, and not that motion is in a body, we ought to say that we are in thought and not that thoughts are in us" (5.289 note). And in 1904, he wrote to Lady Welby: "I abstain from psychology which has nothing to do with ideoscopy" (Hardwick

1977: 25). Ideoscopy, which Peirce sometimes calls phenomenology, but most of the time phaneroscopy, is the proper context of his semiotics, the categories of which are *a priori* conditions for thinking the world. The "idea" (or "phenomenon" or "phaneron") concerned, he warns the reader, is not that of the English philosophers who have given the word "a psychological connotation [ . . . ] which I am careful to exclude" (1.285). It is "all that is in any way or any sense present to the mind, regardless of whether it corresponds to any real thing or not" (1.284). Phaneroscopy, he says further on, "religiously abstains from all speculation as to any relations between categories and physiological facts, cerebral or other" (1.287). This does not mean that these categories cannot have a psychical origin (1.374), but their origin affects their logical nature no more than the psychical origin of numbers (i.e., the fact of their being conceived and thought by a "mind") affects their mathematical nature. Some logicians base logic on the results of psychology: they "confound *psychical* truths with *psychological* truths" (5.485).

It would consequently not be fair to reproach Peirce with maintaining a behavioristic theory, which, even if he did defend it, is not that on which he bases his theory of signs. However, the question may be asked: was Peirce a behaviorist? Historical behaviorism is posterior to the "behavioristic" texts of Peirce. Watson was not yet born when Peirce wrote some of them. This fact being established, it is true that the principle of pragmatism plays a part in Peirce's semiotics, since it was proposed in order to reply to the question that the Cartesian analysis left unanswered when Descartes made clearness and distinctness the test of the meaning of an idea. What is a clear idea? Peirce asks; and his reply is: "Consider what effects, that might conceivably have practical bearings, we conceive the object of our conception to have. Then, our conception of these effects is the whole of our conception of the object" (5.402). If two ideas have the same effects or consequences or bring about an identical action, they are, in fact, only one idea; if one idea has different effects or consequences, it is made up of two or more ideas, as the case may be. For Cartesian intuition, Peirce substitutes scientific experimentation in every sense of the word "experimentation": that carried out in a laboratory as well as the "mental" experimentation of mathematical physics, which is also the testing of a hypothesis or idea. To abandon the intuitive method is to refuse the introspective psychology of states of consciousness in favor of action, and not another psychology, were it behavioristic. What is a sign? Peirce asks; and his reply is: A sign is first and foremost what it does and what it does is its meaning; in other words, it is a rule of action.

Peirce's antipsychologism is the indirect reason of his sociologism, which is connected with his semiotics just as his pragmatism is connected with his criticism of Descartes. It is because the theory of Peirce is not psychological and refuses the subject of discourse that it is social. I shall explain. Peirce constantly defended the social nature of the sign; not by opposing, like Saussure, language to speech, but by eliminating purely and simply the subject of discourse. It is the "I" which speaks, but what it says is not and cannot be "subjective": the "I" is the locus of signs and especially that of interpretants, a locus which is not isolated, but is, on the contrary, in a context—and every context is social.

Unlike the theory of Saussure, that of Peirce is plural and committed (in the political sense or not, according to whether the situation is or is not political). This plural and committed conception of the sign is intrinsic to the very nature of the sign in Peircean semiotics.

The sign is a triadic relation. The Peircean triadicity of the sign has a double origin, mathematical and Kantian. Mathematical:

[ ... ] it is impossible to form a genuine three [ ... ] without introducing something of a different nature from the unit and the pair, [ ... ] (Thus) the fact that A presents B with a gift C is a triple relation, and as such cannot possibly be resolved into any combination of dual relations. Indeed, the very idea of a combination is something which is what it is owing to the parts which it brings into mutual relationship. But we may waive that consideration, and still we cannot build up the fact that A presents C to B by any aggregation of dual relations between A and B, B and C, and C and A. A may enrich B, B may receive C, and A may part with C, and yet A need not necessarily give C to B. For that, it would be necessary that these three dual relations should not only coexist, but be welded into one fact. Thus we see that a triad cannot be analyzed into dyads. (1.363)

Kantian: Peirce's avowed intention in 1867, when he proposed a new list of categories, was to "reduce the manifold of sensuous impressions to unity" (1.546), which can be done only by the means of categories. But, for Peirce, the synthesis could not be achieved, as it was for Kant, in intuition, for the reason that Peirce had already banished intuition and all psychologism, as would appear in the anti-Cartesian articles of 1868. For Peirce, "the unity to which the understanding reduces impressions is the unity of a proposition" (1.548). Now, the logic of relations allows us to distinguish in the proposition: a propositional function, a first, in other words, a relation with no indication of the objects or terms in relation (—loves—); a simple proposition, a second, which indicates that a relation exists between objects or terms which Peirce calls "indices": "Ezekiel loveth Huldah" or *Rij* (2.295); and a complex proposition, a third, which puts propositions in relation (conjunctive, disjunctive, implicative). Whence the three logico-phaneroscopic categories: Firstness, the category of quality which has the generality of the possible; Secondness, the category of existence, of action enacted in its unique singularity here and now; and Thirdness, the category of mediating thought, of instrumental generality. The sign is First when it refers to itself, Second when it refers here and now to its object, Third when it refers to its object through an interpretant. (And the sign taken in itself, its object and its interpretant are themselves signs, and each of them entertains, for that reason, the same triadic relation with itself, its object, and its interpretant.) Peirce coined the word "interpretant" because the sign at this stage in a semiosis plays the role of an interpreter. Thus, "suppose we look up the word *homme* in a French dictionary;

we shall find opposite to it the word *man,* which, so placed, represents *homme* as representing the same two-legged creature which *man* itself represents" (1.553). Peirce adds that it was a requisite, and that consequently a Third was required, only because we receive a diversity of impressions. If we had but one impression, "the conception of reference to an interpretant" would not be required, as there would not be a manifold to reduce to unity (1.554).

It is a fact that the Saussurean theory is dyadic. All the analyses of Saussure are dichotomic: signifier/signified, language/speech, synchrony/diachrony, etcetera. Does this imply that Saussure had a "dichotomic temperament," as Marcel Cohen suggests (Cohen 1958 in Mounin 1968: 38)? In that case, we should have to say that Peirce's temperament was trichotomic. It is true, however, as Marcel Cohen points out, that this dichotomism is "not at all necessary for the study of linguistics" (ibid.). In fact, it is because Saussurean semiology is associationistic that it is dualistic—like all Western philosophy since Plato, including Cartesianism which was continued by associationism. Whereas, for Peirce, semiotics is another name for logic: "the quasi-necessary, or formal, doctrine of signs" (2.227), for Saussure, semiology is a chapter of social psychology and consequently of general psychology. Let us say, however, to avoid any misunderstanding, that what is in question here is the place occupied by the theory of signs among the other "sciences." When I said that the theory of categories explained the Peircean theory of signs, I was alluding to something quite different: the system or explicative context of reference. Although for Saussure, it is psychology which is the locus and point of reference of semiology, one must only distinguish even more carefully between semiology as a psychological science and the psychological philosophy of the associationists which he uses to express his theory of signs. That this philosophy is implicit does not change the situation, unless it be that Saussure, feeling the need of a means of expression other than semiological to describe signs, found himself obliged to use linguistics, which is a part of semiology, as the general pattern of semiology.

It must be admitted, in defense of Saussure, that he fully realized that a psycho-social analysis was not enough for semiology. If we emphasize the viewpoint of the psychologist and the social viewpoint, "the goal is by-passed, and the specific characteristics of semiological systems in general and of language in particular are completely ignored, for the distinguishing characteristic of the sign [ . . . ] is that in some way it always eludes the individual and the social will" (17). If we are to discover the true nature of language, we must learn what it has in common with all the other semiological systems. "It is probable," says Mounin, "that if Saussure had lived longer, his theory of signs would have been the point of departure and of the organisation of his entire doctrine" (Mounin 1968: 50). It is then that the question of its logical foundation would have arisen and could not have been eluded. Would he have renounced dyadic logic? Would he have introduced a third dimension into his theory of signs, as Barthes did? "In meaning, as it has been conceived since the Stoics," Barthes wrote, "there are three things: the signifier, the signified and the referent" (Barthes 1975: 169). We cannot answer this question. What we can be sure of is that a triadic theory of signs is pregnant with a plural and committed semiotics which Roland Barthes could not but approve of and of which Peirce provides a model.

A "same sign" belongs to different categories, types, and classes of signs according to whether it is considered in reference to itself as a first, in reference to its object as a second, in reference to its interpretant as a third. In reference to itself, it is what it is independently of its object and its interpretant. But, as a first, it will be the possibility of a sign: a qualisign; as a second, a given sign (a token): a sinsign; as a third, a codified or archetypal sign: a legisign. In reference to its object, it may either resemble the latter or indicate it or stand for it. In that case, it is respectively icon, index, and/or symbol. In reference to its interpretant, it may be simply conceived or represented (rhema), said or shown (dicisign), or else interpreted by inference in all senses of the word "infer" (argument). Thus, to borrow one of Peirce's examples, "that footprint that Robinson Crusoe found in the sand" (4.531) is in reference to itself a qualisign, the sign of a quality (what it is independently of the fact of being printed in the sand), a sinsign as being the only mark which is there at that particular spot on Robinson Crusoe's island. Although it cannot be a legisign proper, for a legisign is a sign of law and possesses a generality which Man Friday's footprint does not possess, it belongs to a type which enables Robinson Crusoe to say that it is a man's footprint, and not that of any kind of animal he knew. It could be a legisign proper in another context, if, like fingerprints, it could be used to distinguish Man Friday from the other inhabitants of the island, if there were any. In reference to its object, this footprint is a perfect icon, although reversed like the image of a person looking at himself in a mirror. But it is *at the same time* the index of a presence on the island, and not just any presence, but the presence of a human being the shape of whose foot is the "symbol" for the interpretant, which infers from the representation of this shape and what it indicates, that there is another man somewhere on the island. Whence the fact that Peircean semiotics is a semiotics at once of representation, of communication, and of meaning. The sign in itself has its own existence, an existence of a non-sign, one might say, just as an ambassador, although representing his country, is what he is in reference to himself, with his own history which distinguishes him from his predecessor and from the role he assumes at the moment when, for instance, he presents his credentials. The words "role" and "at the moment when" exactly situate the other two levels of the sign—of the same sign. The "role" refers to the meaning which is a rule of interpretation in a system of sign-interpretants. The presentation of credentials is a game which has its own rules and the meaning of the gestures is general. It is valid for every ambassador and for every presentation of credentials. The words "at the moment when" indicate that the game is being played: the communication constituted by the presentation of credentials is being enacted.

Communication is thus a concrete individual action, an event of and in history: it defines the sense of every act of the same type in a given system of signs. (Of course, representation, communication, and meaning may be considered respectively as first, second, and third). This system comprises only symbols; they refer also to (representative) signs which may be (existential) indices of objects; of objects in every sense of the term: possible, existential, or general. The Storming of the Bastille is a symbol in the system of meanings of the history of France. It refers to a certain idea of liberty, the negation or refusal of the arbitrary. But the documents which have reached us (the Bastille having been destroyed), which imagery or our imagination represent, are the indices of a state of France described by history and interpreted by the systems of symbols. However, let there be no mistake, the enactment of action is not limited to a given action, for there is no action which reveals, and, at the same time, constitutes, its meaning. The enactment is at the meeting point, always social, of the three paths of the sign.

\*     \*     \*

Have we to choose between Peirce and Saussure? The question should perhaps be put differently. Does one construct a model—*a priori* conditions for thinking—from experience? Or does one analyze experience in the light of a model whose principles and axioms owe nothing to chance encounters, but everything to the coherence of the choice? In other words, *how* should one choose? Given that a model is autonomous and does not admit of interference from outside, it would be vain to try to describe (and to judge) the semiotics of Peirce in Saussurean terms and Saussure's semiology in Peircean terms. The test of their respective validity resides, in the last analysis, in the coherence of the model on which they are based, and in the fecundity of the analyses they can provide. One cannot choose without committing oneself.

I shall sum up the comparison between Peirce's semiotics and Saussure's semiology in the following table:

| *Saussure's Semiology* | *Peirce's Semiotics* |
|---|---|
| Based on<br>  *philology*<br>  *linguistics*<br><br>  Mill's *empirical psychology*<br>  Durkheim's *sociology* | Based on<br>  *pragmaticism*<br>  *phaneroscopy*<br><br>  *logic of relatives* |
| Man's speech is individual<br>Man is social by nature | Man is social by nature |
| Dualism<br>Psychology/Sociology<br>signified/signifier<br>speech/language | Continuism<br>  Man's mind and the world<br>  are not dissociated |
| Nominalism<br>  Concepts are reducible to<br>  "acoustic images" | Realism<br>  Concepts are general and real |
| Spectator epistemology:<br>  World = "acoustic images"<br>  "acoustic images" = Idea | Actor epistemology:<br>  Pragmatism & Contextualism:<br>  An idea is what it does. |

Table 9.1. Peirce and Saussure—a comparison

## SAUSSURE AND PEIRCE

Although the contexts of Saussurean semiology and Peircean semiotics are radically different, it is possible and even relatively easy to find in the semiology of Saussure some of the fundamental concepts of Peirce's semiotics—which does not mean that they may be assimilated. On the contrary, their respective *a priori* conditions for thinking rule out any assimilation. This being so, my intention is not to "confound" them, as Lady Welby would have said, after opposing them, but to use generally understood Saussurean concepts in order to pave the way for a better understanding, or even acceptance, of Peircean concepts. If we take the Peircean system for my point of reference, it is because its triadic nature allows the introduction into sign-analysis of nuances about which Saussure was sometimes well aware, but which the dyadic nature of his system did not enable him to express.

## Principles of the Theory of Signs

In the first place, one can read in Saussure two principles of Peircean semiotics: First principle. No thought without signs: "Without the help of signs we would be unable to make a clear-cut, consistent distinction between two ideas" (111–112). Second principle. The principle of pragmatism which underlies the Saussurean idea of *difference*. A sign exists in its own right only because it does not coincide with another one: "In language, there are only differences" (120). But "although both the signified and the signifier are purely differential and negative when considered separately, their combination is a positive fact" which generates a system of values which constitutes the effective link between the phonic and psychological elements contained in each sign. "In language, as in any semiological system, whatever distinguishes one sign from the other constitutes it. Difference makes character just as it makes value and unit" (121). This is proved by diachronical facts. "When two words are confused through phonetic alteration [ . . . ] the ideas that they express will also tend to become confused if only they have something in common. A word may have different forms. Any nascent difference will tend to become significant" (121).

Peirce says exactly the same thing, even if he says it differently: "There is no distinction in meaning so fine as to consist in anything but a possible difference in practice" (5.400). How to avoid "the deceits of language" of the kind which consists in mistaking "a mere difference in the grammatical construction of two words for a distinction between the ideas they express" (5.399), Peirce wonders. His answer is that there is no better rule than the following: "Do things fulfil the same function practically? Then let them be signified by the same word. Do they not? Then let them be distinguished" (8.33). This is what Peirce calls the principle or maxim of pragmatism.

## The Analysis of Sign

### The Peircean Analysis

As we noted above, Peirce analyzes signs semiotically in three steps at three different levels of relation: (1) In reference to the representamen: the sign is analyzed as such in reference to itself; (2) in reference to its object; (3) in reference to the sign-interpretant, in other words in reference to the sign or field of signs with which the reader or listener associates the representamen in such a way that the latter refers to an object. The third step, or level 3, semiotically presupposes 2 and 1; the second step, or level 2, presupposes 1. This gives the following well-known table in which the Peircean analysis of signs enables us to distinguish nine types of sub-signs:

|                      | 1         | 2        | 3        |
|----------------------|-----------|----------|----------|
| Representamen (R1)   | Qualisign | Sinsign  | Legisign |
| Object (O2)          | Icon      | Index    | Symbol   |
| Interpretant (I3)    | Rhema     | Dicisign | Argument |

Table 9.2. The nine sub-types of a sign

**The Sign**

LINEARITY OF THE SIGN AND SEMIOSIS

For Saussure, "the linguistic sign [ ... ] unites a concept and a sound-image" (98), a signified and a signifier (99). It is a "two-sided psychological entity" (66). For Peirce, it is a semiosis, a relation which is real, in the sense of existentially active, of the sign. "By *semiosis,* I mean [ ... ] an action, or influence which is or involves a cooperation of *three* subjects, such as a sign (representamen), its object, and its interpretant, this tri-relative influence not being in any way resolvable into actions between pairs" (5.584). There is, in both cases, continuity of the sign, but the similarity stops there, for linearity is temporal and is valid only for "auditory signifiers" of the linguistic sign, and not for "visual signifiers (nautical signs, etc.)" (70); semiosis, although also temporal, is by definition logical and encompasses the whole semiotic process *ad infinitum* (2.303). It must, however, be remarked that Saussure admits that "the linguistic entity exists only through the associating of the signifier with the signified. Whenever only one element is retained, the entity vanishes" (102). That appears to be the case here.

THE ARBITRARINESS OF THE SIGN AND THE
CONVENTIONALITY OF THE INTERPRETANT

The arbitrary sign is unmotivated. It is, in this sense, that we can also understand the interpretant. The interpretant does not interpret freely; it is a translator which says in one language exactly the same thing which is said in another. According to Saussure, the arbitrary sign "should not imply that the choice of the signifier is left entirely to the speaker (we shall see [ ... ] that the individual does not have the power to change a sign in any way once it has become established in the linguistic community)" (69). "The community is necessary if values that owe their existence solely to usage [pragmatic and not practical, given that the community engenders and imposes its rules] and general acceptance [of the community of users (Saussure) or investigators (Peirce)] are to be set up; by himself the individual is incapable of fixing a single value" (113).

THE SYSTEM OF SIGNS, REPERTORY, AREA, AND FIELD OF SIGNS

"To consider a term as simply the union of a certain sound with a certain concept is grossly misleading. To define it in this way would isolate the term from the system; it would mean assuming that one can start from the terms and construct the system by adding them together, when, on the contrary, it is from the interdependent whole that one must start and through analysis obtain its elements" (113). Peirce, for his part, distinguishes three types of systems of signs according to whether the signs are considered in themselves (repertory), in reference to their objects (area), or in reference to their interpretants (field). It will be noticed that, for Peirce, the repertory of representamens, the area of objects, and the field of interpretants are not semiotically separable.

VALUE AND INTERPRETANT

Saussure distinguishes between value and signification. The definition he gives of value in its relation to signification makes it a good equivalent of interpretant. Signification is the counterpart of the sound-image (115).

The value of a word is not limited to the possibility of "exchanging" it for an idea or another word. It comes from the fact that it belongs to a system, or more exactly here to a field of interpretants.

> Its value is [ . . . ] not fixed so long as one simply states that it can be 'exchanged' for a given concept, i.e. that it has this or that signification: one must also compare it with similar values [ . . . ] Its content is really fixed only by the concurrence of everything that exists outside it. (115)

Thus *mutton* and *sheep* have the same meaning, but not the same value, the reason being that English has in its repertory two words for the same animal: *sheep* and *mutton*, while French has only one. In English, it is the repertory of signs which will determine the signification, whereas in French it is the field of interpretants. Saussure neglects the area of objects, as we shall see.

| Repertory of representamens | Area of objects | Field of interpretants |
|---|---|---|
| *Sheep* | *live* | any other meaning |
| *Mutton* | *meat* | *food* |

Table 9.3. Value and interpretant

In the same way, there are two signs or representamens in the German and English repertories (*meten* and *vermeten; to rent* and *to let*) which correspond to only one sign-representamen in the French repertory: *louer,* the signification being supplied by the field of interpretants or, if one prefers, the context (cf. 116). Similar remarks can be made about grammatical entities: the value of a French plural does not correspond to that of a Sanskrit plural which covers the dual and the plural (116).

The signifier–signified relationship "symbolizes signification," but "is only a value determined by its relations with other similar values and [ . . . ] without it signification would not exist" (117). So there is no signification without an interpretant.

**The Three Trichotomies of the Sign**

THE TRICHOTOMY OF THE REPRESENTAMEN

***Signifier, Qualisign, and Sinsign*** For Saussure, as we have seen, "the linguistic sign unites [ ... ] a concept and a sound-image" (98), a signified and a signifier (66). Now the sound-image "is not the material sound, a purely physical thing, but the psychological imprint of the sound, the impression it makes on our senses" (66). The sound-image could thus be a (psychical) qualisign of which the material sound would be the sinsign. We shall see that, in the case of this particular sign, the linguistic sign, a given sound-image (which is in any case a sinsign) is the replica of a legisign.

***Arbitrary Sign and Legisign*** Saussure defines the arbitrary sign when he asks if modes of expression like mime are not the affair of semiology:

> Every means of expression used in society is based, in principle, on collective behavior (in French *habitude*), or what amounts to the same thing,—on convention. Polite formulas, for instance, though often imbued with a certain natural expressiveness [ ... ] are nonetheless fixed by rule; it is this rule and not the intrinsic value of the gestures that obliges one to use them. (67–68)

The global sign (signifier–signified) is thus a legisign, "a law which is a sign" (2.246).

***Replica*** "The signs that make up language are not abstractions, but real objects" (102).

> Linguistic signs, though basically psychical, are not abstractions; associations which bear the stamp of collective approval—and which, added together, constitute language—are realities that have their seat in the brain. Besides, linguistic signs are tangible. (14)

Signs are not abstractions. What Saussure means is that the signifier is nothing without the signified and *vice versa,* as we have already noted. Peirce also insists on the fact that the representamen, the object, and the interpretant by themselves are not signs. It is their conjunction which constitutes the sign.

But what is concrete and tangible is not the linguistic sign, but its replica. Saussure, like Peirce, makes a distinction between the legisign and the replica:

> It is impossible for sound alone, a material element, to belong to language [ ... ]
> All our conventional values have the characteristic of not being confused with the tangible element which supports them. For instance, it is not the metal in a piece of money that fixes its value. (118)

The linguistic signifier is incorporeal (118), i.e., in Peircean terms a "legisign." For instance, says Saussure, "in French, general use of a dorsal *r* does not prevent many speakers from using a tongue-tip trill; language is not in the least disturbed by it; language requires only that the sound be different and not [ ... ] that it have an invariable quality" (119). An identical state of affairs is observable in writing; the letter *t,* for example, may be written in different ways so long as it is not liable to be confused with *l* or *d.* "The means by which the sign is produced is completely unimportant [ . . . ] Whether I make the letters in white or black, raised or engraved, with pen or chisel—all this is of no importance, with respect to their signification" (120).

### THE TRICHOTOMY OF THE OBJECT
Saussurean semiology, which is dyadic, maintains that the linguistic sign unites, not "a thing and a name," but "a concept and a "sound-image" (66), the concept playing the role of an interpretant. However, Saussure does encounter Peirce's index and symbol.

***Difference and Index*** "The value of letters is purely negative and differential. The same person can write *t* in different ways:

The only requirement is that the sign for *t* not be confused in his script with the signs used for *l, d,* etc." (119).

We have already agreed on that in another context, and Peirce would not object. But the way of writing can be an index in another field of interpretants; here, for instance, in graphology. The reasons why Saussure is not interested in the different ways of writing *t* are, first, that a sign does not unite a word and a thing, and, second, that what Saussure is describing is the *linguistic* sign.

***Symbol and Nature*** If Saussure had used the word "symbol," symbol would have been only another term for legisign, and for the same reasons. But as he used the words as they are used in everyday language, Saussure could not use the word "symbol" to designate the linguistic sign because "one characteristic of the symbol is that it is never wholly arbitrary; it is not empty, for there is the rudiment of a natural bond between the signifier and the signified" (68). "The symbol of justice, a pair of scales, could not be replaced by just another symbol, such as a chariot." It is because they have lost their "natural bond" that onomatopoeia and interjections are no longer symbols, but linguistic signs (124).

### THE TRICHOTOMY OF THE INTERPRETANT
Saussure seems to limit the interpretant to the concept of the signified and thus to the rhema. However, the opposition between syntagmatic and associative relations (122–127) could have been a way of distinguishing proposition (dicisign) from concept and argument.

> The syntagmatic relation is *in praesentia*. It is based on two or more terms that occur in an effective series. Against this, the associative relation unites terms *in absentia* in a potential mnemonic series. (123)

But Saussure thought otherwise because although "the sentence is the ideal type of syntagm [ ... ] it belongs to speaking not to language" (124). Does the sentence belong to language or to speech?

> A rather widely held theory makes sentences the concrete units of language: we speak only in sentences and subsequently single out the words. But to what extent does the sentence belong to language? If it belongs to speaking, the sentence cannot pass for the linguistic unit. If we picture to ourselves in their totality the sentences that could be uttered, their most striking characteristic is that in no way do they resemble each other [ ... ] In sentences [ ... ] diversity is dominant, and when we look for the link that bridges their diversity, again we find, without having looked for it, the word with its grammatical characteristics and thus fall back into the same difficulties as before. (106)

The discussion can be summed up in the following table in which the Saussurean terms which might be equivalent to the Peircean semiotic terms are given instead of the latter. The empty spaces indicate either that Saussurean analysis does not enable us to make the corresponding distinctions, or that Saussure did not think this necessary.

| | 1 | 2 | 3 |
|---|---|---|---|
| R | Sound-image | Material element (Support) | Signifier |
| O "Substance" | | | |
| I "Value" | Signified | | |

Table 9.4. Peircean classification of Saussurean concepts

R1—Peirce's qualisign: The sound-image is "not the material sound, a purely physical thing, but the psychological imprint of the sound, the impression it makes on our senses" (66). "The sound-image is par excellence the natural representation of the word as a fact of potential language outside any actual use of it in speaking" (66 n. 1).

R2—Peirce's sinsign: "All our conventional values have the characteristic of not being confused with the tangible element which supports them" (118).

R3—Peirce's legisign: The linguistic signifier is incorporeal (118). It is "unmotivated," i.e., "arbitrary in that it actually has no natural connexion with the signified" (69), "collective habit," "convention," "fixed by rule" (66).

01—Peirce's icon: Nothing corresponds to Peirce's icon in Saussure.

02—Peirce's index: The support can play the part of an index, but, in that case, Saussure does not consider it as a sign, because it is not linguistic.

03—Peirce's symbol: The "symbol" is "natural" for Saussure.

I1—Peirce's rhema: A word which is the link that bridges the diversity of sentences (106).

I2—Peirce's dicisign (such as a sentence): The sentence cannot pass for the linguistic sign: it does not belong to language (106).

I3—Peirce's argument: Nothing corresponds to Peirce's argument in Saussure.

# - 10 -

## Semeiotic and Semiotics

### PEIRCE AND MORRIS

> Peirce's account of signs is embedded in the metaphysics of
> his categories [...] and in the metaphysics of his view of
> mind. These are not secure bases for a scientific semiotics.
> But Peirce himself, in his rejection of the older Cartesian
> mentalism [...] has at least indicated a possible direction
> of advance towards a more adequate account of sign phe-
> nomena.
>
> —Morris (1971: 340)

> The present treatment [by Morris] follows Peirce's empha-
> sis upon behavior rather than his more mentalistic formula-
> tions.
>
> —Morris (1971: 339)

Did Morris read Peirce? The question I am asking is not meant to be a criticism
of Morris. It only implies that I take Peirce as my point of departure and will
judge Morris with reference to his fidelity to Peirce, if he read Peirce.

Morris's tripartition: syntactics, semantics, and pragmatics, is undeniably
Peircean. The separations between these three classes are not. Pragmatics is *con-
tinuistic.*

## PEIRCE'S PRAGMATICS

According to Peirce, the three relations of any sign to its possible object are respectively iconic, indexical, and symbolic. We shall first examine that which is apparently the easiest to understand: the index, of which the index finger of the
hand is the type:

> The index asserts nothing; it only says "There!" It takes hold of our eyes, as it
> were, and forcibly directs them to a particular object, and there it stops. Demon-
> strative and relative pronouns are nearly pure indices, because they denote

things without describing them; so are the letters on a geometrical diagram, and the subscript numbers which in algebra distinguish one value from another without saying what those values are. (3.361)

Indices need symbols to say something, although symbols which are generals, are in themselves empty:

> Without [symbols] there would be no generality in the statements, for they are the only general signs; and generality is essential to reasoning. [ ... ] But [symbols] alone do not state what is the subject of discourse; and this can, in fact, not be described in general terms; it can only be indicated. The actual world cannot be distinguished from a world of imagination by any description. Whence the need of pronouns and indices, and the more complicated the subject the greater need of them. (3.363)

Although logicians are content with these two relations to the object, Peirce goes further in his analysis, showing that by themselves these two relations are insufficient for reasoning. In order to reason, we need a third type of relation, which appears in the form of logical diagrams and sensorial images (mostly visual). These diagrams and images Peirce calls icons:

> With these two kinds of signs alone (symbols and indices) any proposition can be expressed; but it cannot be reasoned upon, for reasoning consists in the observation that where certain relations subsist certain others are found, and it accordingly requires the exhibition of the relations reasoned within an icon. (3.363)

## MORRIS'S PRAGMATICS

Morris's paradigm of knowledge and experience is, according to him, *reductionist:* the only knowable and experienceable objects are spatio-temporal. Morris states his position explicitly: the semiotics developed in *Signs, Language and Behavior* (Morris 1971: 75–398) does not take Peirce as its point of departure. It is based on the quite behavioristic theories of George H. Mead (1863–1931). (I have not found one single reference to Peirce in the complete works of Mead.) Later, says Morris, he studied more seriously "Peirce, Ogden and Richards, Russell and Carnap, and still later, Tolman and Hull" (Morris 1971: 445). Tolman and Hull are behaviorists; Russell and Carnap can be classified as logical empiricists with an atomistic tendency. Peirce, Ogden, and Richards remain.

Morris was convinced that he was faithful to Peirce. When Dewey accused him of misrepresenting Peirce's thought, in particular by substituting the interpreter for the interpretant, Morris obstinately insisted that he was faithful to Peirce—quoting, notably, 5.470–493, in which Peirce discusses the logical interpretant. In actual fact, Morris's reading of Peirce is behavioristic.

# MORRIS'S SEMIOTICS

## Semiosis

[Semiosis] is a five-term relation: $v, w, x, y, z$, in which $v$ sets up in $w$ the disposition to react in a certain kind of $x$, to a certain kind of object $y$ (not then acting as a stimulus) under certain conditions $z$:

$v$ = signs
$w$ = interpreters
$x$ = interpretants (not necessarily with a "subjective" connotation)
$y$ = meanings
$z$ = contexts (401–402)

Morris recognizes that this formulation is behavioristic and valid for all organisms—the case of the human organism is particular only by the fact of its capacity for awareness of its semiotic behavior (401–402).

## Sign

The two definitions of the sign given by Morris in *Signs, Language and Behavior* are behavioristic:

1. "If something, A, controls behavior towards a goal in a way similar to (but not necessarily identical with) the way something else, B, would control behavior with respect to that goal in a situation in which it were observed, then A is a sign" (84).

2. "If anything, A, is a preparatory-stimulus which in the absence of stimulus-objects initiating response-sequences of a certain behavior-family causes a disposition in some organism to respond under certain conditions by response-sequences of this behavior-family, then A is a sign" (87).

Presence or absence of "dynamical" objects? The paradigm of knowledge is, for Morris as for Mead, "presentationistic." Knowledge can only be direct, knowledge by signs is a substitute: "If we present a distant planet, its matter is presented as we would actually sense it if we could place our hands upon it" (Mead: 20).

## Signification

### Preliminary Remarks: "Signification" and "Meaning"

"Signification" by Morris is not used in the ordinary sense of the term. English has the privilege of possessing at least two terms: "signification" and "meaning." What we could say in French to explain what *signification* means is that it is not synonymous with *sens*. The question of "sense" has nothing to do with semiotics, neither in Morris nor in Peirce. Signification is, for Morris, the *significatum*, i.e., "The conditions such that whatever meets these conditions is a denotatum of a given sign" (366). This is not expressible in Peircean terms, for what is "signified" by the sign is the interpretant which refers the sign or representamen to an object.

**Signification**

In discussing the problem of signification, Morris *apparently* adopts a triadic point of view which could be Peircean, but is in fact inspired by Mead and his analysis of an act. According to Mead, the analysis enables one to distinguish four levels of the act: that of the impulse, that of perception, that of manipulation, and that of consummation.

Morris summarizes Mead as follows:

> [ ... ] if an impulse (as a disposition to a certain kind of action) is given, the resulting action has three phases: the perceptual, the manipulatory, and the consummatory. The organism must perceive the relevant features of the environment in which it is to act; it must behave toward these objects in a way relevant to the satisfaction of its impulse; and if all goes well, it then attains the phase of activity which is the consummation of the act. (403–404)

In consequence, Morris goes on, if signs are treated behaviorally (which is apparently what he intends to do), their significations are related to these three aspects of action and so exhibit tridimensionality. A sign is:

1. *designative* insofar as it signifies observable properties of the environment or of the actor;

2. *appraisive* insofar as it signifies the consummatory properties of some object or situation;

3. *prescriptive* insofar as it signifies how the object or situation is to be reacted to so as to satisfy the governing impulse.

It will be noticed that all this is a matter only of the action–object relation. Morris points out that "Mead also speaks of the distance properties of the object, its manipulatory properties, and its consummatory properties" (404). As regards the "formal signs" (logical, grammatical, or structural signs: "or," parentheses, adverbial endings such as "-ly," which Morris had called "formators"), they constitute the fourth dimension of signification: the "formative signification," the other dimensions being the designative, appraisive, and prescriptive significations. Morris wonders how to integrate this fourth dimension in a tridimensional semiotics: by making "formal signs" a particular class of lexical signs, like metalinguistic signs, for instance? The question would not have to be asked if his semiotics was really three-dimensional, in other words, if there were a place for the *legisign* (410–411).

## *Interpretant*

The interpretant is not a sign for Morris. It is *a disposition to react in a certain way because of a sign*. There are three sorts of interpretants, as there are three dimensions of signification: (1) To the designative dimension corresponds a disposition to react to the object designated as if it had certain observable properties; (2) To the appraisive dimension corresponds a disposition to act *toward* a designated object as if it had properties enabling to satisfy or not satisfy the impulse; (3) To the prescriptive dimension corresponds a disposition to act in a *certain way with regard* to the designated object. This tridimensionality of the interpretant has nothing triadic about it either. It is difficult to see how these three sorts of interpretants could be made to correspond with the immediate, dynamic, and final interpretants, even if one called them affective, energetic, and logical, which is not the case with Morris. (It should be remembered that the trilogy of the three interpretants: affective, energetic, and logical is not hierarchized. In other words it is not an ordered series.) In fact, Morris *expressly* rejects triadicity. "Peirce," he says, "always connects processes of mediation, sign-processes, and mental processes. This means that he would not accept any behavioral psychology which attempted to reduce behavior to two-term relations between stimuli and responses" (337). Some behaviorists, he remarks further on, have tried to introduce a third factor, "a 'reinforcing' state of affairs in which a need of the animal is reduced or satisfied" (338).

Even if the process is triadic in this case, this addition cannot satisfy either Peirce or the behaviorist. The behaviorist cannot accept the idea that the conditioned stimulus is a sign—and still less so, in that there are other processes of mediation than conditioning, for instance, the eye or the retinal image. Hence, says Morris, it is preferable to restrict sign-processes "to those in which the factor of mediation is an interpretant" (338).

Peirce would certainly not be content with "reinforcement" as the third term of semiosis, nor with Morris's interpretant. For Morris, the interpretant cannot be a sign:

1. because if it were, one would constantly encounter the empirical question of whether signs always generate new signs;

2. because if it were, a circularity would be introduced in the (theoretical) definition of the sign;

3. because by emphasizing behavior rather than thought, one "avoids the extension of sign-processes to inorganic nature" and this "does not require that all behavior involves sign phenomena" (339).

*Morris's semiotics is thus in reality a distortion of that of Peirce.* The final logical interpretant is admittedly a habit for Peirce, but it is not a *disposition of the interpreter.* Morris defines "disposition" as "[t]he state of an organism at a given time such that under certain additional conditions a given response takes place" (361)—the *interpreter* being "an organism for which something is a sign" and the *interpretant* "the disposition in an interpreter to respond, because of a sign, by response-sequences of some behavior-family" (363).

For Peirce, habit is a rule of action: it is logical (it is not without reason that he calls it "logical interpretant"). Habit is third and because it is third it presupposes an existing second: "the sheriff's arm," as he says, without which the law could not be. Dewey insists on this point in his critique of Morris, which concerns "linguistic signs." Linguistic signs, says Dewey, which constitute thought and belong to thirdness, do not refer, by themselves, to things. This reference to things is the affair of "indexical signs" which pertain to secondness. Dewey quotes Peirce as follows:

> We are constantly bumping up against hard fact. [ ... ] There can be no resistance without effort; there can be no effort without resistance. They are only two ways of describing the same experience. It is a double consciousness. [ ... ] as the consciousness *itself* is two-sided, so it also has two varieties; namely, action, where our modification of other things is more prominent than their reaction on us, and perception, where their effect on us is overwhelmingly greater than our effect on them. And this notion of being such as other things make us, is such a prominent part of our life that we conceive other things also to exist by virtue of their reactions against each other. The idea of other, of *not,* becomes a very pivot of thought. To this element we give the name of Secondness. (1.324)

Consequently, the interpretant is a sign, and as such, triadic: third (final or logical), second (dynamic or energetic), first (immediate or affective). As such, the sign does not require a *faculty of thought.* Thinking is a system of signs (thirdness) which action (secondness) binds to things, not, however, in themselves, but experienced qualitatively in the unity of a global situation (firstness).

Morris takes as reference a Peirce divested of his *mentalism.* By doing so, he divests him of his semiotics. What Morris did not see is that Peirce's theory, although biological and social, is not psychological, but logical and, if the term be allowed, "cosmic," as Dewey rightly remarks: "The organism is an integrated part of the world in which habits form and operate" (Dewey 1946: 94).

I shall conclude with a text by Peirce which I have already quoted in another context (ch. 3) and that Dewey quotes in his paper of 1946, in which the notion of interpreter as an individual separated from society and the cosmos is authoritatively rejected:

> When we come to study the great principle of continuity and see how all is fluid and every point partakes the being of every other, it will appear that individualism and falsity are one and the same. Meantime, we know that man is not whole as long as he is single, that he is essentially a possible member of society. Especially, one man's experience is nothing if it stands alone. [ ... ] It is not "my" experience, but "our" experience that has to be thought of, and this "us" has indefinite possibilities. (5.402 n. 2, in Dewey 1946: 94)

# - 11 -

# Semeiotic and Linguistics

## PEIRCE AND JAKOBSON

[Charles Sanders Peirce] est l'un des plus grands précur-
seurs de l'analyse structurale en linguistique. Peirce n'a pas
seulement établi la nécessité de la sémiotique, il en a aussi
esquissé les grandes lignes. Le jour où on se décidera à étu-
dier soigneusement les idées de Peirce sur la théorie des
signes, des signes linguistiques en particulier, on se rendra
compte du précieux secours qu'elles apportent aux recherches sur les relations entre le langage et les autres systèmes
de signes.

—Jakobson (1963: 27–28)

Philosophers are still divided concerning the importance of Peirce's philosophy.
Nevertheless, if Peirce is accepted today everywhere, and especially in France, it
is thanks to the linguists who followed Jakobson's misreading of Peirce. The
cross-reading I propose here is not intended as a criticism of Jakobson, but as a
kind of clarification of Peirce. The fact that I worked on the French text of Jakobson does not affect the argument.*

We shall deal respectively with Jakobson's reading of Peirce and with a possible Peircean reading of Jakobson.

## JAKOBSON'S READING OF PEIRCE

In the fifties, Roman Jakobson discovered Peirce and wrote that Peirce was one
of the greatest forerunners of structural analysis in linguistics. He said that
Peirce had not only proved the necessity of semiotics, but stated the outlines of
its theory. And he predicted that, when Peirce's ideas on the theory of signs, and
of linguistic signs in particular, were thoroughly studied, the researches on the
relations between language and the other systems of signs would be far easier.

* The Jakobsonian material I used is: Roman Jakobson, *Essais de linguistique générale* (Paris:
Éditions de Minuit, 1963); Roman Jakobson, "A la recherche de l'essence du langage" in *Problèmes
du langage* (Paris: Gallimard, 1966); "Roman Jakobson," *L'Arc,* special issue n° 60 (1975). The translations from the French otherwise mentioned are mine.

From his reading of Peirce, Jakobson concluded (1) that the sign is divided into icons, indices, and symbols, and (2) that this division is "relative" in the ordinary sense of the word. In every sign there is a ratio of icon (resemblance), index (contiguity), and symbol (conventional rule)—"merely a difference in relative hierarchy within individual signs, since in each case one of these factors predominates over the others" (Jakobson 1966: 26–27).

Unfortunately, the definition of the sign and the conception of the "hierarchy" are wrong: there are three trichotomies and not one (i.e., *nine* relational aspects of a sign and not *three*), and the hierarchy is not *relative*, but *ordered.*

## The Conception of the Sign

The fact that Jakobson says that the "totality of signs" is divided into "icons, indices and symbols" (Jakobson 1966: 26) is a genuine misreading. According to Peirce, the division between "icons, indices and symbols" refers only to the sign in relation with its immediate object. It is true, however, that Peirce is not always very clear and that the following way of speaking is misleading:

> Thus we may show the relation between the different kinds of signs by a brace, thus:
>
> Signs: $\begin{cases} \text{Icons} \\ \text{Indices} \\ \text{Symbols} \end{cases}$
>
> (2.282)

The misreading is aggravated when Jakobson introduces Peirce's icons, indices, and symbols between Saussure's signifier and signified.

> It is not the absolute presence or absence of resemblance or contiguity between the signifier and the signified, nor the fact that the usual connection between these constituents would be of the order of the purely factual or the purely institutional, which is at the basis of the division of the totality of signs into icons, indices and symbols, but only the predominance of one of these factors over the others. (Jakobson 1966: 26)

Jakobson is here trying to explain Peirce in Saussurean terms, for example, the use of "signifier" and "signified," without mentioning the "interpretant." Is the signifier Peirce's representamen? Although Jakobson is right concerning the fact that the icon is related to similarity together with the emotional aspect of sign and that the index is related to contiguity together with the action or pragmatic aspect of sign, he does not mention the third relation with the object: the symbol, which is related in the same way to continuity together with the inferential aspect of sign.

We will later encounter the same problem with Umberto Eco's reading of Peirce:

> I am thus asserting that the relationship between *signifiant* and *signifié* (or between *sign-vehicle* and *significatum*, or between *sign* and *meaning*) is autono-

mous in itself and does not require the presence of the referred object as an element of its definition. (Eco 1979: 179)

Although it is a fact that, for Peirce, the "referred object" does not enter in the definition of the sign, the reference to Saussure and Morris is confusing for all concerned.

### Jakobson's "Relative Hierarchy" versus Peirce's Ordinal Hierarchy of the Classes of Signs

Why should we speak in a given case of an icon rather than of an index or a symbol? asks Jakobson. It is simply because of "the predominance of one of these factors over the others" (Jakobson 1965: 26), "the most perfect of signs" being, according to Peirce, those signs "in which the iconic, indicative, and symbolic characters are blended as equally as possible" (4.448).

Two remarks must be made here: On one hand, Jakobson is not speaking from a semiotic point of view, but from a literary or poetical point of view, and using Peircean terms in a loose way. It is understandable, for instance, that in a given sentence the iconic aspect may appear to "predominate" or actually *does* predominate from the point of view of the literary analysis of a poem. But in a semiotic analysis of the Peircean type, it cannot be said that the icon "predominates" over the two other aspects of the sign. On the other hand, "equally" in Peirce's quotation does not mean what Jakobson thinks it means. It means: "in equal proportions" *if and only if* the hierarchical order of each of the three aspects of the sign is respected, as Peirce shows immediately afterwards in the same paragraph: "Of this sort of signs the line of identity is an interesting example" (4.448).

"As a conventional sign, it is a symbol; and the symbolic character, when present in a sign, is of its nature *predominant* over the others" (4.448). The symbol (because of its triadic nature) is hierarchically "predominant" over the index (which is dyadic) and over the icon (which is monadic).

Let us consider the graph of identity between two portions, such as

— is identical with —

[A]s a symbol, [the graph] is of the nature of a *law,* and is therefore general, while here there must be an identification of individuals. This identification is effected not by the pure symbol, but by its *replica* which is a thing. The termination of one portion and the beginning of the next portion denote the same individual by virtue of a factual connexion, and that the closest possible; for both are points, and they are one and the same point. In this respect, therefore, the line of identity is of the nature of an index. To be sure, this does not affect the ordinary parts of a line of identity, but so soon as it is even *conceived,* [it is conceived] as composed of two portions, and it is only the factual junction of the replicas of these portions that makes them refer to the same individual. The line of identity is, moreover, in the highest degree iconic. For it appears as nothing but a continuum of dots, and the fact of the identity of a thing, seen under two aspects, consists merely in the continuity of being in passing from one apparition to another. Thus uniting, as the line of identity does, the natures of symbol, index, and icon, it is fitted for playing an extraordinary part in this system of representation. (4.448)

In other words, hierarchically speaking, an icon by itself cannot act, and consequently be an index, for an index by itself implies an icon, but in itself it has no meaning whatever; it is what it is by sheer chance. That is why a mental sign must be triadic: a symbol, which necessarily includes an index and an icon. One can think of an index, but, if the index is genuine, it cannot be, in any way conceivable, symbolic. The same thing may be said of the icon of a genuine First. It is a sheer possible relation of a possibility.

It is extremely difficult to maintain the delicate balance between the dualistic meanings of the semiological concepts of Saussure and the pragmatic and triadic meanings of the new protocols of Peirce: the protocol of hierarchy and the protocol of degeneracy.

And also the delicate balance between the protocols themselves. The fact that the combination of the two protocols has been made only shows that it would have been better not to do it, although the following passage might seem to imply Peirce's approval of the process:

A *genuine* symbol is a symbol that has a general meaning. There are two kinds of degenerate symbols, the *Singular Symbol* whose Object is an existent individual, and which signifies only such characters as that individual may realize; and the *Abstract Symbol,* whose only object is a Character. (2.293)

Of course, the existent individual is not, properly speaking, an index, nor the character an icon.

Let us remember that the protocol of degeneracy is mathematical and the protocol of the hierarchy of categories is phenomenological or phaneroscopical.

|  | 1 | 2 | 3 |
|---|---|---|---|
| **Firstness** | **Genuine** |  |  |
| Representamen | Qualisign/Tone |  |  |
| **Secondness** | **Degenerate (first degree)** | ← **Genuine** |  |
| Object | Icon | Index |  |
| **Thirdness** | Degenerate (first degree) | **Degenerate (second degree)** | ← **Genuine** |
| Interpretant | Rhema | Dicisign | Argument |

Table 11.1. Protocol of degeneracy

The Protocol of the hierarchy of the three categories has nothing to do with the Protocol of degeneracy. It rests on the value of a "phaneron," whether triadic, dyadic, or monadic.

It is only when one tries to combine the two sets of concepts of the two protocols—which are, properly speaking, uncombinable—that ideas of the following kind can be entertained, such as "the degenerate sign is a deterioration of the triadic relation"; "hypoicons are the degenerate forms of icon"; "symbol has two degrees of degeneracy: icon (first degree), index (second degree)." None of these propositions is true.

1. A degenerate sign is *not* a deterioration of the triadic relation. It is a subdivision of a general relation, such as the definition of a triangle as a figure with three sides, which is a "genuine" triangle, and the isosceles triangle which is a "degenerate" case of the triangle as defined. The proper definition of "degeneracy" is "the condition of a lower stage or type of being obtained by more specification."

2. It is impossible to say that "icon and index are degenerate aspects of the symbol," because the idea of "degenerate" is opposed to the idea of "genuine," and the only genuine categories are First, Second, and Third.

In this context, as we have three genuine categories: Firstness, Secondness, and Thirdness, which are respectively constituted by one, two, and three "indecomposable" elements, Firstness has no degenerate case: Firstness is pure feeling (feeling before it is felt: life provides innumerable cases which you and I have experienced but which cannot be expressed); Secondness with its two elements is genuine as an Index which is Second of a Second, but degenerate as First, as an icon; Thirdness with its three elements is genuine as Third (Third of a Third), for instance the "structures" corresponding to the ideas of implication, law, generality, continuity, but degenerate in the second degree as a case of a structure in action, such as a given "process," *hic et nunc,* and also degenerate in the second degree as "Tertiality" or "Mentality," such as "the way something [a process, in the present case] is thought or represented" (1.534).

Here we should explain why one can think that there are "degenerate" cases of icon, although there are not. Peirce speaks of "hypoicons," which are respectively as a First an image, as a Second a diagram, and as a Third a metaphor. But this division is not what Peirce calls a "pre-scission," because it is not "ordered." Hypoicons are divided in the same manner as "discrimination" and "dissociation," although the idea of the categories stays the same: the idea of First is related to "feeling" (here image), the idea of Second to "action" (here diagram: diagram as drawn, not just thought), the idea of Third as "metaphor," i.e., as "mediation." What is important in Peirce is that a metaphor is not of the nature of an abstract idea, but is really linked with its object as a First, and only thought of as Third as a hypoicon.

It is only out of context and metaphorically that one could say with Peirce that

A *genuine* symbol is a symbol that has a general meaning. There are two kinds
of degenerate symbols, the *Singular Symbol* whose Object is an existent individual, and which signifies only such characters as that individual may realize; and
the *Abstract Symbol,* whose only object is a Character. (2.293)

## A PEIRCEAN READING OF JAKOBSON

As everybody knows, Jakobson's diagram of communication is the following:

Context

Sender       Message       Receiver

Contact

Code

(Jakobson 1963: 214)

Jakobson's diagram can be translated into a Peircean graph without alter-
ing Jakobson's theses on linguistics and poetics. The Message is related by the
Sender to an Object with which the Message has some *contact*. The Message
reaches a Receiver who is in a *context* which may be different from that of the
Sender. Accordingly, the *code* of the Sender and the Receiver being different, the
Receiver may give the sign-representamen of the Sender a different immediate Object or meaning from that of the Sender, as shown in the following Peircean graph:

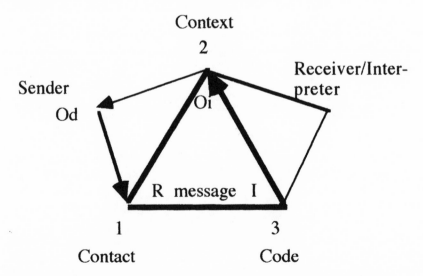

in which the dynamic object (Od) is the reverse of the object (O) and the immediate object (Oi), the obverse of the object (O); the interpreter is the meeting

point of all the interpretants, either sign-representamens or habits in a sign-process or semiosis. The Receiver or interpreter is the τοπος of a Peircean semiosis (Representamen → Interpretant → Object), in a situation or context which is both psycho-physiological (Contact), social (Code), and singular (Context of a subject interpreting).

# - 12 -

# Semeiotic and Communication:
# Peirce and McLuhan

## MEDIA BETWEEN BALNIBARBI AND PLATO'S CAVE

> Objects are unobservable, only relationships among objects are observable.
> —McLuhan (in Stearn 1968: 301)

> The sign can only represent the Object and tell about it. It cannot furnish acquaintance with or recognition of that Object.
> —Peirce (2.231)

In Swift's journey to Balnibarbi, communication is by "things," not by "signs," because "signs" are "things." In Plato's Cave, behind the wall, statues are carried by people whom we do not see nor know. Are they slaves and, in consequence, not human beings? We do not know. What we do know is that we only see images of the statues. Which are the media? The statues or the images? Can we safely say: Images are the media? If we do, what is the nature of a statue? As the answer is outside the Cave, we have to turn away and get out. To find what? Mathematics and, further on, Ideas? What part can they play in helping us to answer the question of the nature of the media? That is the problem we shall try to solve with the help of the doorkeeper of the Cave: Charles S. Peirce.

I shall examine firstly the media in general, secondly Marshall McLuhan's media, thirdly I shall try to locate McLuhan's "Global Village." Where can we find it? In Balnibarbi or in Plato's Cave?

## THE MEDIA

The literature on the media is nowadays considerable. Does it answer the semiotic question of the nature of the media? It is the question we want to examine. A small section of the literature—however great it is—is purely technological and does not give us any direct clue to the question raised. Another section of it—probably the biggest and the only one which attracts the attention of the public—deals with the general problem of the influence (good or bad) of the media. Although more sociological than philosophical, the writings in this section cannot avoid touching the semiotic nature of the media, but most of the time they do it in a very simple and naïve way.

Negatively, the question of the influence of the media has driven most of the commentators in the sixties to the conclusion that, like the tongue of Esop, the media are neither good nor bad. One of them, a French scholar, Francis Balle, gives us the reason why it is so and raises at the same time the very semiotic question which we, as semioticians, are raising:

> So-called mass-communication is still interpreted in mechanistic terms, as a simple and direct relation between transmitters and receivers of messages, according to the behavioristic schema stimulus-response or, if one prefers, according to the univocal relation cause-effect. As if, in the present state of knowledge, it were possible to give so summarily a definite explanation concerning the relations instituted by the media. (Balle 1983: 290–291)

# MARSHALL MCLUHAN

That the media are most of the time dealt with in mechanistic terms is exemplified by the writings of their Godfather: Marshall McLuhan. Although McLuhan's propositions are very rarely convincingly supported, McLuhan was convincing enough to make of the media a new major scientific subject matter. Everybody knows the main books of McLuhan: *The Mechanical Bride: Folklore of Industrial Man* (1951), *The Gutenberg Galaxy: The Making of Typographic Man* (1962), *Understanding Media: The Extensions of Man* (1964), *The Medium is the Massage: an Inventory of Effects* (1967), and *War and Peace in the Global Village* (1968). The main propositions of McLuhan are listed below.

## The Media Are the Extensions of Man

McLuhan's theory is, properly speaking, a "technological determinism." Media are the technological extensions of man, i.e., everything which can extend man's (or woman's) information, action, and power, be it a suit, a car, a newspaper, a radio, or a TV program.

In *The Gutenberg Galaxy*, McLuhan tells the story of Western civilization in terms of the invention of printing. It is, according to him, the movable types which have made nationalism possible, because the mass production of linear types imposes uniformity and continuity, while handwritten messages encourage distinction or division and individualism. Because each Christian could afford to have his own printed copy, the Bible could be read in isolation and "individual revelation" became possible, and therefore Protestantism. Even music was affected by the invention of printing: while Gregorian music required repetition, the printed types rendered possible the linear development and so the symphony.

In short, typography was not only a technological invention, it was a product of technology. It was in itself a natural wealth, just like cotton, wood, or radio; and like any product, it shaped not only the intersensorial relations of the individuals, but also the collective models of interdependence.

In *Understanding Media,* McLuhan passes from the Gutenberg revolution to the electronic revolution with the new technologies of communication: radio, television, telephone, computers, which are similarly reshaping the civilization of the twenty-first century. Even reading is affected. We do not read any longer as before: "People don't actually read newspapers. They get into them every morning like a hot bath" (McLuhan 1964).

## The Medium Is the Message

McLuhan's thesis is "societies have been shaped more by the nature of the media by which men communicate than by the content of the communication." Hence the famous slogan "The Medium is the message" which is the title of the first chapter of *Understanding Media.* "The Medium is the message" means three things:

1. Each medium creates its own public, a public which is more interested in the medium as such than in the medium as a vehicle of information. Television has a public of what we might call "voyeurs," who look at it for the pleasure of looking, just as there were and—fortunately—still are readers who read for the pleasure of reading and people who talk for the pleasure of talking. New technologies have done no more than afford new instrumentalities: instead of reading for oneself, one can listen to a book read by somebody else on cassettes or compact discs, and instead of talking on the street corner, one can talk on the phone.

2. The message of the medium includes everything that the medium has made possible: "The message of the movie medium is that of transition from linear connections to configuration" (McLuhan 1964: 20).

3. The medium itself determines its own content. But all media do not possess the same power of communication. One medium is more suited than another to express an experience. Thus football matches come over better on television than on the radio.

## The Media as "Sensory Ratios" or Qualities

While the previous revolution—the Gutenberg revolution—was essentially a social revolution, the new electronic revolution is a human revolution, both "universal" or rather "global" and "individual" or rather "private." The "sensory ratios" have changed. We are passing from the instrumentalities of communication to the qualities of what is communicated, although McLuhan still thinks that the content is far less important than the medium of communication. The traditional media appealed essentially to the separate senses: books and paintings to sight, music to hearing. The new media call simultaneously upon all the senses including that of touch which "consists of a meeting of the senses."

Each medium seems to possess a hidden mechanism of appreciation. McLuhan divides these mechanisms into two classes which he uses to distinguish between people as well as things, or, more technically, between media-receivers and media-senders. These two classes are "hot" media and "cool" media. They are described in the second chapter of *Understanding Media,* "Media Hot and Cold." A "hot" medium has a "high definition," which means that it has a highly individualized character as well as a rich content. A "cool" medium is poor in quality and quantity. This distinction is reminiscent of John Stuart Mill's empiristic distinction between "connotation" and "denotation," except that the rule of inverse proportionality does not apply. Let us note something that will be referred to again later, that this distinction has no sense if one does not take into account both sender and receiver. Because a "cool" medium has a "poor" sender, it requires a "rich" receiver. For instance, "a cartoon is low in information, simply because very little information is provided" (McLuhan 1964: 31) and accordingly more outside participation is required. On the contrary, "any 'hot' medium allows less participating than a cool one, as a lecture makes for less participation than a seminar, and a book for less than a dialogue" (McLuhan 1964: 32). Print and radio, photography and paintings are, according to McLuhan, "hot" media. But television is a "cool" medium.

The participation in a "cool" medium, although necessary, is variable, because the receivers may be either "cool" or "hot." Take two "cool" media: a cartoon and a TV serial. The first one requires a "hot" reader, while the second one is at its best with a "cool" viewer.

In short, Marshall McLuhan was the prophet of a new age, that of the Global Village. If the new technologies have not kept the promises that McLuhan made in their names, it is not the fault of the new technologies of communication in themselves, but of the erroneous conception that people, and not least McLuhan, have of their capacities.

## WHERE CAN WE LOCATE THE TERRITORY OF THE "GLOBAL VILLAGE"? IN BALNIBARBI OR IN PLATO'S CAVE?

Balnibarbi would not be a bad place, if we follow Jonathan Swift's description (Swift 1939: 229–231), without forgetting that, in the mind of Swift, it was a critical parody of philosophy at its worst. Here we have a territory from which Gutenberg was banished, for the scientists had "a scheme for entirely abolishing all words whatsoever." It is the very project of McLuhan, only refined to avoid the difficulty of the Balnibarbi system. In the latter, "an expedient was [ . . . ] offered, that since words are only names for things, it would be more convenient for all men to carry about them such things as were necessary to express the particular business they are to discourse on" (Swift 1939: 229). To avoid the burden of carrying things, McLuhan has proposed to use the new technologies to do the job:

the new media reach the things and bring them as images to any debating community. With the new media, in the "Global Village" which they have created, everything is at hand instantaneously.

Another great advantage proposed by this invention, adds Swift—an advantage which is even greater in McLuhan's system—is "that it would serve as an universal language to be understood in all civilised nations whose goods and utensils are generally of the same kind, or nearly resembling, so that their uses might easily be comprehended" (Swift 1939: 231).

Of course, the new system is more mechanistic and no less nominalistic, because things have been replaced by their images, more so because nobody knows if an image is the image of the thing people mean.

Are we better off with Plato's Cave? Plato describes it in *The Republic*, as follows:

> Picture men in an underground cave-dwelling, with a long entrance reaching up towards the light along the whole width of the cave; in this they lie from their childhood, their legs and necks in chains, so that they stay where they are and look only in front of them, as the chain prevents their turning their heads round. Some way off, and higher up, a fire is burning behind them, and between the fire and the prisoners is a road on higher ground. Imagine a wall built along this road, like the screen which showmen have in front of the audience, over which they show the puppets.

> Then picture also men carrying along this wall all kinds of articles which overtop it, statues of men and other creatures in stone and wood and other materials; naturally some of the carriers are speaking, others are silent. (Plato 1942: 207–210)

Of course, what they do see is only the shadows "of themselves or of each other" and of the "things carried along the wall," thrown by the fire on the wall of the cave opposite to them, but "they would suppose what they [see] to be the real things" and that the voices they hear, which are mere echoes from the opposite wall, do come from "the shadows passing before them." And "the only truth that such men would conceive would be the shadows of those manufactured articles" and of themselves and their co-prisoners.

In short, Plato's Cave, although far less comfortable than Balnibarbi's debating societies, has a place not only for things, but also for "sense data," with a way of feeling the latter (sensation: αἴσθησις) and believing the former (belief: πίστις or opinion which is a habit of thinking in a certain way: δόξα). The three elements being respectively in Peirce's semeiotic: Firstness (sense data), Secondness (things as object or subject matter of belief), and Thirdness (belief). McLuhan would agree, except that he is concerned neither with the "content" nor with any kind of epistemological problems.

Plato does not stop there:

> Let us suppose one of them released, and forced suddenly to stand up and turn his head, and walk and look towards the light [ . . . ] I fancy that he would need

time before he could see things in the world above. At first he would most easily see shadows, then the reflections in water of men and everything else, and, finally, the things themselves. (Plato 1942: 208)

Plato is not satisfied with the things of the Cave and the media thanks to which they are known. He wants his prisoner to experience the world outside the Cave, not through sense data and belief or habit, but through discursive knowledge (ἐπιστήμη) and contemplation or Pure Thought (νοῦς). Discursive knowledge whose object is mathematics is a necessary step towards the apprehension of the supreme Object: Pure Ideas.

Of course, McLuhan has nothing to do with the World Above. The ascent toward the World Above was too arduous for him and mathematics was of no help. He was content with metaphorical definitions such as "The spoken word: Flower of evil," "The written word: An eye for an ear," "The printed word: Architect of nationalism," "Photograph: The brothel-without-walls." Peirce, on the contrary, had the courage to get out of the Cave and painfully, step by step, to master mathematics and see the Sun.

However, Peirce was braver than Plato, and was courageous enough to go back to the Cave and liberate his fellow-prisoners, not by helping them to escape, but by introducing into the Cave the freedom of reasoning and of analyzing Being into the categories of the Cave: Possibility (Firstness) of Being "here-now-mine" (Jean Wahl) (Secondness), according to Conditional, i.e., contextuality of the Cave, laws (of inference) (Thirdness). Plato seems to describe Peirce's venture in the following passage of *The Republic:*

> [...] suppose that he had again to take part with the prisoners there in the old contest of distinguishing between the shadows, while his sight was confused and before his eyes had got steady (and it might take them quite a considerable time to get used to the darkness), would not men laugh at him, and say that having gone up above he had come back with his sight ruined, so that it was not worthwhile even to try to go up? And do you not think that they would kill him who tried to release them and bear them up, if they could lay hands on him, and slay him? (Plato 1942: 209–210)

They tried and did not succeed. That is why we are here speaking of the "Semiotics of media." Semiotics is the story of Plato back in the Cave. Would he have been on speaking terms with McLuhan? Maybe. But he would have needed a "translator," as McLuhan puts it in another metaphor: "Media as translators." And, of course, the translator would have been Charles S. Peirce.

But the dialogue would not have been easy because McLuhan, although considered "a scholarly nuisance and agitated protagonist" (Stearn 1968: 23), was actually quite mild and modest. To any objection, he would answer:

> I am an investigator. I make probes. I have no point of view. [...] The explorer is totally inconsistent. He never knows at what moment he will make some star-

tling discovery. And consistency is a meaningless term to apply to an explorer. If he wanted to be consistent, he would stay home. (Stearn 1968: 23)

Peirce, on the contrary, as a logician explorer, although also "a scholarly nuisance and agitated protagonist," is consistent. Would he have conceded that Mc-Luhan's theories on the media are worth being semiotically examined? We are not sure, but, when we are back in the Cave, a few things can be said:

1. McLuhan's method is pragmatic. McLuhan can be considered an American pragmatist, be it only of the James tribe, since McLuhan is concerned with media as man's tools in a given context. His method is experimental and like James's more physiological, in the sense of Claude Bernard, than philosophical, in the sense of Charles S. Peirce.

On the contrary, *experience* implies, according to the same physiologists, the idea of a variation or of a disturbance *intentionally* introduced by the investigator in the conditions of the natural phenomena. [ ... ] For that purpose, an organ of the living body is suppressed by section or ablation and, according to the disturbance produced in the entire organism or in a special function one can know the use of the suppressed organ. (Bernard 1965: 62–63)

McLuhan states his *profession de foi* in an interview in the following way:

Literally, *Understanding Media* is a kit of tools for analysis and perception. It is to *begin* an operation of discovery. It is not the completed work of discovery. It is intended for practical use. [ ... ] A structural approach to a medium means studying its total operation, the *milieu* that it creates—the environment that the telephone or radio or movies or the motor car created. One would learn very little about the motor car by looking at it simply as a vehicle that carried people hither and thither. Without understanding the city changes, suburban creations, service changes—the environment it created—one would learn very little about the motor car. The car then has never really been studied structurally, as a form. (Stearn 1968: 316)

2. The medium as representamen. In the last quotation, two words have to be underlined: "perception" and "structural." Peirce would have agreed with McLuhan. Semiotically, the percept is what Peirce calls a "representamen." The representamen has, categorially organized, three ways of being:

1° the act of representing a (mediate) object of the mind; 2° the representation, or, to speak more properly, representamen, itself as an (immediate or vicarious) object exhibited to the mind; 3° the act by which the mind is conscious immediately of the representative object, and, through it, mediately of the remote object represented. (Hamilton 1863: 877)

This was not written by Peirce, but by William Hamilton from whom Peirce borrowed the idea of "representamen," together with the distinction between "immediate object" and "dynamic object" (the mediately conscious remote object of Hamilton). The "representamen" became in Peirce's theory of signs: Qualisign as First, Sinsign as Second, and Legisign as Third. The "legisign" is McLuhan's "structure."

According to McLuhan—in Peircean terms—media are vehicles of sinsigns. Although media may have a short range like the sense of touch and a long range like vision, especially when it is "extended" by television, the sinsign has the same logical nature or rather definition: it is a dyadic image which can only stand for an immediate object.

An image is a sinsign which refers to an immediate object. It is an indecomposable dyad:

| | 1 | 2 |
|---|---|---|
| R | R1 | R2 |
| O | O1 | O2 |

Table 12.1. Image as a dyad

In other words, it has neither legisign nor interpretant. It is a mere happening which obeys no rule whatsoever and cannot be interpreted as such. There is no difference between the typographical world of Gutenberg and the world of the new media.

3. The medium as content. The representamens as sinsigns (or percepts, if one prefers) can only be interpreted, according to Peirce, within another semiosis, which by definition, must be triadic. It is a *sine qua non* condition of the possibility for media to carry any meaning or structure.

Most of the time, McLuhan speaks as if the medium was the content. He does not make any difference between the legisign (or "structure," which is the "type" of the linguists) and the sinsign (or "individual instances" or "occurrences," which is the "token" of the linguists).

Without denying the part played sociologically and psychologically by the media, the media cannot logically in any way be legisigns: ideas, thoughts, "designs or patterns" (McLuhan 1964: 16), or whatever, as McLuhan thinks they can:

> The electric light is pure information. It is a medium without a message, as it were, unless it is used to spell out some verbal ad or name. This fact, characteristic of all media, means that the "content" of any medium is always another medium. The content of writing is speech, just as the written word is the content of print, and print is the content of the telegraph. If it is asked "What is the content of speech?," it is necessary to say, "It is an actual process of thought, which is in itself non-verbal." An abstract painting represents direct manifesta-

tion of creative thought processes as they might appear in computer designs.
(McLuhan 1964: 15–16)

McLuhan is committing here the same typical mistake of the whole Western
philosophical tradition: to think in terms of quantity as if by adding media to
media, extending the range of media or accelerating the pace of media, one
could change the "pattern" conveyed by the media. Peirce himself worked on
this line for a long time and tried hard to help induction to do the job by refining
the theory of probabilities, until he gave up induction for abduction—quantity
for quality. The choice between the two is not *ad libitum*. It is the duty of the
semiotics of the media, to use abduction as a tool or method, instead of induction, for, as René Thom reminded us, "the theory of probabilities is fundamentally an imposture" (Thom 1995: 14).

4. The media as interpretants, hot and cool. McLuhan seems to avoid part of
the consequences of determinism with the concepts of "hot" and "cool" which
are obviously qualitative; more so than Peirce would admit, because they give
the interpretant a psychological dimension and that Peirce is not ready to accept.
According to Peirce, the interpretant is logical. It cannot be expressed in terms
of "feeling"; on the contrary, it must be expressed in terms of "rules." The "interpretant" is formally a "sign." Just as the representamen is the sign of the
sender, the interpretant is the sign of the receiver.

However, Peirce himself resorted to the concept of "interpretant" in another
sense. When a semiosis is concluded, it either creates a new habit or reinforces
or modifies an old one. In this case, Peirce says that the interpretant is no longer
a sign, but a "logical final interpretant," which is another name for "habit," not
as *routine,* but as incorporated and spontaneous rule.

Peirce would have agreed that this kind of interpretant could be "hot" or
"cool," provided those qualities were logically defined. In McLuhan's theory,
they depend on the "whimsy" of the author. Which McLuhan recognized in an
interview:

> Perhaps I should have set up polarities on media rigid and frigid. It's very diffi-
> cult to have a structure of any sort without polarities, without tension. For ex-
> ample, the triangle is the most economic way of securing an upright object.
> Without polarities [ ... ] there is no progression, no structure. [ ... ] I must
> know how media are structured to discover what they are doing to me and my
> environment. *Media, hot* and *cool* are not classifications. They are structural
> forms. (Stearn 1968: 332)

Contrary to Peirce, McLuhan is not concerned with "systems," but with
"systems development": " 'Systems development' is a structural analysis of pres-
sures and strains, the exact opposite of everything that has been meant by 'systems' in the past few centuries. [ ... ] It is concerned with the inner dynamics of
the form" (Stearn 1968: 333). Is this not a good Peircean definition of the
semiotics of the media?

5. Media: The role of the individual versus the power of society. The last question I should like to ask concerns the misinterpretation of the interpretant for the interpreter which the distinction between "hot" and "cool" is bound to convey.

In fact, McLuhan and Peirce are very close to one another here: they both propose a "community": a "community of inquirers" in the case of Peirce, a "community of users" in the case of McLuhan, to which McLuhan gives the name of "Global Village." If there is a difference, it is a difference, not of range, but of place in the semiotic process. Both of them recognize the part played by the individual in semiosis in spite of the predominance of the environment or *milieu*.

I shall conclude the present chapter by saying that, in spite of many technological discrepancies, Peirce has proposed the best theory of signs which can fit McLuhan's theory of the media, not only because they are both pragmatic, but because they both reconcile continuity and discontinuity: social uniformity and individual creativity.

To the objection that no genius could have a place in the new electronic age, McLuhan answers that, because the media are the extensions of man, they are *ipso facto* the extensions of man's will, although man "never intends the cultural consequences of any extension of himself" (Stearn 1968: 315).

To the objection that the mass media uniformity of the Global Village created by the new technologies kills man's creativity, McLuhan answers that "there is more diversity, less conformity under a single roof in any family than there is with the thousands of families in the same city. The more you create village conditions, the more discontinuity and division and diversity" (Stearn 1968: 314), and, consequently, creativity.

Continuity and discontinuity are not incompatible for Peirce. They are two of Peirce's cosmological categories: synechism, the category of continuity, and tychism, the category of "happening" which is by definition "individual." But no happening can take place out of context: no creativity without continuity (Peirce 1931: 5.402 n. 2). The future of the semiotics of media is still "open."

# - 13 -

# Semeiotic and Epistemology

## PEIRCE, FREGE, AND WITTGENSTEIN

> All testing, all confirmation and disconfirmation of a hy-
> pothesis takes place already within a system. And this sys-
> tem is not a more or less arbitrary and doubtful point of de-
> parture for all our arguments: no, it belongs to the essence
> of what we call an argument. The system is not so much the
> point of departure, as the element in which arguments have
> their life.
>
> —Wittgenstein (1969: §105)

By "epistemology," we mean the critique of the principles of the logic of scientific research, be it the logic of science or formal logic. As we know, semiotics is
another name for logic, according to Peirce, a comprehensive, inferential logic,
which is both experimental and formal.

This may seem original, but it is not. For the Greeks (see ch. 7), logic was
already a theory of inference from signs, and it still is today, as well for Wittgenstein as for Frege. The difference between the latter two and Peirce is that for
Peirce logic is not only a theory of inference from signs, but an inference from
signs *through signs.* The theories of Frege and Wittgenstein are dyadic and dualistic; that of Peirce is triadic and dialectic.

I shall try to describe the basic axioms of Peircean epistemology, compare
its concepts with those of Frege and Wittgenstein, and draw its methodological
implications in the context of the philosophy of science today.

## FREGE, WITTGENSTEIN, PEIRCE

Frege, Wittgenstein, and Peirce are logicians and semioticians.

1. From the historical point of view, Frege can undoubtedly claim priority to
Peirce. The first version of Frege's propositional calculus dates back to 1879.
Peirce's first systematic expositions of "the algebra of logic" were written in 1880
and 1885. Peirce's work on the tables of truth (1902) is prior to Wittgenstein's
(1922).

On Peirce's side, three independent inventions must be noted: that of the quantifiers, that of the Sheffer-function (1880), named after its re-inventor (1921), which stipulates that all the Boolian operations can be reduced to the negation of the alternative disjunction "neither—, nor—"; and that of trivalent logic (1909), ten years before Lukasievicz (Deledalle 1990: 59).

2. The pragmatistic tone of Wittgenstein's work, from the *Tractatus logico-philosophicus* onward, is surprising. The question may be asked: did Wittgenstein know Peirce's work? In fact he did, but this does not mean that he read all that Peirce wrote; far from it. He came across two of the main ideas of Peirce. One was through Frank P. Ramsey, co-translator with Charles K. Ogden, of the *Tractatus,* the same Ogden who, with I. A. Richards, was to give a certain publicity to Peirce's semiotics in *The Meaning of Meaning* (1923). This theory is epistemological, properly speaking, and we shall come back to it later on. The other, which also seems to have reached Wittgenstein through Ramsey, is pragmatic: a critique of Cartesian doubt and a definition of meaning by action. Peirce's theory can be read in "The Fixation of Belief" (1877) and "How to Make Our Ideas Clear" (1878). The definition of meaning by action can be read everywhere in Wittgenstein's writings after 1933–1934, from the *Blue and Brown Books* to the *Investigations,* and the question of doubt is studied in great detail in *On Certainty,* which was the last book Wittgenstein was to write (see ch. 8).

## THE AXIOMS OF PEIRCE'S EPISTEMOLOGY

The basic theses of Peircean epistemology can be stated in the three following propositions:

1. A sign or representamen is a First which cannot furnish acquaintance with nor recognition of its object;

2. A law (a Third) without an occurrence (a Second) is empty; an occurrence without a law is blind;

3. A proposition is the individuation of a "general" (a Third) by an index (a Second).

a. The first Peircean thesis is fundamental: it maintains that the sign or representamen is not the copy of its object. The sign represents its object as an ambassador represents his country in a *foreign* country. If we develop the metaphor, it is obvious that this ambassador has been appointed by someone having the power to do so. The object thus "determines" the sign, in a sense of the word, but without leaving its mark on it. The nature of the sign-representamen appears clearly in Peirce's definition of "percept." Can the "percept" be identified with the "sign-representamen"? One could very well do so, without being taxed with psychologism, which is Peirce's *bête noire,* because the "percept" is not a psychical phenomenon. It is "physical," providing one does not oppose this term to "psychical," but understands it as meaning that it is there in the world:

It has no generality; and without generality there can be no psychicality. [ . . . ]
The percept brutally forces itself upon us; thus it appears under a physical guise.

It is quite ungeneral, even antigeneral—in its character as percept; and thus it does not appear as psychical. The psychical, then, is not contained in the percept. (1.253)

Consequently, the presence of a percept in consciousness does not make it a cognition.

Direct experience is neither certain nor uncertain, because it affirms nothing— it just is. There are delusions, hallucinations, dreams. But there is no mistake that such things do appear, and direct experience means simply the appearance. It involves no error, because it testifies to nothing but its own appearance. For the same reason, it affords no certainty. It is not *exact,* because it leaves much vague; though it is not *inexact* either; that is, it has no false inexactitude. (1.145)

Only perceptual judgment is cognition, because it confers on knowledge the generality or thirdness (5.150) which enables us to give an object, or, as Frege says, a sense (*Sinn*) to the representamen.

Comparing Peirce's and Frege's theories helps to clarify both. According to Frege, a sign (*Zeichen*) "stands for" (*bedeutet*) its objects in exactly the same way as the sign represents its object for Peirce. Moreover, it has for Frege as for Peirce, two objects: a dynamical or referential object (*Bedeutung*) and an immediate object or sense (*Sinn*). The referential object (the number or the evening star) is not what the sign represents (the immediate object or sense). And lastly the problem of the mode of existence of both arises and seems to be solved in the same way by both Frege and Peirce. There is indeed something outside the sign, but it is in and by the sign (semiosis or discourse) that it is said: the number figures in arithmetical propositions exactly as the evening star does in propositions of astronomy.

b. The second Peircean thesis expressed in semiotic terms is very clear. A legisign—a Third—a grammatical rule, for instance, is empty if no occurrence (or single replica) of this rule exists. It is the distinction between "type" and "token" adopted by all the linguists. In a page of English an average of twenty replicas or *tokens* of the definite article are to be found, but the definite article as a legisign or *type* can never figure there: it is the law which governs this determinative function in English and, as a law, because it is general, it cannot be written. Occurrences which obey no law have, of course, no sense.

This Peircean distinction is very useful for the understanding of Wittgenstein's propositional sign. According to Wittgenstein in the *Tractatus logico-philosophicus,* the propositional sign is a sentence (*Satz*) which as fact (*Tatsache*), expresses a sense (*Sinn*) and constitutes the picture (*Bild*) of an "atomic" situation or state of things (*Sachverhalt*); and which, as perceived (perceptible sign) is the projection of the picture of a possible situation or state of things (*Sachlage*).

We owe to Ramsey the clarification of Wittgenstein's thought in terms of Peirce's distinction between legisign (or *type*) and replica (or *token).* I quote from Ramsey's review of the *Tractatus* which appeared in *Mind* in 1923:

A *propositional sign* is a sentence; but this statement must be qualified, for by "sentence" may be meant something of the same nature as the words of which it is composed. But a propositional sign differs essentially from a word because it is not an object or class of objects, but a fact, "that fact that its elements, the words, are combined in it in a definite way" (3.14). Thus "propositional sign" has type-token ambiguity; the tokens (like those of any sign) are grouped into types by physical similarity (and by conventions associating certain noises with certain shapes) just as are the instances of a word. But a *proposition* is a type whose instances consist of all propositional sign tokens which have in common, not a certain appearance, but a certain *sense*. (Ramsey 1923: 468–469)

Wittgenstein's aphorism: "Philosophy does not result in philosophical propositions, but rather in the clarification of propositions" (4.112) is often quoted. The question of what a clear proposition may be, is rarely asked. But Wittgenstein's distinction between the propositional sign as fact and the propositional sign as perceptible sign should incite us to ask it. Is a clear proposition a perceptible sentence? Ramsey gave us the answer by again resorting to Peirce's distinction between legisign (type) and replica (token). The following quotation sums up his conclusions:

I think that a written sentence is "clear" in so far as it has *visible* properties correlated with or "showing" the internal properties of its sense. According to Mr. Wittgenstein the latter always show themselves in internal properties of the proposition; but owing to the type-token ambiguity of "proposition" it is not immediately clear what this means. Properties of a proposition must, I think, mean all the properties of its tokens; but, the internal properties of a proposition are those properties of the tokens which are, so to speak, internal not to the tokens but to the type; that is, those which one of the tokens must have if it is to be a token of that type, not those which it is unthinkable that it should not have anyhow. (Ramsey 1923: 476)

c. The third Peircean thesis concerns the nature of the proposition. We shall not here go back to the analysis of the proposition into subject, copula, and predicate. I shall confine myself to a logico-semiotic description, the main interest of which is another possible comparison between Peirce and Frege.

Peirce trichotomizes the sign-interpretant into rhema (a First), dicisign (a Second), and argument (a Third). We shall examine the nature of the rhema and the dicisign.

## Rhema, Predicative Function, and Proposition

The rhema is not the Aristotelian "term." It is not the subject of a proposition. The rhema is a predicate in the modern sense of the word, i.e., a verb: "is red" is the predicate of a possible proposition: "This rose is red." The dicisign is a dyadic relation of which the proposition is only a particular kind, one might say a species, of which the dicisign is the genus. Thus a portrait with the name of the person written below it is a dicisign in the same way as the proposition. A dicisign (and hence a proposition) is composed of a rhema and an index in the Peircean semiotic sense: an effective or rather dynamical relation that a sign-representamen has with its object.

Frege distinguishes between three sorts of signs: the singular term, the function, and the sentence (*Satz*). Frege's functions correspond in Peirce's logic of relatives to the monadic relation (predicate) and the dyadic relation (dual expression). Nothing corresponds in Frege to the triadic relation, not even the functional expression. Frege is a dualist.

The correspondence between the rhema and the propositional function is the most interesting. For Peirce, the rhema is a propositional function. It is a predicate and it is, in Frege's terminology, "unsaturated." The proposition is "saturated" by a singular term for Frege, i.e., an index for Peirce. It is important to point out that Frege uses *andenten* (to indicate) in the same *indexical* sense as Peirce (which means that one cannot translate *bedeuten* by "indicate" as Russell does). Peirce goes further than Frege in his analysis of the proposition. In "This is red," there is not an attribution of a "redness" which would already be there to "this," but the production of a "red object" by the index of saturation "this." Any "subject" (this rose, these tomatoes) is an index of saturation or "principle of individuation," in Peirce's terminology (5.107) (see Deledalle 1986: 35–40).

It is the entire traditional conception of the proposition which is at stake, as Ramsey had also realized:

> In "Socrates is wise," Socrates is the subject, wisdom the predicate. But suppose we turn the proposition round and say: "Wisdom is a characteristic of Socrates," then wisdom formerly the predicate is now the subject. [ ... ] They are not, of course, the same sentence, but they have the same meaning. [ ... ] Which sentence [ ... ] has nothing to do with the logical nature of Socrates and wisdom, but is a matter entirely for grammarians. [ ... ] (T)he above argument throws doubt upon the whole basis of the distinction between particular and universal. [ ... ] (N)early all philosophers, including Mr. Russell, have been misled by language [ ... ] (in) mistaking for a fundamental characteristic of reality, what is merely a characteristic of language. (Ramsey 1925: 404–405)

## THE TRUTH OF THE SIGN AS OBJECT

Does Frege entirely share this Peircean conception which we have expressed in Fregean terms? We cannot say so, for the reason already given, that Frege's logic is dualistic. This is obvious from the stands taken by the two logicians concerning the object of a proposition. According to Frege, the predicate has as referent (*Bedeutung*) the concept (*Begriff*) which is, like the relation, an "objective" function, the value of which must be true if it has a sense; and the sentence or proposition, whatever it may be, has as object its truth-value. According to Peirce, a rhema can be neither true nor false; hence, truth or falsity cannot be its object— *the object is what is produced by truth* (which, in the long run, will be reality).

However, one can read in a draft which Peirce wrote in 1900 or 1901 when he was preparing his articles on logic for Baldwin's *Dictionary,*

> [I]n a narrower sense, logic is the science of the reference of symbols to their objects. For logic in this narrower sense, all symbols which have precisely the same possible objects, are identical,—a limitation which must not be overlooked. Hence, according to Boole, and those who follow him, every symbol has one or two *values,* according as it does or does not, represent the object intended. All true assertions are equivalent, and all false assertions are equivalent. (Ms 1174 A)

## PEIRCE'S EPISTEMOLOGY OF INVENTION

From the three theses or axioms which we have just examined, and which have taken us back to the origins of contemporary logic, numerous consequences result. We shall refer only to those which coincide with some of the epistemological positions defended today. But it will really be a matter of encounters, not influences, and in most cases, if not in all, of coincidence of consequences, rather than of agreement on principles.

### *Abduction, Induction, Deduction*

The first consequence is the questioning of the nature of scientific research. If the sign-representamen is a First, and if its object is a construction of the sign-interpretant, science can discover nothing; it can only invent. Induction cannot be a method of discovering pre-existing laws by observation of occurrences of singular cases. The principle of the hierarchy of categories would be enough to make us abandon the idea: one cannot pass from secondness to thirdness—in other words, from occurrences, cases, or instances, however numerous they may be—to the law which governs them. Induction is *a priori* an invalid method. Besides, things never happened like that. Hence, the introduction of another method: abduction, which is not substituted for induction, but introduces a supplementary stage into the experimental process of invention.

Peirce, who first proposed this concept, describes abduction as "a method of forming a general prediction without any positive assurance that it will succeed in the special case or generally, its justification being that it is the only possible hope of regulating our future conduct rationally, and that induction from past experience gives us strong encouragement to hope that it will be successful in the future" (2.270).

Abduction is opposed to induction. Induction infers from similar phenomena, abduction infers something different from what is observed and "frequently something which it would be impossible for us to observe directly" (2.640). But nevertheless, as we have said, abduction is not substituted for induction. The great mistake of the logic of science has been not to distinguish their "essentially different characters" (7.218). This was, of course (and it is clearly the explanation), in conformity with the dualistic conception of the world: matter on one side, spirit on the other side. The traditional conception of the relation between induction and deduction being phaneroscopically untenable (from the singular, no general or universal whatever can be inferred), the production of the general or universal must be explained in another way. Abduction is the answer to the question. Abduction is thus a stage in the process of research which now has three stages: abduction, which "furnishes all our ideas concerning real things, beyond what are given in perception, but is mere conjecture, without probative force" (8.209); deduction, which "is certain but relates only to ideal objects" (8.209, see 6.474) (whether it be necessary [8.209] or probable [2.785]); lastly, induction, which "gives us the only approach to certainty concerning the real that we can have" (8.209).

In brief, abduction suggests hypotheses or general ideas that deduction develops, and that induction, in a sense entirely different from the classical sense, verifies or rather tests.

Karl Popper would have said "falsifies" instead of "tests," but the term used by Popper, although infelicitous, in my opinion, does not affect the process, and, of all contemporary epistemologists, he is certainly the closest to Peirce, without having undergone his influence. His *Logic of Scientific Discovery* (1959) is a logic of the invention of hypotheses which has many points in common with Peirce's logic of inference, the difference being unfortunately that Popper's schema remains dualistic: on one hand, the *a priori* acceptability of the hypothesis with its *a priori* tests; on the other hand, the *a posteriori* acceptability with its empirical tests.

## EPISTEMOLOGY:
## CONTINUITY OR DISCONTINUITY?

Another contemporary epistemologist, Nelson Goodman, defends a theory which is close to Peirce's. Goodman's approach, like Peirce's, is prospective. Although Goodman does not use the term "abduction," the problem of the "projectibility" of hypotheses is given a similar solution (in his book *Fact, Fiction, and Forecast* [1954]) to that proposed by Peirce, and leads to a theory of the "entrenchment" of hypotheses comparable to Bachelard's "rupture épistémologique" and Kuhn's "paradigms" (see Deledalle 1983: 307–313).

Comparison does not imply influence here either, and still less "reason." Science is certainly prospective for Peirce. It depends on time (and space), without the shadow of a doubt. But must it be inferred from this that science is discontinuous? Confronted by Kuhn, and more especially by Feyerabend, Peirce would have certainly maintained with Popper that scientific theories are not "incommensurable" and that there are no absolute truths. The idea of discontinuity, whatever its name—"rupture" or "paradigm"—is incompatible with the idea of experimental research. Research is the continuous invention by the community of investigators, of the ultimate adequation of reality and truth:

The opinion which is fated to be ultimately agreed to by all who investigate, is what we mean by the truth, and the object represented in this opinion is the real. (5.407)

Truth is that concordance of an abstract statement with the ideal limit towards which endless investigation would tend to bring scientific belief, which concordance the abstract statement may possess by virtue of the confession of its inaccuracy and one-sidedness, and this confession is an essential ingredient of truth. (5.565)

# PART FOUR

# *Comparative Metaphysics*

> [T]he only successful mode [of metaphysical research]
> yet lighted upon is that of adopting our logic as our meta-
> physics.
> —Peirce (7.580)

> Metaphysics [ . . . ] ought to be expounded side by side with
> the history of society, of government, and of war; for in its
> relations with these we trace the significance of events for
> the human mind.
> —Peirce (8.9)

Peirce's semeiotic is based on a scientific or "laboratory" metaphysics which is
better understood when it is compared to Western classical or rather "seminary"
metaphysics, such as Scholasticism. The unity and originality of Peirce's philosophy of signs appear in all the domains of metaphysics: in his pragmaticist theory
of a self-controlled constructive knowledge (ch. 14), in his ontological theory of
transcendentals without Being (ch. 15), in his synechistic cosmology where
chance combines chaos and order within continuity (ch. 16), and in his conception of the reality of a Triune God (ch. 17).

# - 14 -

# Gnoseology:
# Perceiving and Knowing

## PEIRCE, WITTGENSTEIN, AND GESTALTTHEORIE

The problem of perception is less the problem of knowing what we perceive than that of knowing whether the way in which we describe perception does not predetermine our reply. Wittgenstein said: "Tell me *how* you think and I shall tell you *what* you think." What must first be examined is the *how*, not the *what*.

What do we perceive? A Form or an individual object? Very quickly nearly everybody agrees: the eye sees the individual object, the mind perceives the form. How?

Most of the theories which were widespread in the West from antiquity up to the end of the nineteenth century were derived from the Aristotelian Thomistic theory, including all the empiricist doctrines from Locke to Watson. Not until the advent of Dewey's instrumentalist psychology and the *Gestalttheorie* was the question at last asked anew in a fresh perspective.

For over two thousand years, the Aristotelian conception was continually being refined, distorted and imposed, from Thomas Aquinas to John Poinsot *alias* John of St. Thomas in the seventeenth century and Jacques Maritain in the twentieth.

In *Les Degrès du savoir*, Jacques Maritain put forward an admirable defense of the Thomistic theory. His position can be summed up in a simplified (and somewhat simplistic) way by making an analogy with the functioning of the camera. On one side we have the body (the camera or cine-camera) and on the other what is photographed or filmed. The film is first exposed. This stage corresponds exactly to that at which the senses receive impressions of the thing as object. The intellect is not affected. The film is then developed. This is the stage at which the impress form of the external sense is transformed into the express form of the imagination. The active intellect then extracts the essence of the object now imagined, and projects it, so to speak, on to the screen of the passive intellect which is the mind. The operation can be expressed in the following schema:

|  | Body | | Soul (animus) | |
|---|---|---|---|---|
| Essence | *Forma impressa* (external sense) | *Forma expressa* (imagination) | Active intellect | Passive intellect |
| Filmed sequence | Film not yet developed | Film developed | Projector projecting | Screen on which the concept appears: the audience *sees* the essence (i.e., what was filmed) |

Table 14.1. Thomistic theory of knowledge

Cartesianism was to consecrate the separation of the two worlds, and to give birth to idealism by locating knowledge in the mind alone. Later, English empiricism, although derived from Cartesianism, emphasized the sensorial data. Still later, American behaviorism insisted on the reaction or response of organism to physiological stimuli of the outside world (S–R).

It must be pointed out that in France the textbooks of philosophy which were the most widely used from the beginning of the twentieth century (Armand Cuvillier) or from the end of the Second World War (Denis Huisman and André Vergez) up to the 1970s continued to use this schema.

In a famous article of 1896, "The Arc Reflex Concept in Psychology," John Dewey criticized the various forms of the classical conceptions of knowledge down to the Arc reflex notion:

1. Sensation is not first; what is first is the *act:* the act of seeing, for instance, and not the sensation of light.

2. The stimulus does not appear *ex nihilo;* it appears in a *context.* A "same" sound is different depending on whether one is reading, hunting, watching a deserted place at night, or carrying out some chemical experiment. Thus, not only is the sound not a pure stimulus, *it is* the act of hearing and *it happens* in an act, for instance the act of reading, in a *"whole-act."*

There is thus neither sensation or perception proper nor arc reflex, but an organic circuit in which the motor response determines the stimulus in exactly the same way as the sensory response determines movement (Dewey 1972: 96–109).

*     *     *

Dewey was not alone. *Gestalttheorie* also went counter to the traditional conception. In *La psychologie de la forme,* Paul Guillaume wrote:

> In classical treatises it was first the materials, the data of sensibility that were studied, then in the following chapters more and more complex "syntheses" of these: perceptions, memories, judgements, etc. But if one rejects the idea that the materials can exist prior to any organisation, one will immediately find oneself confronted by structures. Certain forms of organisation belong in a primitive way to perception; they are not constructions whose origin has to be traced. The so-called higher functions have not the privilege of organisation. (Guillaume 1937: 48)

Like Dewey, W. Köhler, one of the most well-known representatives of Gestalt psychology, is anti-behaviorist. To the mechanistic model S–R (which Bloomfield transposed into linguistics), Köhler, like Dewey, opposes "a dynamic model of human behaviour which emphasises the active role of organisation in perception." Dewey's "action in context" has its analogue in Köhler's "segregated whole," and "as Köhler often puts it, an 'organized whole,' forms the basis of Köhler's anti-behaviourist psychology" (Monk 1990: 509). But he goes still further, as we have seen with Guillaume: Form is "a concrete, individual and characteristic entity, existing as something detached and *having* a shape or form as one of its attributes" (Köhler 1930: 148).

*     *     *

We have now reached a turning point and must make a stop. If the "Gestalt" is not a property of things, how can this "concrete, individual and characteristic entity" be explained? A first reply—or attempt at one—was given by Wittgenstein.

Let us take Jastrow's duck-rabbit picture (Jastrow 1971: Fig. 19):

Figure 14.1.  Jastrow's duck-rabbit

It may be taken for a rabbit's head or a duck's head. And I have to make a distinction between the "continuous seeing" of an aspect and its "dawning." It may be that I have been shown this picture and have seen only a rabbit.

> I am shown a picture-rabbit and asked what it is; I say "It's a rabbit." Not "Now it's a rabbit." I am reporting my perception.—I am shown the duck-rabbit and asked what it is; I may say "It's a duck-rabbit." But I may also react to the question quite differently.—The answer that it is a duck-rabbit is again the report of a perception; the answer "Now it's a rabbit" is not. Had I replied "It's a rabbit," the ambiguity would have escaped me, and I should have been reporting my perception. (Wittgenstein 1953: 194c–195c)

The question of the recognition of one object (the rabbit), or of one rather than the other (rabbit rather than duck) is used by the Gestaltists to maintain the objectivity of form. Paul Guillaume writes:

> Against any theory which (attributes all the organisation of perception to the influence of memory) one can set an argument of principle. Memory can bring to new experience only what existed in old experience. A first inorganic perception, a pure sum of "sensations" could not serve to organise a second. How could an object emerge for the first time from the chaos of sensations? The existence of primitive structures must be admitted. (Guillaume 1937: 71)

This argument of principle rests on another principle which is, however, rejected by Guillaume; namely, that the "primitive structures" are "given." Are they?

Wittgenstein does not think so, for two reasons:

1. Between the passage from the *perception* of the rabbit to the recognition of the duck, or *vice versa* the "aspect" is "dispositional." In *Lectures on Philosophical Psychology,* Wittgenstein develops his argument as follows:

> Suppose I show it [the figure of the duck-rabbit] to a child. It says "it's a duck" and then suddenly "Oh, it's a rabbit." So it recognises it as a rabbit.—This is an experience of recognition. So if you see me in the street and say "Ah, Wittgenstein." But you haven't an experience of recognition all the time.—The experience only comes at the moment of change from duck to rabbit and back. In between, the aspect is as it were dispositional. (Wittgenstein 1976: 104)

2. There are two uses of the word "see":

> Two uses of the word "see."
>
> The one: "What do you see there?"—"I see *this*" (and then a description, a drawing, a copy). The other: "I see a likeness between these two faces"—let the man I tell this to be seeing the faces as clearly as I do myself.
> The importance of this is the categorical difference between the two 'objects' of sight. (Wittgenstein 1953: 193e)

How, if we take account of this distinction, can we maintain at the same time that the "Gestalt" is in things *and* in the mind? But that is what Köhler does: for him the "organisation" of an object *belongs* to that object as much as do its colors and shape. *Shape* must be distinguished from *form* or *Gestalt:*

> If you put the "organization" of a visual impression on a level with colours and shapes, you are proceeding from the idea of the visual impression as an inner object. Of course this makes this object into a chimera; a queerly shifting construction. (Wittgenstein 1953: 196e)

Indeed, according to Köhler, we are not always confronted by the same "visual reality." For instance, Figure 14.2 represents two unknown objects crossed by a horizontal line:

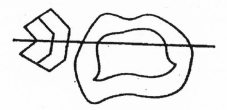

Figure 14.2. The hidden 4

Köhler writes:

> When I tell the reader that the number 4 is before him in the field, he will undoubtedly find it; but if he is not influenced by theoretical prejudices, he will confess that the form of the 4 did not exist as a visual reality at first and that, if it began to exist later on, that meant a transformation of visual reality. (Köhler 1930: 153)

To which Wittgenstein objects:

> Now Köhler said: "you see two visual realities." As opposed to what? To interpreting, presumably. How does he do this? [i.e., how is this established?] It won't do to ask people. Köhler never says it will; but he says "If you're not blinded by theory you'll admit there are two visual realities." But of course, he can't mean only that those who don't hold a certain theory will say "There are two visual realities." He must intend to say that whether or not you're (1) blinded by theory, or (2) whether or not you do say one thing or the other, you must, to be right, say "there are two visual realities." (Wittgenstein 1976: 329–330)

In the case of ambiguous representations (duck–rabbit, the hidden 4), there is indeed a problem. But if one cannot find a reply which does not contradict the theory, it is perhaps the theory which should be reconsidered. This is in conformity with Wittgenstein's method: to show that the problem should not be raised. Should it?

## PERCEPT AND PERCEPTUAL JUDGMENT

Peirce distinguishes between percept and perceptual judgment:

> The percept brutally forces itself upon us; thus it appears under a physical guise.
> It is quite ungeneral, even antigeneral—in its character as percept; and thus it
> does not appear as psychical. (1.253)

It cannot be otherwise, because "without generality there can be no psychicality" (1.253). The percept has no element of "Thirdness," but only elements of "Secondness" and "Firstness" (7.630). Only perceptual judgment professes to *represent* something and accordingly involves "Thirdness." On the other hand, the mere presence of a percept in a conscience cannot be an act of knowledge. Perceiving—i.e., *having* a percept—is not knowing. "Direct experience is neither certain nor uncertain, because it affirms nothing—it just *is*" (1.145). Only the perceptual judgment can be an act of knowledge. Only perceiving—i.e., "determining one thing to refer to another" (7.630)—is knowing, because it gives an object to a percept.

## PERCEPT AND PHANERON

The "phaneron" is the "aseptic" (if one may use the term) expression of the "phenomenon":

> [The phaneron is] the collective total of all that is in any way or in any sense
> present to the mind, quite regardless of whether it corresponds to any real thing
> or not. (1.284)

As Arthur Büchler wrote in a letter to the author, the "phaneron" is "whatever is the case" (whatever can be dealt with), whereas the "phenomenon" is what appears. In other words, the "phaneron" is logical, the "phenomenon" psychological.

The phaneron is triadic. This triad which Peirce represents as:

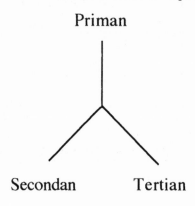

Priman

Secondan          Tertian

is *indecomposable.* Each of its elements is a form of the hierarchically organized phaneron. It is not a description of psychological facts.

## PEIRCE AND WITTGENSTEIN

Is the percept "dispositional"? For Wittgenstein, there is a contradiction in being and not being. His system does not possess the category of "Firstness."

The distinction between seeing a "visual reality" and seeing a likeness is interesting. But Wittgenstein does not make use of it; whereas we do find in his system the fecund distinction between percept and perceptual judgment.

## PEIRCE AND SCHOLASTICISM

It is to Scholasticism that Peirce comes closest. We can establish a parallel between the priman and the impress form, the secondan and the express form, the tertian and the concept-modification of the subject (expressed by the) concept.

The difference resides in the splitting up, supposed by the Scholastics but unnecessary, of this (indecomposable) triad into a dyad of the world (a dyad reduced to the secondan: impress and express form—no priman) and a monad of the mind.

Knowledge is a copy or *thought,* i.e., *conceptual form* of a *real form* incarnated in things.

## KNOWLEDGE ACCORDING TO PEIRCE

Peirce does not presuppose any splitting up of the world and the mind. For him, there is only *one continuous universe.* By "continuous" is not meant a continuity of two worlds, but *indistinction,* or, one might say, a universe which is *indecomposable* like the triad. For the sake of clarity one may distinguish elements, but this will be no more than a pedagogical device.

For Peirce, there is collateral knowledge (or experience) and knowledge by signs in the sense of semiosis (inference by signs from signs) which presupposes collateral knowledge (namely the relation of a sign and an object in a given context for a given individual).

This distinction has been made at different moments in the history of philosophy, and can be found in Plato as well as in Spinoza. It is commonly made use of in English, "knowledge by acquaintance" being distinguished from "knowledge about" (Grote, James, Russell, Dewey).

The following passage is Peirce's iconic expression:

> Suppose I chance to overhear one man at a club say to another "Ralph Pepperill has bought that mare Pee Dee Kew." Never having heard before either of Ralph Pepperill or of Pee Dee Kew, it means to me only that some man has bought some famous trotter; and since I knew already that some men do make such purchases, it does not interest me. But the next day I hear somebody inquire

where he can find a copy of Steven's edition of Plato; to which reply is made that Ralph Pepperill says he has a copy. Now although I never was knowingly acquainted with any purchaser of crack trotting horses, yet I should not have supposed that such a person would be aware of possessing an old edition of Plato whose chief value is due to the circumstance that modern citations from the Dialogues usually refer to it. After this I begin to pay attention to what I hear of Ralph Pepperill; until, at length, that which the name means to me probably represents pretty fairly what it would mean to an acquaintance of the man. This imparts not merely an interest, but also a meaning to every little scrap of new information about him;—to scraps that would have conveyed no information whatsoever, had they first introduced his name to my ears. Yet the name itself will remain a designation devoid of essential signification, and so much of the accidental kind as it may at any time have acquired will not have been derived, in however slight measure from the utterer of any sentence which it may furnish with informatory interest,—at least, not from him in his capacity as utterer of that sentence. (Peirce, 1907 Ms 318: 23–25)

Once the place of collateral experience has been clearly marked out, one can proceed more easily to the analysis of semiosis, knowledge by signs from signs.

Thus we have the solution not only to the problem raised by the division of the universe into two distinct worlds of which one is the temporal copy of the other, eternal, one, but also to the problem raised by Wittgenstein: that of the existence of "two visual realities" which are concomitant and different: semiosis is prospective, not retrospective invention; it takes place in time, and cannot be reduced to a simple process of producing each and every day a copy of eternal forms.

# - 15 -

# Ontology: Transcendentals *of* or *without* Being

PEIRCE VERSUS ARISTOTLE AND THOMAS AQUINAS

The Transcendental is defined as what can be found in all kinds of Being. The list of Transcendentals, always three in number, varies from one period to another. For Thomas Aquinas, the three Transcendentals of Being are the One, the True, and the Good. The Beautiful, which for the Modernists, is a Transcendental *proprio sensu* in place of the One, is for Thomas Aquinas a Transcendental derived from the Good. Peirce also adopted the True, the Good, and the Beautiful, except that he does not call them Transcendentals, but ultimate categories, respectively, of logic, of ethics, and of aesthetics.

## DISTINCTIONS

Aristotle is the initiator of the division of Being into Transcendentals. But for him there is only one Transcendental: the One, which is identical with Being. The True is, in a sense, only a subjective, let us say human aspect of the apprehension of Being, but its cause is Truth in the highest sense of the word (Aristotle 1966: α 1, 993b 26–31). The Good is at the root of action, but, although Aristotle says nothing of its relation to Being, it is difficult to conceive that the Prime Mover is not Being as Being (Aristotle 1966: λ 6).

According to Thomas Aquinas, the Transcendentals are distinctions of reason. These distinctions differ from real distinctions in that they are proposed by our intelligence, whereas real distinctions do not depend on what we think about them.

Thomas Aquinas divides distinctions of reason into distinctions of reasoned reason and distinctions of reasoning reason.

1. The distinction of reasoned reason has a foundation in reality, and is sub-

divided into (1a) the major or perfect distinction of reasoned reason which can contain the other only potentially: kind and species, and (1b) the minor or imperfect distinction of reasoned reason which can contain the other only virtually in act: Being and two of its Transcendentals: the True and the Good.

2. The distinction of reasoning reason is a pure artifice of thought. This is the case of the Transcendental One which is identical with Being.

Here the Transcendentals are not obtained by deductive reasoning, as with the idealists, but by the integration of the most general aspects of the given in the sense of the existential real. For Thomas Aquinas they are based on the principle of the universal analogical intelligibility of Being.

As, according to Duns Scotus, all being is univocal and not analogical, the Thomistic distinctions are insufficient for him. He replaces them by the following ones:

1. The *real* distinction between two absolute *beings* capable of existing separately. These beings, simple or compound, are absolute individuals depending exclusively on the divine Will and fully intelligible owing to formal distinctions.

2. The distinction of *reason* between two ways of expressing a same essence like the identity of unity.

3. The formal *a parte rei* distinction between two essences, *formally distinct,* but *incapable of existing separately,* such as animality and rationality.

According to Ockham, Scotist univocality leads to the infinite multiplication of real distinctions. In order to limit them, Ockham proposes his principle known as "Ockham's razor": *Non sunt multiplicanda entia sine necessitate.* Necessity not being a criterion of universal intelligibility as it was for Thomas Aquinas, he resorts to the principle of separability, which Peirce will adopt, in order to determine the real, in the sense of existential, character of a distinction; all the other distinctions, including the formal *a parte rei* distinctions, being distinctions of reason for Ockham if not for Peirce.

Francis Suarez tried to reconcile the Thomistic and Scotistic oppositions by admitting modal distinctions which are in fact *a parte rei,* but not as with Duns Scot simply conceptual, but "objectively" necessary. Suarez was a Jesuit, Thomas Aquinas a Dominican, and Duns Scot a Franciscan.

Finally, Descartes, who studied at the Jesuit college of La Flèche in France, kept the three distinctions made by Suarez:

1. Real distinctions valid for substances. A substance is a reality of which we have a clear and distinct idea: two substances, the objects of two clear and distinct ideas, are *really distinct.* The "I" of "I think therefore I am" is a substance.

2. Distinction of reason valid for the attributes of the substance from which they are inseparable. One cannot have a clear and distinct idea of being without the idea of essence which is its attribute. The attribute of "I" is "thought": *cogito ergo sum.*

3. Modal distinction. The modes are qualities which are not necessary to the idea that we have of a substance, such as feeling, wanting, willing, which are the modes of the thinking *ego,* the "moi pensant."

Charles S. Peirce introduces three types of distinction which can be compared with the preceding ones:

Dissociation is a real distinction in Ockham's sense.

Discrimination is a distinction of reason.

Prescission is a formal *a parte rei* distinction in a *more* Ockhamistic than Scotistic sense. In effect, for Ockham this distinction is one of reason; whereas Peirce maintains like Duns Scotus that it is a distinction of reason, but founded *in re*. It is thus formal *a parte rei*, on the condition that one insists upon its role of unifying both the real distinctions and those of reason: no Third (category of reason) without a Second (category of existence *in re*) nor First, (a category peculiar to Peirce, but which can be compared to the modal distinction of Suarez and Descartes). However, only Peirce introduces between these distinctions a hierarchy both *a parte rationis* and *a parte rei.*

## THE TRANSCENDENTALS

### *The One*

The idea of the One goes back to Parmenides: Being is, and it is One. It is associated with the theory of Pythagoras, for whom the numerical unity is constitutive of the idea of Being as One. Thomas Aquinas adopts a diametrically opposed position which argues against the Platonico-Pythagorean position taken by Avicenna.

> These opinions rest on the supposition that there is identity between the One which is convertible with Being and which is the principle of number, and there is no other Multiple than number which is a species of quantity. Which is clearly false. It is a fact that division is the cause of the Multiple, and unity the cause of indivision. Thus the One and the Multiple must be judged according to the "reason" of the division. (Aquinas 1259/1263: q. 9, a. 7)

Peirce is in entire agreement with this: The One is not of the kind of the discrete quantity. The One is for Peirce, as for Aristotle and Thomas Aquinas, an attribute of Being, the only difference being that according to him, there are three ontological attributes or, more precisely, three ordinal categories of Being: the First, the Second, and the Third, of which the Transcendentals are the normative expressions: aesthetics, ethics, and logic.

### *The True*

If the One is for Thomas Aquinas a distinction of reasoning reason, which it is not for Peirce, the True implies for both a distinction of reasoned reason because it is based on something real: *intelligence.* The True is that towards which knowledge tends. For Thomas Aquinas this something real is *appetite* (*appetitum*, ὀρεξις) which, in a reasonable being, is intellectual: the desire to know. Aquinas distinguishes the logical True from the ontological True. Thus, logically, artifacts are said to be true with relation to our intelligence: a true house is one which attains resemblance to the idea which is in the architect's mind, and a true speech is true insofar as it is the sign of a true thought (Aquinas 1267/1273: 1, q. 16, art. 1); and in the same way, ontologically, natural things are said to be true insofar as they attain resemblance to ideas which are in the mind of God: a true stone is one in which the proper nature of stone is realized, in conformity with the anterior conception of the divine intelligence (ibid.). Whereas Augustine tends to objectify truth in God, Aquinas thinks that truth is first in the intelligence, and in things only by derivation. Is this not also what Peirce suggests when he situates the immediate object in the sign and the dynamical object out of the sign?

## The Good

The Good, which is, according to Aristotle, *quod omnia appetunt*—that toward which all tends—is based on appetite, which in the reasonable being is the will to seek for Good as apprehended by the intelligence. It is thus also a distinction of reasoned reason. It will be noted that the True and the Good have the same foundation outside Being: the nature of that other which man is. The Good (*bonum*, τὸ ἀγατόν) is that which satisfies the desire of which the apprehension is the Beautiful (*pulchrum*, τὸ καλόν). Thus Peirce does not separate, for this very reason, the Good, the True, and the Beautiful. Whereas it is only a derived Transcendental for Aquinas, the Beautiful is, for Peirce, the foundation of the Good and the True.

## The Beautiful

Peirce is, however, in agreement with Aquinas: the beautiful cannot please without reason:

> So, then, we appeal to the esthete to tell us what it is that is admirable without any reason for being admirable beyond its inherent character. [ ... ] If he replies that it consists in a certain quality of feeling, a certain *bliss,* I for one decline altogether to accept the answer as sufficient. [ ... ] I cannot without strenuous proof admit that any particular quality of feeling is admirable without a reason. (1903: 1.612)

# THE HIERARCHY OF THE TRANSCENDENTALS

The Beautiful is thus inseparable from the Good and the True. After writing in his *Private Thoughts* that "the soul is that which can move. [ ... ] But what puts the soul in this active state? Beauty" (W1: 6, 12 August 1856)—which would make it appear that the Beautiful is the ultimate Transcendental—Peirce wrote his very first article: "The Sense of Beauty Never Furthered the Performance of a Single Act of Duty" (W1: 10, Ms 12, 26 March 1857), which confirms this impression.

Charles Peirce was then eighteen. After quoting Ruskin: "Schiller, in his Es-

thetic Letters, observes that the sense of beauty never furthered the performance of a single act of duty," Peirce comments: "If he [Ruskin] had read the letter
which follows the one to which he refers he would have found the words: Beauty
is in the highest degree fruitful with respect to knowledge and morality."

> [A] false beauty [ . . . ] sometimes misleads experience. We must seek then a
> pure idea of beauty, by which we can test experience.* Such an idea of beauty, if
> it exists is to be inferred from what our nature renders possible, and beauty will
> discover itself to be a necessary condition of humanity. It will be necessary, then,
> in the first place, to develop the purely *a priori* idea of humanity.
>
> Man consists of Person and Condition—analysis can go no further. Now, from
> these elements of humanity arise two impulses: from Person the impulse which
> produces form [ . . . ] from Condition, the *sensuous impulse,* which insists upon
> absolute reality, and would convert all pure ideas into manifold realities, and
> make all dispositions apparent. The first impulse gives laws, the second creates
> cases. [ . . . ] Since [these impulses] do not conflict in the same objects they can
> easily coexist, and in perfect harmony, whence arises a third impulse, the result
> of the perfect balance of the other two, which [ . . . ] may be regarded as the
> impulse which creates beauty. [ . . . ] Now it will be observed that beauty gives
> the mind no particular direction or tendency—hence it can have no result either
> for the intellect or the will, and can help us to perform no single duty. On the
> other hand, it places the mind in a state of "infinite determinableness" so that
> it can turn in any direction and is in perfect freedom, hence beauty is in the
> highest respect fruitful with respect to knowledge and morality. (W1: 10–12)

Peirce's first intellectual act in 1857 was thus to maintain explicitly that
Beauty—a pure possible which places the mind in a state of "infinite determin-
ableness"—is the first Transcendental which can produce neither a true proposition, nor a good act, but on which are based Truth and Goodness. The Procrus-
tean bed of the trichotomy was ready for use (cf. 1910: 1.568–172).

It is the same doctrine which will be found in *Minute Logic* (1902) and *A
Syllabus of Certain Topics of Logic* (1903) in which Peirce deals with the normative sciences: logic, ethics, and esthetics. In the latter text he writes:

> Esthetics is the science of ideals, or of that which is objectively admirable with-
> out any ulterior reason. [ . . . ] Ethics, or the science of right and wrong, must
> appeal to Esthetics for aid in determining the *summum bonum.* It is the theory
> of self-controlled, or deliberate conduct. Logic is the theory of self-controlled,
> or deliberate, thought; and as such, must appeal to ethics for its principles.
> (1.191)

For Peirce, logic is based on ethics which is based on esthetics. If the object
of logic is Truth, that of ethics Goodness, and that of esthetics Beauty, the scientific hierarchy of the categories is as follows:

---

* It should be noted here that Peirce does not appeal to experience to test an idea, as in 1877,
when he will introduce the pragmatic method. He is writing in 1857.

1. Beauty
2. Goodness
3. Truth

This confirms that the categorial distribution of the Transcendentals: Beauty First, Goodness Second, Truth Third, is correct or, shall we say, justified? Ultimate Truth is indeed Third, Goodness Second (with reference to agapism), and Beauty is therefore First. But questions arise: Truth as testable is Second, Beauty as the Harmony of proportions Third, and Goodness as a source may well be First. What hierarchy of categories should be chosen?

Furthermore, what is the place of the One? It must be remembered that the Thomist order of the Transcendentals is: the One, Truth, Goodness, and Beauty which is a Transcendental derived from Goodness. Herbert Schneider held that the *Summum Bonum,* being above ultimate Beauty, Goodness, and Truth, is a categorical imperative which he calls Fourthness (Schneider 1952: 209–214). It is true that Peirce says expressly in 1.191 that it is esthetics, whose object is Beauty, which determines the *summum bonum.* Is it necessary to refer to Kant as Schneider does? Could the *summum bonum* not be rather the One of Aristotle and Aquinas? One part of the problem would thus be solved, but the question of the categorical classification of the Transcendentals would remain. For, according to Aquinas, if it is admitted that the *summum bonum* is the One, the scientific hierarchy is the same as that of Peirce, but in inverse order, as appears in the following table:

| *Summum Bonum* Being as One | | | |
|---|---|---|---|
| Aquinas | 1 | 2 | 3 |
| | Truth | Goodness | Beauty |
| Peirce | 3 | 2 | 1 *Summum Bonum* |

Table 15.1. Hierarchy of the Transcendentals

## THE TRANSCENDENTALS AND THE TRINITY

The question of the Transcendentals has always been linked, at least in Christianity, consciously or not, with the question of the Trinity. The most explicit instance is that of the Catalan philosopher Ramón Llull.

The four causes being the Creator, matter, form, and the final cause, it is clear that the Creator occupies a privileged place:

Intellectually we understand that your wisdom knew, before man existed, what he would do with matter, form and the final cause. (Llull 1991: "Contemplació," *L'art bref,* 265)

This reduction from four causes to three is obviously linked to the mystery of the Trinity:

Lord, your virtues, which we call essential virtues, and that the intellect (in catalan: *enteniment,* in latin: *intellectus*) understands as a unique substance, mean that there are in your substance three persons, which is signified by three forms. (Llull 1991: 179, 2)

Lord, the first of these three meanings is itself triple: infinity, life, eternity mean that you are in three persons; the second meaning is also triple: power, wisdom, love mean that in you there are three persons; the third meaning is also itself triple: your simplicity, your glory, your perfection mean that three persons are in you. (Llull 1991: 179, 2)

Lord, as memory means one thing, understanding means another thing, and will, still another one, understanding, infinity, power, simplicity mean Paternity in your glorious substance; life, wisdom, glory mean Filiation; eternity, love, perfection mean Procession. (Llull 1991: 246, 23)

[That is why] when the intellect understands what infinity, life, eternity signify of your Trinity, memory remembers, and will loves, your infinity, your life and your eternity. (Llull 1991: 317, 19)

As Augustine said in the *De Trinitate,* God, who is, for us, the sovereign Good (*Deus est nobis summum bonum*) is Three: Loving, Loved, and Love: *Tria sunt: amans, et quod amatur, et amor.*

It was also in a theological context that Peirce was to explain for the first time his triadic theory of the sign, as will be shown later. In this context, he elaborates the triadic nature of any sign, namely: the object second, the interpretant third, and the ground, later replaced by the representamen, first. Like Being, which in order to be can be only One, the Unity of God recognized by the Christian can be only the triadic Unity of the Father, the Son, and the Holy Spirit.

# - 16 -

# Cosmology: Chaos and Chance *within* Order and Continuity

## PEIRCE BETWEEN PLATO AND DARWIN

The question of the relation between chaos and order can be dealt with from many viewpoints, theoretical and practical. From Greek cosmogony to the scientific thought of today, it is the same question which is raised when Western man wants to picture the world he lives in. Our way of thinking has changed since the Greeks and one can hardly compare Greek philosophy and American philosophy, let alone Plato's cosmogony and Peirce's cosmology. However, even if their answers are different, Plato's and Peirce's question is the same and represented in almost identical fashion.

## GREEK GODS AND COSMOLOGICAL PRINCIPLES

According to Greek mythology, as expressed by Plato in the *Symposium* (*Le banquet* in French), the first three gods were Chaos, Gaea, and Eros. Chaos (Χάος) was born first without any father or mother. Gaea (Γαῖα)—the Goddess Earth—sprang from Chaos, and then Eros ("Ερος), whose creative capacity, by uniting and dividing, shapes every being and thing. Thus, the essential mythological Triad represents and illustrates respectively the three cosmological principles: Chaos the principle of potentiality, Gaea the "unshakeable and eternal foundation of all things" (Plato), and Eros the category of Love as mediator.

Peirce's triadic cosmology rests on the same categories: First the category of *potentiality*, illustrated by *chaos;* Second the category of *actuality*, illustrated by the *cosmos* as it is; Third the category of *regularity* or "order," illustrated by "love" as *agape*, not *Eros*. We will come back to that point later.

## EPISTEMOLOGY AND MYTHOLOGY

Right from the beginning, the Greek philosophers do not sever image from thought. They do not advance any special epistemology, idealist or empiricist. They simply borrow from the Greek mythology the necessary images to express their philosophy. It is the very conception that Charles S. Peirce proposed when idealism and empiricism failed to explain the relations between the concepts and their representations.

> The only way of directly communicating an idea [concept] is by means of an icon [representation]; and every indirect method of communicating an idea must depend for its establishment upon the use of an icon. Hence, every assertion must contain an icon or set of icons, or else must contain signs whose meaning is only explicable by icons. The idea which the set of icons (or the equivalent of a set of icons) contained in an assertion signifies may be termed the *predicate* of the assertion. (1902: 2.278)

The resort to diagrams gives substance or rather existence to all kinds of abstractions and especially mathematical abstractions. It is a pedagogical device, as old as the Greeks, that Peirce will justify in his *chef d'oeuvre,* the theory of Existential Graphs:

> The term *(Existential) Graph* will be taken in the sense of a Type; and the act of embodying it in a *Graph-Instance* will be termed *scribing* the Graph (not the Instance), whether the Instance be written, drawn, or incised. (Charles S. Peirce 1906: 4.537)

## HOW DO WE PASS FROM CHAOS TO ORDER? THE GREEK CONNECTION

Plato's cosmology rests on a static and rather dualistic ontology:

> What is that which always is and has no becoming [the Ideas as Patterns or Forms]; and what is that which is always becoming and never is [the things which are the copies of Ideas? [ . . . ] That which is apprehended by intelligence and reason is always in the same state; but that which is conceived by opinion with the help of sensation and without reason, is always in a process of becoming and perishing and never really is.

According to Plato in *Timaeus,* Chaos and Order are linked by the sensible and the intelligible. But the sensible and the intelligible are not the only ontological "forms"; there is a third "form" (εἶδος), the *chôra* (χώρα) without which the intelligible—the Idea—could not be copied in a sensible image—icon. As the Chôra is the spatial gap, the τοπος, the "hole" through which the sensible can be reached by the intelligible, there is another "hole" through which the eternal character of the Ideas can be instantiated in copies. This "hole" is called Exaphnès (Ἐξαίφνης): "Instantaneous" (Mattéi 1996: 191–216. See Wahl 1951: 167–172).

| Chaos (Χάος) | | | | Order (Εἶδος) [or Λόγος] |
|---|---|---|---|---|
| | Sensible | Chôra (Χώρα) | Intelligible | |
| | Instant | Exaphnès (Ἐξαίφνης) [Time] | Eternity | |

Table 16.1. Plato's Cosmology

## COSMOLOGY IN PEIRCE'S CONTEXT: PURITANISM, EVOLUTIONISM, AND PHANEROSCOPY

### Puritanism and Evolutionism

When Columbus discovered America, he did not do only that, but provided a new opportunity to look at Western civilization from the point of view of puritanism, on one hand, and from the point of view of evolutionism, on the other hand. Which explains, firstly, that love as *agape* was substituted by Peirce to love as *Eros;* and, secondly, that the static world of the Greeks was replaced by Darwin's evolutionary cosmology. Of course there were other conceptions of evolution. Peirce himself was more inclined to a Lamarckian conception than a Darwinian conception, in spite of the fact that in the end he surrendered to Darwin's solution.

According to Peirce, there are "three modes of evolution": evolution by fortuitous variation (*tychastic* evolution in Peirce's terminology), evolution by mechanical necessity (*anancastic* evolution), and evolution by creative love (*agapastic* evolution), which is summed up in Table 16.2.

I shall limit my comments to Peirce's denial of the evolution by "necessity," especially Weismann's, and to the "third method" "enwrapped in the theory of Lamarck."

### Weismann

Weismann, unlike Peirce, opposed evolution by chance and favored "a mechanical necessity to which the facts that come under their observation do not point."

| Possible modes of evolution | Names of the modes (and related doctrines) | Names of the principles |
|---|---|---|
| Darwin's solution "fortuitous variation" (6.302) | Tychasm (discontinuity: τύχη = hazard) [Tychasticism] | Tychism "absolute chance [as] severally operative in the cosmos" (6.302) |
| Weismann's solution "mechanical necessity" (6.36 sq., 34, 143, 302) | Anancasm (repetitive continuity: ἀνάγκη = necessity) "Tychasm and anancasm are degenerate forms of agapasm" (6.303) [Anancasticism] | Anancism "mechanical necessity [as] severally operative in the cosmos" (6.302) |
| Peirce's solution "creative love" (6.302) | Agapasm (creative continuity: ἀγάπη = love) (6.302) [Agapasticism] | Agapism "the law of love [as] severally operative in the cosmos" (6.302) Agapism: degenerate form of synechism |

Table 16.2. Peirce's Evolutionary Cosmology
Discriminative Classification

He held "that all forms are simple mechanical resultants of the heredity from two parents" (6.298).

**Lamarck**

Lamarckian evolution is this "evolution by the force of habit," according to which "all that distinguishes the highest organic forms from the most rudimentary has been brought about by little hypertrophies or atrophies which have affected individuals early in their lives, and have been transmitted to their offspring" (6.299). It is true that Peirce was inclined to explain the Cosmos in terms of Lamarck, although he confessed that the sentence "evolution by the force of habit" "slipped off my pen" (6.300).

> Of course, it is nonsense. Habit is mere inertia, a resting on one's oars, not a propulsion. Now it is energetic projaculation (lucky there is such a word, or this untried hand might have been put to inventing one) by which in the typical instances of Lamarckian evolution the new elements of form are first created. Habit, however, forces them to take practical shapes, compatible with the struc-

tures they affect, and, in the form of heredity and otherwise, gradually replaces the spontaneous energy that sustains them. Thus, habit plays a double part; it serves to establish the new features, and also to bring them into harmony with the general morphology and function of the animals and plants to which they belong. (6.300)

But this account of Lamarckian evolution coincides exactly with Peirce's description of the action of love, although it is only its first step: "The first step in the Lamarckian evolution of mind is the putting of sundry thoughts into situations in which they are free to play" (6.303).

### Phaneroscopy

Peirce's cosmology rests on his phaneroscopy which we have already discussed on several occasions. "Chance is First, Law is Second, the tendency to take habits is Third. Mind is First, Matter is Second, Evolution is Third" (6.32). Hence the three steps: One variety of tychasm, two varieties of anancasm, and three varieties of agapasm.

Here again, as in ontology, cosmology can be referred to theology:

Men who seek to reconcile the Darwinian idea with Christianity will remark that tychastic evolution, like the agapastic, depends upon a reproductive creation, the forms preserved being those that use the spontaneity conferred upon them in such wise as to be drawn into harmony with their original, quite after the Christian scheme. (6.304)

## THE PEIRCEAN CONNECTION

Peirce's cosmology not only raises the same question as Plato's, but sometimes with the same concepts, if not always with the same words. The result is, however, a totally new dynamic philosophy which one cannot help thinking is the philosophy which Plato would have proposed, had he lived in Peirce's context. Such is at least Peirce's opinion:

In short, if we are going to regard the universe as a result of evolution at all, we must think that not merely the existing universe, that locus in the cosmos to which our reactions are limited, but the whole Platonic world, which in itself is equally real, is evolutionary in its origin, too.

Thus, according to Peirce, the cosmos lies, as in Plato, between Chaos and Order. "In the original chaos, where there was no regularity, there was no existence" (ca. 1897: 1.175). "The original chaos, therefore, where there was no regularity, was in effect a state of mere indeterminacy, in which nothing existed or really happened" (*A Guess at the Riddle,* ca. 1890). Order does not exist either. But without it, as Aristotle said, "We cannot know anything except it be a uniformity." To which Peirce adds the following comment: "I am simply suggesting first that an event altogether out of order and presenting no regularity could not come to our knowledge at all, and second, that only in respect to its being orderly can we know it" (*Grand Logic*, 1893).

The three principles of cosmology are:

1. Tychism, the principle of chance (τύχη). "Tychism must give birth to an evolutionary cosmology" (6.102). "Tychism is only a part and corollary of the general principle of 'synechism'" (Peirce's letter to W. James, Perry II: 223).

2. Agapism, the principle of love (ἀνάγπη) which is "the great evolutionary agency of the universe" (6.287). (Agapism is a degenerate form of synechism.)

3. Synechism, the principle of continuity (συνέχεια). Synechism is a "regulative principle of logic" (6.173) "which insists upon the idea of continuity" (6.169). Continuity is the absence of ultimate parts in that which is divisible (6.173). "Once you have embraced the principle of continuity no kind of explanation of things will satisfy you except that they *grew*" (1.175).

Most of the misunderstandings concerning Peirce's cosmology arise from taking the cosmological trichotomies—chance, love, and continuity—as the three hierarchical terms of a triad. Properly speaking, they belong to Secondness. They nevertheless are indispensable if we want to understand our own Western conception of the world as elaborated by the Greek philosophy (concept) and mythology (representation). That is why Order means generality, rather than physical regularity. Cosmologically, "physical regularities" are continuous processes; what Plato called the Chôra. On the other hand, chance is linked to Chaos by the "instantaneous," the Exaphnès:

> [I]n the beginning—infinitely remote there was a chaos of unpersonalized feeling, which being without connection or regularity would properly be without existence. This feeling, sporting here and there in pure arbitrariness, would have started the germ of a generalizing tendency. Its other sportings would be evanescent, but this would have a growing virtue. Thus, the tendency to habit would be started; and from this, with the other principles of evolution, all the regularities of the universe would be evolved. At any time, however, an element of pure chance survives and will remain until the world becomes an absolutely perfect, rational, and symmetrical system, in which mind is at last crystallized in the infinitely distant future. (1891: 6.33)

Let us conclude with a vivid description by Peirce of the *cosmos* as continuous and instantaneous.

Peirce starts by saying that there is no Time without existing change:

> Time with its continuity logically involves some other kind of continuity than its own. Time, as the universal form of change, cannot exist unless there is something to undergo change and to undergo a change continuous in time there must be a continuity of changeable qualities. Of the continuity of intrinsic qualities of feeling we can now form but a feeble conception. (6.132)

| 1 | 2 | 3 |
|---|---|---|
| **Chaos**<br><br>[Feeling] | **Chance** (τύχη)<br>[Instantaneous]<br><br>— — — — — — — — — — — — —<br><br>**Love** (ἀγάπη)<br><br>is "the great evolutionary agency of the universe" (6.287).<br><br>[Processes]<br><br>— — — — — — — — — — — — —<br><br>**Continuity** (συνέχεια)<br><br>is "the absence of ultimate parts in that which is divisible" (6.173). "Once you have embraced the principle of continuity no kind of explanation of things will satisfy you except that they *grew*" (1.175).<br><br>[Space] | **Order**<br><br><br><br><br><br><br><br><br><br><br>[Generality] |

Table 16.3. Peirce's Principles of Cosmology

Consider a gob of protoplasm, say an amoeba or a slime-mould. It does not differ in any radical way from the contents of a nerve-cell, though its functions may be less specialized. There is no doubt that this slime-mould, or this amoeba, or at any rate some similar mass of protoplasm, feels. That is to say, it feels when it is in its excited condition. But note how it behaves. When the whole is quiescent and rigid, a place upon it is irritated. Just at this point, an active motion is set up, and this gradually spreads to other parts. In this action, no unity nor relation to a nucleus, or other unitary organ can be discerned. It is a mere amorphous continuum of protoplasm, with feeling passing from one part to another. Nor is there anything like a wave-motion. The activity does not advance to new parts just as fast as it leaves old parts. Rather, in the beginning, it dies out at a slower rate than that at which it spreads. And while the process is going on, by exciting the mass at another point, a second quite independent state of excitation will be set up. In some places, neither excitation will exist, in others each separately, in still other places, both effects will be added together. Whatever there is in the whole phenomenon to make us think there is feeling in such a mass of protoplasm—*feeling,* but plainly no *personality*—goes logically to show that that feeling has a subjective, or substantial, spatial extension, as the excited state has. (6.133)

Then Peirce passes to the role of Space in the evolutionary process:

Since space is continuous, it follows that there must be an immediate community of feeling between parts of mind infinitesimally near together. Without this,

I believe it would have been impossible for minds external to one another ever to become coördinated, and equally impossible for any coördination to be established in the action of the nerve-matter of one brain. (6.134)

But with this he ventures to conclude that "everybody can see that the statement of St. John is the formula of an evolutionary philosophy, which teaches that growth comes only from love" (6.289)—that Love which unites Space and Time, Continuity and Chance.

Is this description "scientific" or "metaphorical" like Greek mythology? Peirce's answer is clear: "In the very nature of things, the line of demarcation between the three modes of evolution is not perfectly sharp. That does not prevent its being quite real; perhaps it is rather a mark of its reality" (6.306). But the two main questions are not there. The first one is "whether three radically different evolutionary elements have been operative," and the second question is "what are the most striking characteristics of whatever elements have been operative" (6.306)?

# - 17 -

# Theology: The Reality of God

PEIRCE'S TRIUNE GOD AND THE CHURCH'S TRINITY

Peirce was born a Unitarian. Unitarians believe that only God the Father is God; Jesus, the Son of God, and the Holy Spirit are the first among the creatures. One of Peirce's fellow students at Harvard, Charles Fay, had a sister, Harriet Melusina, who not only had become an Episcopalian, and consequently a Trinitarian, but was a kind of American suffragette, a feminist who had advanced a conception of the Trinity in which the Holy Spirit represented the Woman in the triune Divinity:

> A Divine Eternal Trinity of Father, Mother and Only Son—the "Mother" being veiled throughout the Scriptures under the terms "The Spirit," "Wisdom," "The Holy Ghost," "The Comforter" and "The Woman clothed with the sun and crowned with the stars and with the moon under her feet." (Max Fisch in W1, Introduction: xxxi)

Charles S. Peirce married Melusina in the Episcopalian Church and adopted Melusina's triune conception of God:

> Here, therefore, we have a divine trinity of the object, interpretant, and ground. [ ... ] In many respects, this trinity agrees with the Christian trinity; indeed I am not aware that there are many points of disagreement. The interpretant is evidently the Divine *Logos* or word; and if our former guess that a Reference to an interpretant is Paternity be right, this would be also the *Son of God.* The *ground,* being that partaking of which is requisite to any communication with the Symbol, corresponds in its function to the Holy Spirit. (W1: 503)

Peirce gave later in 1907, although he had been separated from Melusina for more than thirty years, an even more feminist conception: "A Sign mediates between its *Object* and its *Meaning*. [ . . . ] Object the father, sign the mother of meaning." "That is," Max Fisch comments, "he might have added, of their son, the interpretant" (w1: xxxii).

## DOES GOD EXIST?

The question was dealt with by Peirce in a convincing paper published in the *Hibbert Journal* in 1908, under the title "A Neglected Argument for the Reality of God." Peirce's positive answer has a very important consequence. It shows that answering the question is possible on the sole condition that God is Triune.

Peirce's way to God is not argumentative, nor historical; it is sheer wandering of the mind in the Universe of Firstness through "musement." "Musement" is "Pure Play." "Pure Play has no rules, except this very law of liberty. It bloweth where it listeth. It has no purpose, unless recreation" (6.458). It takes many forms: "aesthetic contemplation," "castle-building," or that form "of considering some wonder in one of the [three] Universes, or some connection between two of the three, with speculation concerning its cause," which is, properly speaking, the "musement" which "will in time flower into the N.A. [Neglected Argument]" (6.458).

Peirce was not only born a Unitarian, he was born an empiricist. Historically, Peirce was first, from 1851 to 1867, an out-and-out empiricist and thus a nominalist: only Seconds—concrete individual existents—were real. Reality and existence were then synonymous. In 1857, he wrote: "Reality [refers] to the existence of the object itself" (W1: 18).

From 1867 onward, more precisely during the winter of 1867–1868, in an unpublished item in which he criticized positivism, Peirce distinguished between existence and reality. What is real is "that which is independently of our belief and which could be properly inferred by the most thorough discussion of the sum of all impressions of sense whatever" (W2: 127).

It will be remarked that this kind of reality, although general, is not properly a Third in the sense in which Peirce will use the term in 1908. Then, a Third will not be a generalization of Seconds, that is of singular cases, but of operative rules, *a priori* empty, of the type "if *p*, then *q*."

It was not until about 1890 that Peirce conceded that Firsts are also real. In 1891, he wrote: "In the beginning [ . . . ] there was a chaos of impersonalized feeling, which being without connection or regularity would properly be without existence." However, "this feeling, sporting here and there in pure arbitrariness, would have started the germ of a generalizing tendency" (6.33). How to interpret the reality of the Firsts is not easy. If we say that they are *in potentia*, how can they be entirely without existence? If they are not *in potentia*, they must be general without *ground*, contrary to Thirdness, which is a rule expressing the logical relation between "arguments," such as $p$ and $q$. Thus there must be another kind of "general." This generality is something "vague" and undetermined, which can only be "realized" by sheer chance. One of the best commentators who was also editor, with Paul Weiss, of the *Collected Papers* of Peirce, Charles Hartshorne, insisted on this point in a chapter of his *Logic of Perfection:* "Ten Ontological or Modal Proofs for God's Existence." Since perfection is not a state, Hartshorne argues, an *actus purus,* but a destiny, perfection is perfectibility:

> The absolute infinity of the divine potentiality might also be called its *coincidence with possibility as such.* (Perhaps "coextensiveness" with possibility would be more accurate.) To be possible is to be a possible object of divine knowing. But it immediately follows that one thing is not possible—the non-existence of the divine knower. For no subject can have knowledge of the fact of its own non-existence, certainly not perfect, infallible knowledge. Thus either the non-existence of the perfect knower is impossible, or there is one possibility whose actualization the perfect knower could not know. But the second case contradicts the definition of perfection through the coincidence of "possible" and "possible for God." (Hartshorne 1962: 38)

As, on the other hand, according to modal logic, to say that "$p$ is possible" is to say that "necessarily $p$ is possible," and to say that "it is possible that $p$ is necessary," is to say that "necessarily $p$ is necessary," the ontological argument is valid and God is real, in the Peircean sense; that is to say: God as Triune—the father, the Son, and the Holy Spirit—"exists." Hartshorne's complete logical argumentation is worth quoting:

> To squeeze this modal complexity into the mere dichotomy, "existent versus non-existent," is to fail to discuss what Anselm was talking about. He repeatedly expressed the principle that "contingently-existing perfect thing" is contradictory in the same way as "non-existing perfect thing." However, since what is not exemplified in truth is certainly not necessarily exemplified ($\sim p \rightarrow \sim Np$), and since what is not necessary could not be necessary ($\sim Np \rightarrow N\sim Np$), to exclude contingency (this exclusion being the main point of the Argument) is to exclude factual non-existence as well as merely factual existence, leaving, as the only status which the idea of perfection can have (supposing it not meaningless or contradictory), that of necessary exemplification in reality; and it then, by the principle $Np \rightarrow p$, "the necessarily true is true," becomes contradictory to deny that perfection is exemplified. (Here, and throughout, we use the arrow sign for strict, not material, implication.) (Hartshorne 1962: 50)

## THE REALITY OF GOD

The "reality" which Peirce has in mind when he speaks of the reality of God is the reality of Firstness. But it is not enough to oppose "reality" as First and "existence" as Second, because there are not two but three Universes of Experience which are not separate universes, but fundamental modalities of Being: Firstness or the mode of Being as "felt" which is more than a simple "feeling": it tends to get united with other "feelings" in time and space, in other words to "exist" *hic et nunc;* "existing" *hic et nunc* is the mode of Being of Secondness; the interactions of "feelings" give birth in the long run to a third mode of Being: Thirdness which includes habits and laws.

The first Universe is that of Possibility; "the second Universe is that of the Brute Actuality of things and facts"; the third Universe is that of the Sign, "not the mere body of the Sign, but "the Sign's soul, which has its Being in its power of serving as intermediary between its Object and a Mind" (6.455).

Which "reality" is the reality of God? It is the "reality" of Firstness which can be reached through the action of the Mind which Peirce calls "musement." The play of Musement is neither the play of deduction (Thirdness) nor the play of induction (Secondness), but the play of retroduction or rather abduction. It is only "musement," the play of Firstness, which can reveal the reality of God; not the existence of God, because "existence" can be shown only through "induction"; nor the reality of God as Holy Spirit, which can be proved only through deduction.

Consequently, Peirce's answer to the question of the existence or rather reality of God implies that God is triune: God the Father has the reality of Firstness: He is, but does not exist, while God the Son, although also real as First, did exist as Second in the "Person" of Jesus. As to the reality of God as Third or Organizer of the World, it is personified in the Holy Spirit.

To conclude this first part, I should like to insist on the originality of Peirce's argument. It is the first argument ever founded on the category of possibility whose argumentative *scientific* expression is neither induction on which all the proofs of the "existence" of God rest, nor *a priori* deduction, very often used by metaphysicians since Saint Anselm, which for sure leads to God's "reality," a "reality" which implies "existence"—a terminological contradiction denounced by Peirce and Duns Scotus—but retroduction or abduction, the only argument which can "show" the "reality" of God without imposing on Him the "haecceity" of existence. This conception is not incompatible with God's incarnation as Second in the historical existence of Jesus Christ, nor with the reality of God as First through the mediation as Third of the Holy Spirit.

## PEIRCE'S TRIAD AND THE MYSTERY OF THE TRINITY

Peirce was not interested in the Mystery of the Trinity of God proper. The reason why I wanted to deal with this problem is that, on one hand, when I read Peirce, I was surprised that he had experienced and dealt with the same problem of the Unicity of God and His triune nature as the Christian Church, and, on the other hand, that Peirce's position was closer to the Eastern interpretation of the decisions of the Councils than the Western one.

The word "Trinity" was proposed initially by Theophilus of Antioch about

180 AD, as a synonym for the word "Triad," in the course of a theological dispute. It was also in a theological context that Peirce exposed his triadic theory for the first time, in 1866, at the end of the eleventh Lowell Lecture. Here is the main passage already quoted above:

> Here, therefore, we have a divine trinity of the object, interpretant and ground. [ ... ] In many respects, this trinity agrees with the Christian trinity; indeed I am not aware that there are any points of disagreement. The interpretant is evidently the Divine *Logos* or word; and if our former guess that a Reference to an interpretant is Paternity be right, this would be also the *Son of God.* The *ground* being that partaking of which is requisite to any communication with the Symbol, corresponds in its function to the Holy Spirit. (W1: 502–503)

Paradoxically enough, Peirce's conception of God as a hierarchical Triunity is better understood when it is read in the context of the history of the quarrels around the mystery of the Trinity whose reasons are not the mystery itself, but (1) the interference of the political power, (2) the different—Eastern or Western—mental representations of the concepts, with (3) their political implications, the two latter partially due to (4) the language used—Greek or Latin.

## *Political Interference*

The first Council which met in 325 at Nicea (Iznik in Turkey), was summoned by the Emperor Constantine, who presided. In accordance with the Emperor's wishes, the Council pronounced the condemnation of Arianism. Arius, a priest of Alexandria (ca. 280–ca. 336) had taught that the divine persons cannot be equal nor assimilated: the Father, un-created and un-engendered cannot communicate with the world; the Son engendered for all eternity is the ordinator of the world in lieu of the λόγος or divine power. The Son is subordinate and inferior to the Father. The Council decided that the Son was consubstantial (ὁμοούσιος) with the Father (ὁμο meaning "same" and οὐσία "substance"): "Jesus Christ is the Son of God, engendered and not created, consubstantial with the Father."

Soon disagreements appeared concerning the synonymity of "consubtantialis" and ὁμοούσιος, as we shall see. As the Emperor Constantius II (317–361) was against the "consubstantiality" of the Son with the Father, the Councils of Rimini (West) and Seleucia (East) condemned the Western interpretation, because such was the order of the emperor.

When Constantius II died in 361, the new Emperor Julian the Apostate, who was to write the treatise *Adversus Christianos,* reestablished the freedom of speech and discussion in matters of religion which had been prohibited by Constantius II.

After Julian's death, the Council of Constantinople summoned in 381 by Theodosius I (ca. 346–395), the last emperor of the Eastern and Western Empire

(374–395), put a temporary stop to the discussion by confirming the doctrine proclaimed by the Council of Nicea.

## Definitions and Representations

Definitions of dogmas *without representations* raise only problems of formal coherence, but no difficulties of adhesion if they are coherent. To believe in a dogma is another problem, because to believe is to believe in the representation one makes of it. It must be remembered that, on dualistic principles, Euclidean geometry does not require, any more than does the Trinity, a figured representation, but that non-Euclidean geometries have their point of departure in a criticism of the representation of Euclidean geometry. All philosophers, however, from Plato (who made use of myths) to Peirce (who used diagrams and existential graphs), have "illustrated" their discourse.

The problem arises when the same definition leads to different representations. Which is what happened when Constantine tried to unify Christian doctrine. If Christianity had no difficulty in agreeing on the formal definition of the Trinity, the Eastern and Western Churches were in disagreement about the representations they made of it. By "formal definition," I mean in plain English, "the Unity of God in three Persons: the Father, the Son and the Holy Spirit." By "representation" I mean the "image" in every sense of the word: the "mental" image and the "corporeal" image. The mental image refers to the "values" given to the terms, implicit or explicit, of the definition: in this case, the way in which the unity (of God) is divided into three. The corporeal image was to be at the center of the quarrel about images which broke out at the beginning of the eighth century. In both cases, it appears clearly that, although it is true that one cannot think without images, thought unites, while images divide.

The quarrel concerning the filiation of the Holy Spirit from the Father *and the Son*—the quarrel of the *filioque*—between Rome and Constantinople, has its root in the doctrine of the ὁμοούσιος character of the Son which did not satisfy the Eastern Church. If it is true that, for Philo (Alexandria, 13 BC–54 AD), ὁμοούσιος really means what the Council intended it to mean, the word was associated in the κοινή with the idea of metal. The word ὁμοούσιος was used only to mean that, for instance, two pieces of gold jewelry were of the same kind of material or substance. The word had thus a material and concrete implication which could not be fitting in speaking of God. The Western representatives had not the same "interpretants" and consequently were ready to accept the "word" and the doctrine.

Eusebius of Caesarea (today in Israël) (265–340) reformulated the doctrine without using the word ὁμοούσιος: "The Father is the beginning of the Son who takes his divinity from Him. There is thus only one God without beginning and unengendered. As to the Son, He is the image of the only true God, He alone who is God by Himself." But this was only coming back to the subordinationism of Arius, for whom in fact Eusebius had some sympathy. Besides, it did not eliminate completely the ὁμοούσιος character which reappeared in the idea of "image" inseparable from the idea of "resemblance."

The Eastern Churches found still other ways of avoiding the word ομο-ουσιος. The first was to reject any resemblance between the Father and the Son; this was what Aetius and his disciple Eunone proposed. The second one was to accept a certain resemblance while affirming the inequality of the divine persons or, in other words, to use the Greek term, by maintaining the thesis of the *anomeism* of the persons (ἀνόμοιος meaning "unlike").

After Julian's death, at Antioch, Aetius and Eunone renewed the philosophical reflection on the Trinity. As it was the essence of God to be unengendered, only the Father was God and thus the Son was fundamentally dissimilar (ἀνόμοιος) from the Father. Whence a hierarchized conception of the Trinity which was very well exposed by Eunone: The essence of God unengendered (ἀγεννησία), which is by definition incommunicable, cannot have been communicated by the Father to the Son. What the Father does communicate is his creative power—his ἐνέργεια—which makes the Son the intermediary between God and the world of existence. The Holy Spirit comes last and has no divine character.

The decisions of the Councils of Rimini and Seleucia were strikingly "hierarchical": "Unicity and Solitude of the Father, Subordination of the Son to the Father, and of the Holy Spirit (minister and servant) to the Son." The Son was declared to be "similar" (ὅμοιος) to the Father without further precision. If the resemblance were neither substantial nor essential, it could only be external.

After long discussions between East and West, the Council of Constantinople restated in 381 the doctrine proclaimed by the Council of Nicea. The Holy Spirit regained his questioned divinity. The only Son of God is "true God of true God, engendered, but not created, and of the same substance of the Father," the Holy Spirit "emanates from the Father [but not from the Son] and is worshipped and glorified together with the Father and the Son." This rejection of the *filioque* is the consequence of the constant reluctance of the Eastern Church to accept the ὁμοούσιος character of the Father and the Son. In this connection, Peirce would have sided with the Eastern Church. God the Father by Himself certainly is *Ens Necessarium* and creator of all, but He cannot as Such act in time, because He is out of time; He "probably has no consciousness" (6.489), no mind, properly speaking, and no purpose, except "in a vague sense" potentially (see 6.505–509). Thus the *filioque,* the existential necessity of the Son.

Seventy years later, in 451, The Emperor Marcianus summoned the Council of Chalcedon (Kadiköy in Turkey). Marcianus (396–457), the second Emperor of the Eastern Empire, had succeeded Theodosius II (the eldest son of Theodosius I and the author of the Theodosian Code) whose sister Pulcheria he had married. The Council of Chalcedon reopened the question of the relation of the Father and the Son and elaborated the doctrine in order to combat two other errors: that of Nestorius who maintained that there were two persons in Christ: a divine person and a human person (an error which had already been condemned by the Council of Ephesus in 431), and that of Eutyches who maintained that there was only one nature in Christ and that was the divine nature. Against Nestorius, the Council proclaimed that there was only one Person (ὑπόστασις) in Christ and against Eutyches that this unique person has two natures: one divine and one human: Jesus Christ is the Son of God and of Mary.

It may be noted in passing that Tarek Aziz, the present Deputy Prime Minister of Iraq, is a Nestorian, and that Islam maintains that there is only one nature in Jesus Christ, the human nature. Something more important and intriguing is the agreement of 1994 between Pope John Paul II and Patriarch Mar Dinkha IV, Head of the Eastern Assyrian Church which is Nestorian; an agreement by which they conjointly declared that "Christ was not a man in the ordinary sense of the word, chosen by God as 'His body' and as somebody to inspire, as it had been the case with the Just and the Prophets, but the very Verb of God, engendered by the Father before all the centuries, without beginning according to His divinity, and born recently from a mother without father, according to His humanity."

This agreement does not solve the mystery of the Trinity. The mystery of the Trinity, which is at the core of the misunderstanding between East and West, is still unresolved. In sum:

1. For Easterners, the mystery is that of one **Being** (Οὐσία) in three **hypostases** (ὑπόστασεις), a formula smacking of Arianism for Westerners;

2. For Westerners, the mystery is that of one Substance (**Substantia**) in three persons (**personae**), a formula redolent of Sabellianism for Easterners. Sabellius of Cyrenaica (beginning of the third century) maintained that the distinctions between the Father, the Son, and the Holy Ghost do not affect the unity of God, because they denote only modes or aspects of God.

## Political Implications

The dispute is not yet at an end—and, as before, the theology of the Trinity is the spiritual arm of worldly power. When in the eighth century resistance in Spain against Arabo-Berber occupiers began to be organized under the influence of the acculturated Visigoths, who had been in power there since the great invasions until 711, it was in the name of orthodoxy (to which the Visigoth kings adhered only in 589, having until then been partisans of the Arianist heresy) that the "resistants" through their spokesman the monk Beatus of Liebana (the author of the famous *Commentary on the Apocalypse*) fought against the "collaborators" personified by the Bishop Elipand who preached "adoptianism," a variety of Arianism which also denied the consubstantiality of the Father and the Son. This could only be acceptable to the Moslem occupier, since it is the same doctrine as that revealed in the Koran: Jesus is a prophet like Moses and Mohammed. Here again the Trinity helped to mobilize the Christians against their enemies. It made possible the Reconquest of Spain and . . . the conquest of America (of which Christendom celebrated the 500th anniversary in 1992)—America where the Unitarians persecuted in England found refuge in 1620. . . .

## From Greek to Latin

The misunderstanding between East and West concerning the mystery of the Trinity was not only semantic, but syntactic, and probably more a question of culture expressed in two different languages than a question of theology. The translation from Greek to Latin was the syntactic source of all the confusions which I would explain by the difference between Greek and Latin cultures: Greek culture is philosophical and all of *esprit de finesse,* and Latin culture juridical and of *esprit de géométrie,* to use Pascal's distinction. For instance, ὑπόστασις is a good translation of the idea of "substance" although the latter has a passive connotation in Latin and an active connotation in Greek. But Latin speakers translated ὑπόστασις (hypostasis) as *persona* (person) and translated as *substantia* the Greek term ουσια which is something which changes. But *persona* denotes an actor's mask and by derivation (1) role, (2) individuality, (3) person (in grammar). It is in the second derived sense that *persona* translates ὑπόστασις.

The equalitarian Trinitarism of the West has no origin but the geometrical juridicism of the Latin language.

And this applies not only to the mystery of the Trinity, but to Western philosophy in general, when Greek philosophy is read in the Latin translations originated by Cicero and reproduced by all the Western philosophers. Descartes is as good an example as any as was shown by the American philosopher John Herman Randall Jr.:

> It is significant that when Descartes asked, "What is Substance?" he was asking for what persists unchanged throughout change, what it is in change that does not itself change. And in Locke and in Kant, in fact, throughout modern philosophy, "substance" has been taken as the unchanging, the permanent in change, whether Locke's "I know not what," or Kant's "permanent in relation to phenomena." But for Aristotle, who since he gave the technical meaning to the term *ousia* rendered into Latin as *substantia,* ought to know, *ousia* or *substantia* is defined precisely as that which undergoes change in change, what is at the end of any process different from what it was at the outset. And in the most important and fundamental kind of change of all, *genesis kai phthora,* "generation" and "corruption," a new *ousia* or substance is present at the end that was not there at all in the beginning, or a substance has disappeared completely. Thus it is clear, Aristotle's pattern of motion and change is a pattern of novelty that emerges in process. (Randall Jr., 1960: 112–113)

*       *       *

Linguistics can also explain strange theological conceptions, such as the "feminist" personification of the Holy Spirit in the Virgin Mary, which Melusina shared.

One can read in the *Gospel of the Hebrews* (*Écrits apocryphes chrétiens,* 1997: 460–461) that the Holy Spirit is the "Mother of Jesus" (Saint Jerome), and that "the Savior said: my Mother, the Holy Spirit, took me by one hair and transported me onto the Great Mount Tabor" (Origen).

Of course, this feministic reading has nothing to do with feminism, per se. It was a current iconic association with the feminine gender of the Semitic word designing "Spirit" in this Gnostic environment: Mary was fully woman and virgin, but only apparently mother of God.

## WHY HAS THE MYSTERY OF THE TRINITY NOT YET BEEN SOLVED BY THE CHURCH?

It will have been noticed that the Councils were more concerned with the relation of the Father and the Son than with the question of the Trinity. The Holy Spirit is hardly mentioned except accessorily. Moreover, in order to refute Arius, the Councils had recourse to a dualistic philosophy: the Aristotelian philosophy of substance.

As already pointed out, to understand the mystery of the Trinity, the mystery must be situated in the politico-cultural context of the time, which is that of the opposition between East and West. The Councils of Nicea and Constantinople, which imposed the doctrine which is still in force today in the Roman Church, were summoned, respectively, by the first and the last emperors of the Eastern *and* Western Empire.

However, between these two Councils, and also outside them and after them, two philosophies are opposed: the Aristotelian philosophy and the Neo-Platonist philosophy; the West favoring the former and the East preferring the latter.

It was in an Aristotelian spirit that the Councils of Nicea and Constantinople defined the Trinity: God in three persons *equally* divine.

All the Eastern interpretations of the decisions of these Councils are Neo-Platonist. I shall note two points of doctrine which are never defended for themselves, but which are ever-present and that we noticed in Peirce's conception of God as Triune.

1. The conception of a demiurge, the creator of the world, which in the definition of the Trinity becomes that of a solitary Father having no communication with the world, and that of a Son, engendered but not created, creator of the world.

2. The Platonist conception of the procession of being. Plotinus (Lycopolis, now Assiout in Egypt, 205–270) was a commentator of Plato and especially of the *Parmenides.* Neo-Platonism was derived from his commentaries in the famous *Enneades.*

Schematically, Being, which is inaccessible, has its expression in a process (πρόοδος, translated by the word "procession"), a downward procession in three hypostases:

First hypostasis: the One absolute,
Second hypostasis: the One multiple = intuitive intelligence,
Third hypostasis: the One and the multiple = the soul or discursive reason.

It is in this way that the Eastern Church understands the Trinity: One God in three hypostases. Proceeding from God the Father, the Son loses the fullness of being possessed by the Father, but he can communicate with the world—which the Father cannot do. Proceeding from the Father and the Son, the Holy Ghost, without quite losing his divine being (although Eunone maintains the contrary) plunges the divine being into the multiplicity of the empirical world whose foundation is the pure multiple or pure matter.

## PEIRCE'S SOLUTION

The position that Peirce was to develop is closer to that of Plotinus than that taken by the Councils of Nicea and Constantinople: The Son proceeds from the Father out of time, but precedes Him in time. He is a "hypostasis" in the Greek sense adopted by the Eastern Church, not a "substance" in the Latin sense of the Western Church, while possessing both a divine nature and a human nature. The "procession" moves downward: what it gains in multiplicity, it loses in unity: the Father is First, the Son is Second, the Holy Spirit is Third.

In a letter to his brother Herbert, written before the publication of the Neglected Argument, Peirce had recognized that the Church's conception of God was close to his own, without entering into details:

> [V]arious great theologians explain that one cannot attribute *reason* to God, nor perception (which always involves an element of surprise and of learning what one did not know), and, in short, that "mind" is necessarily [ . . . ] unlike ours, [and] that it is only negatively [ . . . ] that we can attach any meaning to the Name. (6.502)

If they had been pragmatists, Peirce concludes, the Neglected Argument would have enabled them not "to think any thought of God's," of course, but to "catch a fragment of His Thought, as it were" (6.502), and to answer the question "whether there is such a being":

> Let a man drink in such thoughts as come to him in contemplating the physico-psychical universe without any special purpose of his own; especially the universe of mind which coincides with the universe of matter. The idea of there being a God over it all of course will be often suggested; and the more he considers it, the more he will be enwrapt with love of this idea. He will ask himself whether or not there really is a God. If he allows instinct to speak, and searches his own heart, he will at length find that he cannot help believing it. (6.501)

# Conclusion: Peirce

## A LATERAL VIEW

There are as many Peirces as philosophers who read him. Of course, this does not contradict Peirce's semeiotic. On the contrary, it confirms it. However, one would like to be sure of the correctness of one's interpretation. That is why I thought of studying Peirce's *Contributions to "The Nation"* as if they were the only writings by Peirce in our possession. But I realized immediately that it could not work because I knew Peirce too well—I mean I knew my knowledge of Peirce too well. So I decided to make a list of Peirce's main philosophical doctrines and see how he deals with them in *The Nation*. I shall describe the result of my inquiry in three parts. The first one will be concerned with Peirce's phaneroscopy, semeiotic, epistemology, and metaphysics. The second one will be incidental and stress some remarks made by Peirce which throw light on some points of doctrine we meet in his other writings. The third one will be devoted to pragmatism or rather pragmaticism which is *The Nation*'s philosophy, with or without italics.

## I

How to express one's philosophy is Peirce's main concern: one should use a terminology not likely to be misinterpreted by the reader. In the first review that Peirce wrote in *The Nation*, March 18, 1869, he says:

> New terms can be constructed in accordance with the principles of it [the terminology of a system] which may be understood by anyone who is acquainted with these principles. (A024*)

* References are to the edition of the three volumes of *Contributions to "The Nation,"* ed. Kenneth Laine Ketner and James Edward Cook, Lubbock, Texas Tech Press, 1975, 1978, and 1979.

This rule suffers exceptions only "in cases in which it [our terminology] fails us" (A024) to express new principles.

As philosophical or psychological terminologies do not differ from the terminologies of other sciences,

> the only possible basis for a universally accepted scientific terminology lies in a strict adherence to the rule that the word proposed as the scientific designation of a concept into science, shall be adopted unless there are very solid objections to it. (B166)

This was written on August 25, 1898. The next year (on February 2, 1899), Peirce insists:

> The only way to keep scientific terminology free from confusion is to recognize the right of him who introduces a given conception into science to confer upon it its scientific designation and symbol, which should never be rejected nor changed except for really substantial reasons, such as the previous use in another signification of the word chosen. (B184)

And again on October 24, 1901, concerning philosophical terminology, Peirce writes:

> Our first rule, subject, perhaps, to a few general but well-defined classes of exceptions (the fewer the better), will certainly be that every technical term of philosophy ought to be used in that sense in which it first became a technical term of philosophy. (C053)

Which new terminology has Peirce in mind? One would think that it is his own, or that he is not economical. However, the only terminology he mentions in every case when he treats the subject is Scholastic terminology. It was the case in the first review he wrote and it is the case in the last review where he deals with the same topic on July 7, 1901. It is not only Scholastic terminology which is here advocated, it is the Thomistic terminology, and not just any kind of Thomism, but "Leonine Thomism." The book reviewed (William Turner's *History of Philosophy*), Peirce writes, produces upon us "the impression that Leonine Thomism" is "a decidedly favorable standpoint from which to survey the course of philosophy" (C173).

And, Peirce adds, "there is a reason why it should be so: the adherent of any modern school is a nominalist" (C173).

What about Peirce's Ethics of terminology and his own terminology? I read the *Contributions* and found hardly any mention of Peirce's neologisms in the new fields he introduced in philosophy: phaneroscopy, semeiotic, and in the new doctrines he advanced in epistemology and metaphysics.

---

The Index constitutes a fourth volume which was published in 1987. The first letter refers to the volume, the following figures to the page in the volume. For instance, A024 reads vol. 1, page 24.

"Phaneroscopy" is never mentioned, nor "phaneron." Even the word "phenomenology" does not appear. Of course, Peirce speaks of Hegel and the "three stages of thought," but it is in relation with Lady Welby's three kinds of meaning. The categories Firstness, Secondness, Thirdness are never mentioned nor is the distinction between "genuine" and "degenerate." The last term appears once applied to a monkey: a "degenerate monkey" (C017). But the theory is there, not the phenomenology of Hegel, at least as interpreted by his followers: Harris, Wallace, Hibben, Everett, and others, who misinterpreted it. According to them, Hegel's system "is anti-evolutionary, anti-progressive, because it represents thought as attaining perfect fulfilment of any rational life except progress towards further fulfilment" (C124).

"The 'Logik'," Peirce goes on, "is supposed to mirror the history of mind" (C124). This is enough to explain why Peirce's phaneroscopy has nothing to do with Hegel's phenomenology. To quote Peirce:

> [ . . . ] It is evident enough that all Hegel's categories properly belong to his third grand division, the *Begriff*. What, for example, could be more monstrous than to call such a conception as that of Being a primitive one; or, indeed, what more absurd than to say that the *immediate* is *abstract?* (C124)

Peirce concludes that "a powerful and original study of what the true Hegelian doctrine of *Wesen* should be, according to our present lights, might breathe some real life into a modified Hegelianism, if anything could have that effect" (C125).

And something can have that effect: to be faithful to traditional scholastics and especially to Scotism according to which there are three modes of being:

> [M]atter, or the positively possible; form, or that whose being in its general governing of what in any way is; and hecceities, or positive elements of individual existence. (C174)

"Unfortunately," Peirce remarks, "no considerable Scotistic school is now extant. Only a pragmatist, here and there, has a sort of affinity to Scotus" (C174).

Let us note that the order in which the categories are given is the order in which they appear in a semiosis: First, Third, and Second; and also that the terminology used is not Peirce's, but the traditional and misleading Aristotelian terminology: matter First, form Third, to which is added Scotus's hecceity Second. Of course, one can object that the Aristotelian terminology is not at all misleading, because "matter" stands for "a general mode of being, a positive, substantial possibility, or potentiality, over and above actual existence, or *exsistence*" (C173–174). But "that there are three stages in the comprehension of phenomena is now generally admitted," Peirce says, "whether this be a mere logical division, or represent a subjective tendency to divide by three, or whether it is an objective law as Comte seems to think it is" (C170). And also Aristotle and Peirce himself.

"Semeiotic" is never dealt with. Its existence is alluded to quite by accident when Peirce speaks of the foundations of logic. He writes:

> One appeals chiefly to mathematics, another to metaphysics, a third to the general notion of a sign, a fourth and a fifth to this and that branch of psychology, a sixth to linguistics, a seventh to the history of science; and still the list is incomplete. (C279)

As for Peirce, semeiotic is another name for logic. It is not at all certain that, by "the general theory of a sign," he meant his own semeiotic. It is a fact that in the *Contributions* there is not a word on the triadic division of the sign into representamen, object and interpretant. There is nothing on the nine subdivisions into qualisign, sinsign, legisign, . . .

The word "sign" appears here and there, but not significantly except once in a review of Baldwin's *Thought and Things* in 1907:

> [ . . . ] the author frequently speaks of the "meaning" of an "object." It appears to us that meaning belongs exclusively to signs; and a sign, as the medium between two minds or between an object and an idea, and being so regarded, however obscurely, must involve a triplet. (C290)

It is the only expression of the fact that Peirce's theory of signs is triadic. That the relation between a sign (representamen), an idea (interpretant), and an object is a semiosis is precisely expressed, without the term being used, in a review of Windelband's *History of Philosophy* in 1894 *à propos* the translation of the Περὶ Σημείων καὶ Σημειώσεων of Philodemus into "On Signs and Designations."

> He who reads the text finds to his amazement that the title cannot, agreeably to the contents, be understood to mean "On Signs [i.e., words and the like] and designations," but, on the contrary, must be rendered "On Signs [i.e., facts symptomatic of other facts] and their significance [i.e., their inferential value]"; and further that the substance of the treatise bears not the remotest affinity with the "supposition" of nouns, but is a discussion of the philosophy and value of inductive reasoning! (B074)

Σημείωσις or semiosis is thus the Greek or Anglicized term for an inference or inductive reasoning.

Other remarks are also interesting in relation to semeiotic, provided the reader has some knowledge of the doctrine. In 1893, in a review of Spencer's *Principles of Ethics* (Parts V and VI), one can read an intriguing paragraph on likenesses or icons:

> [Spencer] represents every operation of the mind as a recognition of a likeness or the recognition of an unlikeness. [ . . . ] it implies that all relations can be analyzed into likenesses and unlikenesses, the falsity of which has been recognized

by every analyst who has seriously examined the question. Spencer says that sequence is unlikeness in order. Undoubtedly, a sequence is an unlikeness, but that is no sign that it is nothing but unlikeness, or nothing but a compound of likenesses and unlikenesses. It clearly cannot be so, for when A is like or unlike B, B has that same relation to A; while when A is followed by B, B is *ipso facto* not followed by A. Spencer is therefore tiresome, with his old-world psychology of likeness and unlikeness; it is particularly unfavorable to clear conceptions of evolution, which demand a recognition of the distinction between temporal relations and the mere acervations of the crudest form of generalization. (A192–193)

This logical conception of "likeness" is expressed in another review of 1902 wherein the author of a book on classification is congratulated for thinking that "*Likeness,* as the ground of the putting together of things in classification is, in brief terms, interchangeability" (C061).

"Epistemology" is in the background of many reviews, because Peirce was given mostly scientific books to review. However, the word "abduction" never appears. "Induction" is the key word. But, for Peirce, "induction" is this "inferential reasoning" by which expression he translated semeiosis in terms of a triadic process which includes the relation between a First and a Third (abduction), the relation between this Third and other Thirds in a system of Thirds (deduction), and the relation between a deduced Third and a Second (induction).

All that appears very clearly applied to mathematics in a review of Spinoza's *Ethics.*

[ ... ] the real procedure of mathematical thought is not merely syllogistic [ ... ]. Mathematical thought advances chiefly by generalization; and the generalized conclusions are made rigorously logical by the device of correspondingly generalizing the premises. [ ... ] Let the predicates be relational, and generalization means organization, or the building up of an ideal system. Mathematical reasoning consists in thinking how things already remarked may be conceived as making part of a hitherto unremarked system, especially by means of the introduction of the hypothesis of continuity where no continuity has hitherto been thought of. (B085)

So that, Peirce writes a few months later in another review,

Mathematics advances, just as the physical sciences do, by observation and generalization. Its observations are, it is true, only observations of the mind's own constructions, but they often have that *startling* quality which indicates that they *are* observations. (C102)

The three stages of an inferential or inductive process are there: abduction as generalization, deduction as organization, induction as observation or experimentation of a deduced proposition.

"Scientific metaphysics" is everywhere in the *Contributions.* But while "tychism" is mentioned, there is not a single allusion to "agapism" or "synechism," although, as we have just seen, for Peirce, continuity is a major hypothesis of explanation.

Tychism is mentioned twice, in 1899 and 1906. In 1899, it is, so to speak, the classical tychism:

> There remain two opinions less deterministic than the common one. One of these, which has been called Tychism, is that there are minute departures in nature from any general formula which can be assigned, so that there is a certain element of absolute chance. This is the position maintained by C. S. Peirce a few years ago in the *Monist.* (B208)

In 1906, Peirce proposes a tychism less classical. He writes:

> The deepest revolution of scientific conception [is that which reduces] matter from the rank of primordial substance to that of a special state of electricity. After that, we shall be prepared for anything, even for experimental demonstration of the Tychist's doctrine that electricity is a psychical phenomenon. (C255)

## II

It is astonishing, in a way, to see Peirce defend the doctrine that electricity is a psychical phenomenon, when one knows his constant anti-psychologism. However, the *Contributions* give a clue to this apparent contradiction and to several other questions.

As to psychology, Peirce has always distinguished between the "psychic" or "psychical" and "psychology." One is a fact, the other a theory. Peirce's anti-psychologism is explicitly justified in his review of James's *Principles of Psychology* (1891) and Wundt's *Principles of Physiological Psychology* (1905).

The appeal to "facts" is "the principle of the uncritical acceptance of data to which Prof. James clings." It is a departure from accepted methods of sciences in general (A106). The method of any science takes for model the science of dynamics and it is in this sense that the word "dynamic" must be understood in the writings of Peirce, not just "fact" but the testing of phenomena in the light of a hypothesis. And it is because the "psychic" cannot be tested in this way that "logic, ethics, and philosophy [cannot] be securely based on that special science": psychology (C232). How can we "diagnose the malady of psychology"? Easily enough: "There is nothing which for the psychical wing of science fulfils that function which the science of dynamics fulfils on the physical side" (C230).

This function is that of a semeiotic inference:

> Every attempt to explain any phenomenon physically consists in first proposing some hypothesis [abduction] as to the existence of designated dynamical conditions from which, according to the principle of dynamics, phenomena such as

have been observed would take place [deduction], and then going on to put the hypothesis to the test of making it the basis of predictions concerning untried experiments [induction]. (C230)

# III

Nowhere does Peirce describe more clearly why he rejects psychology, what "dynamic" means, what his epistemology is—and what the principle of pragmatism consists of.

Pragmatism is *The Nation*'s philosophy. I do not mean the philosophy of the editors, but the philosophy of Peirce—pragmatism or rather pragmaticism—which was to become the philosophy of the nation: America.

It is not the place here to show that a philosopher of American nationality is an American philosopher if and only if he is a pragmatist, or should I say a pragmaticist or rather a speculative pragmatist.

To conclude my comparative essays between Peirce's pragmaticist thought and the thought of the main Europeans who dealt with the same topics, I shall sum up Peirce's pragmatism and his reactions to the works of the great philosophers of the Golden Age of American philosophy: James, Royce, Dewey, Mead, Santayana. Peirce was certainly a genius, but, so to speak, by accident, but fortunately he was accident-prone. What I mean is that he had not that kind of intelligence which characterizes the American Mind, an intelligence open to other people. When one reads his comments on James, Dewey, Santayana, and even Royce—he never mentioned Mead, and it was reciprocal: Mead never referred to Peirce—one is astonished to see that he was unable to foresee or even to see the epoch-making contributions of James's *Principles of Psychology* and of Dewey's *Studies in Logical Theory.*

Santayana is a half-hearted American, as everybody knows. Although he is in a way a pragmatist or, if one prefers, a half-hearted pragmatist, Peirce does not see that. For him, "Professor Santayana's volumes [the first two volumes of *The Life of Reason*] are anything but commonplace. They are all that Boston has of most *précieux*" (C222). "They are extremely handy and agreeable to the eyes," Peirce goes on.

James is rewarded, as "a tribute of respect" (A104), with a lot of negative comments: His terminology is "unsuitable" (A104); his originality is "destructive"; he has a "general incomprehensibility of things" (A105); he is a materialist; he inclines towards "Cartesian dualism"; he suspects evolution; he is anti-intellectualist, anti-associationist, anti-spiritualist (A105). His originality is positive in only one case: his positivism, although he does not use it properly.

Dewey had two books reviewed by Peirce: *The Psychology of Number* and *Studies in Logical Theory.* The comment on the first book is negative: Measuring does not teach us "to improve our general conceptions" (B114). But it allows Peirce to give his own opinion which is worth quoting:

It is useful to distinguish the different purposes of numbers, because a distinct system of numbers, each with its distinct modification of logic, is used for
each purpose. For *counting,* we must use cardinal numbers; for the *assignment
of places in cycles,* we use limited series (the names of the days of the week is
such a system of numbers); for *dating,* in series running indefinitely both ways
(like the years BC and AD), we require negative as well as positive integers; for
*measurement,* we need rational fractions; for *reasonings about continua,* where
first the idea of a limit comes in, we need surds; for *comparing functions,* we
need imaginaries; for *four-dimensional continuous numerotations,* quaternions.
(B115)

On the *Studies* which are the platform of instrumentalism, a branch of pragmatism very close to his own, closer in any case than James's or Royce's, Peirce
has only one thing to say: The members of the Chicago school "are manifestly in
radical opposition to the exact logicians, and are not making any studies which
anybody in his senses can expect, directly or indirectly, in any considerable degree, to influence twentieth-century science" (C185).

Although Peirce does not think that all the positions of Royce in *The World
and the Individual* are "perfectly demonstrated" (C082), he is sympathetic with
Royce's kind of pragmaticism. He accepts Royce's distinction between "internal
meaning" and "external meaning," which he traces back to John of Salisbury's
distinction between signification which is intrinsic and denotation which is ex-
trinsic. This distinction does not differ much from Peirce's distinction between
"immediate object" and "dynamic object," if we follow Peirce.

Another writer, a quarter of a century ago, proposed this maxim: "Consider
what effects that might conceivably have practical bearings we conceive the object of our conception to have. Then our conception of those effects is the *whole*
of our conception of the object." Carrying this pragmatistic spirit a trifle further, Professor Royce holds that the internal meaning of an idea is a Purpose,
instead of regarding it, with his predecessor [Peirce] as a germinal purpose.
(C082)

Who are then, apart from himself, the true pragmatists? Peirce's answer
takes us back to Europe: The Founding Fathers of the doctrine are Spinoza and
Berkeley, with the help of Scotus and Kant.

Spinoza, who "thoroughly recognized as a fundamental truth that the substance of what one believes does not consist in any mere sensuous representation, but in how one would be disposed to behave" (C178).

Berkeley is the father of all modern philosophy. "It is he, more than any
other single philosopher, who should be regarded as the author of that method
of modern pragmatism—i.e., the definition, or interpretation, of conceptions by
their issues" (C036). But there were two weaknesses in Berkeley. One of these is
that existence is a form to be conceived. Thanks to Scotus, and Kant in that matter, existence is now "a compulsive force to be experienced" (C037). The other

weakness of Berkeley, "shared by Kant in a lesser degree," is "his Ockhamism, or refusal to acknowledge any being *in futuro,* or any mode of being whatever except that of individual existence" (C037).

A last remark. When he had the opportunity of publishing a paper, Peirce used to write about everything he thought important to convey without much consideration for the topic of the paper. Why did he not do the same thing in his contributions to *The Nation*? Whatever the answer, it is a fact that, in spite of his ethics of terminology, he did not impose on *The Nation*'s readers his own doctrines, or at least his terminology in the fields in which he knew he was a pioneer, and in which he is now universally recognized to be one: phaneroscopy, logic, semeiotic, epistemology, and scientific metaphysics. On the contrary, his main theories are more insinuated than exposed; except pragmatism, which is properly *The Nation*'s philosophy, but not just any kind of pragmatism—not James's, nor Dewey's, not even Royce's—but his own brand of pragmaticism, the kind of speculative pragmatism which in retrospect, or from outside or laterally, appears to be the philosophy of the American nation.

It was the destiny of America to unite what was divided in Europe and give birth to a new philosophy: pragmatism, thanks to Peirce, without whom philosophy would not be what it is, not only in America, but the world over.

# BIBLIOGRAPHY

*The present bibliography is also used as references for the notes in the text.*
*In addition, see "Original Papers by the Author."*

*Écrits apocryphes chrétiens.* 1997. Paris: Gallimard, Bibliothèque de la Pléiade.
*L'Arc,* special issue on Roman Jakobson. 1975, n° 60.

*

Aquinas, Thomas. [1259/1263] *Questiones disputatae de Potentia,* ed. Fretté. Paris: Vivès.
———. [1265/1268] *In Metaphysicam Aristotelis Commentaria,* ed. Cathala. Turin.
———. [1267/1273] *Summa theologica,* ed. Pecci. Paris: Lethielleux.
Aristotle. 1831. *Prior Analytics,* Greek ed., *Aristotelis Opera,* Berolini apud Georgium Reimerum.
Balle, Francis. 1983. "Médias et pouvoirs," *Universalia 1983.* Paris: Encyclopaedia Universalis: 289–292.
Barthes, Roland. 1975. *Barthes par lui-même.* Paris: Éditions du Seuil.
Benedict, George A. 1979. "What is a Representamen?" Third International Congress of IASS, Vienna.
Bernard, Claude. 1965 [1865]. *Introduction à l'étude de la médecine expérimentale.* Paris: Hachette. Quoted in McLuhan 1967.
Bianchi, Cinzia. 1995. *Su Ferruccio Rossi-Landi.* Napoli: Edizioni Scientifice Italiane.
Bonfantini, Massimo A. 1987. *La semiosi e l'abduzione.* Milano: Bompiani.
Bouquet, Simon. 1997. *Introduction à la lecture de Saussure.* Paris: Payot.
Buchler, Justus. 1939. *Peirce's Empiricism.* London: Kegan Paul.
Calvet, Louis-Jean. 1975. *Pour et contre Saussure.* Paris: Payot.
Cohen, Marcel. 1958. "Linguistique et idéalisme," *Recherches internationales à la lumière du marxisme.*
Cuvillier, Armand. 1927. *Manuel philosophique.* Paris: Armand Colin.
D'Alembert. 1751. *Discours préliminaire de l'Encyclopédie,* § 71. Quoted by Lalande 1947: 698.
De Lacy, Estelle. 1964. "The Empirical Metaphysics of Epicurus," in *Process and Divinity: The Hartshorne Festschrift,* ed. William L. Reese and Eugene Freeman. LaSalle, Ill.: 377–401.
Deledalle, Gérard. 1964. "Charles S. Peirce et les maîtres à penser de la philosophie européenne d'aujourd'hui," *Les Études philosophiques:* 283–295.
———. 1969. "Charles S. Peirce: La nature du pragmatisme," *Revue philosophique,* January–March: 31–60.
———. 1972. "Présence du pragmatisme," *Revue internationale de philosophie:* 21–41.
———. 1978. *Charles S. Peirce, Écrits sur le signe.* Paris: Éditions du Seuil.
———. 1979. *Théorie et pratique du signe, Introduction à la sémiotique de Charles S. Peirce.* Paris: Payot.
———. 1981. "English and French Versions of C. S. Peirce's 'The Fixation of Belief' and 'How to Make Our Ideas Clear.'" *Transactions of the Charles S. Peirce Society* (Spring): 140–152.
———. 1983. "L'actualité de Peirce: abduction, induction, déduction," *Semiotica,* 3/4: 307–313.

——. 1984/1985. "Du fondement en sémiotique peircienne," *Semiosis.*

——. 1985. "Charles S. Peirce, Introduction à un traité de logique," *Kodikas/Code.*

——. 1986. "La philosophie du quantificateur existentiel selon Charles S. Peirce," in *Déterminants: syntaxe et sémantique,* ed. Jean David and Georges Kleiber: 35–40.

——. 1990a. *Charles S. Peirce: An Intellectual Biography,* translated from French and introduced by Susan Petrilli. Amsterdam/Philadelphia: John Benjamins.

——. 1990b. "Victoria Lady Welby and Charles S. Peirce: Meaning and Signification," in *Essays on Significs,* ed. H. Walter Schmitz. 1990: 133–149.

——. 1998. *La Philosophie américaine (1620–1996).* Bruxelles: De Boeck Université.

Descartes, René. 1952. *Oeuvres complètes,* Bibliothèque de la Pléiade. Paris: Gallimard.

Dewey, John. 1910. *The Influence of Darwin on Philosophy.* New York: Henry Holt & Co.

——. 1929. *Experience and Nature,* 2nd ed. New York: George Allen and Unwin.

——. 1946. "Peirce's Theory of Linguistic Signs, Thought, and Meaning," *The Journal of Philosophy* (February 14, 1946): 85–95.

——. 1972. *The Early Works.* Carbondale, Ill.: Southern Illinois University Press. Vol. 5.

Eco, Umberto. 1976. *A Theory of Semiotics.* Bloomington: Indiana University Press.

——. 1979. *The Role of the Reader.* Bloomington: Indiana University Press.

Eco, Umberto, and Thomas A. Sebeok, eds. 1983. *The Sign of Three.* Bloomington: Indiana University Press.

Eco, Umberto, and Costantino Marmo, eds. 1989. *On the Medieval Theory of Signs.* Amsterdam/Philadelphia: John Benjamins.

Eschbach, Achim. 1983. "Significs as a Fundamental Science," in Welby, Victoria Lady. 1983: ix–xxxii.

Fisch, Max. 1982. "Introduction" to the first volume of the *Writings:* xv–xxxv.

——. 1986. *Peirce, Semeiotic, and Pragmatism,* ed. Kenneth Laine Ketner and Christian J. W. Kloesel. Bloomington: Indiana University Press.

Foucault, Michel. 1972. *Power/Knowledge.* New York: Random House.

Godel, Robert. 1957. *Les sources manuscrites du cours de linguistique génerale de Ferdinand de Saussure.* Geneva: Droz and Paris: Minard.

Goodman, Nelson. 1983 [1979]. *Fact, Fiction, and Forecast.* Cambridge: Harvard University Press.

Greenlee, Douglas. 1973. *Peirce's Concept of Sign.* The Hague: Mouton.

Guillaume, Paul. 1937. *La psychologie de la forme.* Paris: Flammarion.

Hamilton, William. 1863. *The Works of Thomas Reid,* 6th ed. Edinburgh: Maclachlan and Stewart.

Hardwick, Charles S., ed. 1977. *Semiotic and Significs: The Correspondence Between Charles S. Peirce and Victoria Lady Welby.* Bloomington: Indiana University Press.

Hartshorne, Charles. 1962. *The Logic of Perception.* LaSalle, Ill.: Open Court.

Huisman, Denis. 1957. *Manuel de philosophie.* Paris: Nathan.

Jakobson, Roman. 1952. "Results of a Joint Conference of Anthropologists and Linguists."

——. 1963. *Essais de linguistique générale.* Paris: Éditions de Minuit.

——. 1966. "A la recherche de l'essence du language," in Émile Benveniste et al. *Problèmes du langage.* Paris: Gallimard.

——. 1974. *Coup d'oeil sur le développement de la sémiotique.* Research Center for Language and Semiotic Studies. Bloomington: Indiana University Press.

Jastrow, Joseph. 1971 [1901]. *Fact and Fable in Psychology.* Freeport, N.Y.: Books for Libraries Press.

Köhler, Wolfgang. 1930. *Gestalt Psychology.* New York: G. Bell & Sons.

Lalande, André. 1947 [1926]. *Vocabulaire philosophique.* Paris: P.U.F. Translation mine.

Llull, Ramón. 1991. *L'Art bref,* translated into French and introduced by Armand Llinarès. Paris: Éditions du Cerf.

Locke, John. 1690. *An Essay Concerning Human Understanding*. London: George Rout-
    ledge and Sons.
Manetti, Giovanni. 1987. *Le teoriee del segno nell'antichità classica*. Milano: Bompiani.
Maritain, Jacques. 1939. *Les Degrés du savoir*, 3rd ed. Paris: Desclée de Brouwer.
Marquand, Allan. 1883. "The Logic of the Epicureans." *Studies on Logic by Members of
    the Johns Hopkins University*, 1–11. New edition by Achim Eschbach. Amster-
    dam/Philadelphia: John Benjamins, 1983.
Mattéi, Jean-François. 1996. *Platon et le miroir du mythe*. Paris: Presses Universitaires de
    France.
McLuhan, Marshall. 1951. *The Mechanical Bride: Folklore of Industrial Man*.
———. 1962. *The Gutenberg Galaxy: The Making of the Typographic Man*. The University
    of Toronto Press.
———. 1964. *Understanding Media: The Extensions of Man*. New York: Sphere Books Edi-
    tion.
———. 1967. *The Medium is the Massage: an Inventory of Effects*.
———. 1968. *War and Peace in the Global World*.
Mead, George H. 1938. *The Philosophy of the Act*. Chicago: University of Chicago Press.
Mill, John Stuart. 1843. *A System of Logic*. London: George Routledge and Sons.
Monk, Ray. 1990. *Ludwig Wittgenstein*. London: Vintage.
Morris, Charles. 1946. "Signs, Language and Behavior," in Morris 1971: 175–397.
———. 1971. *Writings on the General Theory of Signs*. The Hague: Mouton.
Mounin, Georges. 1968. *Saussure ou le structuralisme sans le savoir*. Paris: Seghers.
———. 1970. *Introduction à la semiologie*. Paris: Éditions de Minuit.
Ogden, Charles K., and I. A. Richards. 1946 [1923]. *The Meaning of Meaning*. London:
    Routledge and Kegan Paul.
Parret, Herman. 1983. *Semiotics and Pragmatics*. Amsterdam/Philadelphia: John Ben-
    jamins.
Peirce, Charles S. 1931–1935. *Collected Papers*, vols. 1–6, ed. Charles Hartshorne and Paul
    Weiss. Cambridge, Mass.: Harvard University Press.
———. 1953. *Charles S. Peirce's Letters to Lady Welby*, ed. Irwin C. Lieb. New Haven.
———. 1958. *Collected Papers*, vols. 7–8, ed. Arthur Burks. Cambridge, Mass.: Harvard
    University Press.
———. 1975. *The Contributions to* THE NATION, vol. 1, ed. Kenneth Laine Ketner. Lubbock:
    Texas University Press.
———. 1976. *The New Elements of Mathematics*, ed. Carolyn Eisele. Atlantic Highlands,
    N.J.: Humanities Press.
———. 1978. *The Contributions to* THE NATION, vol. 2, ed. Kenneth Laine Ketner and James
    Edward Cook. Lubbock: Texas University Press.
———. 1979. *The Contributions to* THE NATION, vol. 3, ed. Kenneth Laine Ketner and James
    Edward Cook. Lubbock: Texas University Press.
———. 1982. *Writings of Charles S. Peirce*. Vol. 1 1984, Vol. 2 1986, Vol. 3 1988, Vol. 4 1990,
    Vol. 5 1998. Peirce Edition Project. Bloomington and Indianapolis: Indiana Uni-
    versity Press.
———. 1985. "Introduction à un traité de logique" (ed. Deledalle), *Kodikas/Code*.
Pelc, Jerzy. 1993. "Several Questions to Experts in Peirce's Theory of Signs," in *Peirce in
    Italia*, ed. M. A. Bonfantini and A. Martone. Napoli: Liguori Editore: 63–84.
Petrilli, Susan. 1991. "From Peirce (via Morris and Jakobson) to Sebeok," in Sebeok,
    Thomas A. 1991.
———. 1992. "Social Practice, Semiotics and the Sciences of Man: The Correspondence
    Between Charles Morris and Ferruccio Rossi-Landi," *Semiotica*: 1–36.
———. 1998. *Su Victoria Welby*. Napoli: Edizioni Scientifiche Italiane.
Philodemus. 1978 [79 AD]. *On Methods of Inference*, edited with English translation and

comments by Phillip Howard De Lacy and Estelle Allen De Lacy. Naples: Bibliopolis.

Plato. 1942 [1935]. *The Republic,* trans. A.D. Lindsay. London: Everyman's Library.

Ponzio, Augusto. 1990. *Man as a Sign.* Berlin/New York: Mouton de Gruyter.

Popper, Karl. 1959. *The Logic of Scientific Discovery.* London: Hutchinson.

Proni, Giampaolo. 1990. *Introduzione a Peirce.* Milano: Bompiani.

Ramsey, Frank P. 1923. "Critical Notice of Wittgenstein's *Tractatus logico-philosophicus,*" *Mind:* 465–478.

———. 1924. "Review of Ogden and Richards: *The Meaning of Meaning.*" *Mind:* 108–109.

———. 1925. "Universals," *Mind:* 404–445.

———. 1931 [1926]. "Truth and Probability," in *Foundations of Mathematics and Other Logical Essays,* ed. R. B. Braithwaite. London: K. Paul, Trench and Tribner.

Randall Jr., J. H. 1960. *Aristotle.* New York: Columbia University Press.

Reid, Thomas. 1863. *The Works of Thomas Reid, D.D.,* 6th ed. Edinburgh: Maclachlan and Stewart.

Santayana, George. 1920. *Character and Opinion in the United States.* New York: Charles Scribner's Sons.

Savan, David. 1976. *Peirce's Semiotic.* Toronto Semiotic Circle, Victoria College: Toronto.

Schmitz, H. Walter. 1985. "Victoria Lady Welby's Significs: The Origin of the Signific Movement," in Welby, Victoria Lady 1985: iv–ccxxxv.

———, ed. 1990. *Essays on Significs.* Amsterdam/Philadelphia: John Benjamins.

Schneider, Herbert W. 1952. "Fourthness," in *Studies in the Philosophy of Charles Sanders Peirce,* ed. Wiener and Young. Cambridge, Mass.: Harvard University Press.

Sebeok, Thomas A. 1976. *Contributions to the Doctrine of Signs.* Bloomington: Indiana University Press.

———. 1981. "The Images of Charles Morris," in *Zeichen über Zeichen über Zeichen,* ed. A. Eschbach. Tübingen: Gunter Narr: 267–284.

———. 1991. *American Signatures,* ed. Iris Smith. Norman: University of Oklahoma Press.

———, ed. 1977. *A Perfusion of Signs.* Bloomington: Indiana University Press.

Sebeok, Thomas A., and Jean Umiker-Sebeok. 1979. "You Know My Method: A Juxtaposition of Charles S. Peirce and Sherlock Holmes," *Semiotica:* 203–250. Reprinted in Eco and Sebeok 1983: 11–54.

Sextus Empiricus. 1933–1949. Heinemann in four volumes, Greek ed. and English trans. Vol. 1, *Outlines of Pyrrhonism,* Vol. 2, *Against the Logicians.* London: The Loeb Classical Library.

Stearn, Gerald E., ed. 1968. *McLuhan, Hot and Cool.* London: Penguin Books.

Swift, Jonathan. 1939 [1727]. *Gulliver's Travels.* London: Macmillan & Co.

Tejera, Vittorino. 1991. "Has Eco Understood Peirce?"

Thayer, Horace S. 1968. *Meaning and Action: A Critical History of Pragmatism.* Indianapolis/New York: The Bobbs-Merrill Company: 304–313.

Thom, René. 1995. *Le Monde,* July 22–23.

Valéry, Paul. 1973. *Les Cahiers.* La Pléiade, vol. 1. Paris: Gallimard.

———. 1974. *Les Cahiers.* La Pléiade, vol. 2. Paris: Gallimard.

Wahl, Jean. 1944. *Existence humaine et transcendance.* Neuchatel: La Baconnière.

———. 1951. "La troisième hypothèse," in *Etudes sur le Parménide de Platon.* Paris: Vrin: 167–172.

Welby, Victoria Lady. 1892. "The Use of the 'Inner' and 'Outer' in Psychology: Does the Metaphor Help or Hinder?" For private circulation.

———. 1893. "Meaning and Metaphor," *The Monist 3,* 4: 510–525. Facsimile published in *Significs and Language,* 1985.

———. 1896. "Sense, Meaning, and Interpretation," *Mind,* 5: 17: 24–37 and 18: 186–202. Facsimile published in *Significs and Language,* 1985.

———. 1983 [1903]. *What is Meaning?* Amsterdam/Philadelphia: John Benjamins.

———. 1985 [1911]. *Significs and Language*. Amsterdam/Philadelphia: John Benjamins.

Wittgenstein, Ludwig. 1953. *Philosophical Investigations*, ed. G. E. M. Anscombe and R. Rhees; trans. G. E. M. Anscombe. Oxford: Blackwell.

———. 1961 [1922]. *Tractatus logico-philosophicus*, new English trans. D. F. Pears and B. F. McGuinness. London: Routledge and Kegan Paul.

———. 1969. *On Certainty*, ed. G. E. M. Anscombe and G. H. von Wright; trans. Denis Paul and G. E. M. Anscombe. Oxford: Blackwell.

# INDEX

GÉRARD DELEDALLE (born 1921) holds a Doctorate in Philosophy from the Sorbonne. Research Scholar, Columbia University, New York, and Attaché at the Centre National de la Recherche Scientifique, Paris, he was also successively Professor of Philosophy and Head of the Philosophy Department of the universities of Tunis (1963–1972), Perpignan (1974–1990), and Libreville (1977–1981). He was appointed Director of the Institut Franco-Japonais in Tokyo from 1972 to 1974. He has been Visiting Professor in Japan (Waseda University), China (Beijing and Wuhan), the United States (Bloomington), and Canada (UQAM). Deledalle has written extensively on American philosophy, Charles S. Peirce, John Dewey, pragmatism, and semiotics. In 1990 he received the Herbert W. Schneider Award "for distinguished contributions to the understanding and development of American philosophy."